DATE DUE

DEMCO, INC. 38-2931

HELPS AND HINDRANCES TO PERFECTION

Helps and Hindrances
to PERFECTION

THOMAS J. HIGGINS, S.J.

THE BRUCE PUBLISHING COMPANY
MILWAUKEE

NIHIL OBSTAT:

    JOHN A. SCHULIEN, S.T.D.
    Censor librorum

IMPRIMATUR:

    ✠ ALBERT G. MEYER,
    Archiepiscopus Milwauchiensis

August 11, 1955

Rosary College Dewey Classification Number: 248

Library of Congress Catalog Card Number: 55–12063

Preface

IN MY earlier book *Perfection Is for You*, I attempted to set forth the chief features of the doctrine of Christian perfection. There, too, I insisted that high holiness is truly intended for all Christians. It has been gratifying, therefore, to learn that my effort was not totally in vain. The thought that all aspirants to perfection are not in the cloister or the priesthood was confirmed by this letter from a stranger:

Dear Father,

I enjoyed so much your book *Perfection Is for You* that I would like to thank you for writing it.

As a Mother Superior (postulant and novice), I too believe that perfection is for each and *all* members of Christ's Mystical Body, because the world is crying for saints. I do not like being Mother Superior of this order of one — Kitchen Contemplative. Novice is easy, but being the boss is hard; so much depends on Mothers (in and out of orders). I happen to be Mother of five wonderful, healthy, self-willed, delightful, bright, and sometimes *very* trying children and wife to an equally wonderful husband.

I especially loved the chapters on humility and mortification. There are some things I do not understand. I believe Father Caussade speaks of the prayer of aspirations as a form of prayer very close to God. Now one whose mind and heart always are raised to God in this manner would, it would presuppose, have a certain amount of virtue. My own poor heart is raised to God in all my waking moments. Unconsciously or consciously, all day long my mind is saying, "Jesus, how good You are, how fair Your lovely Mother. Oh God the Father, thank You for Your Son and Our Mother, and Holy Spirit, thank You that I know them. Thank You for the beauty of Your saints and the grace and glory of You that shines in them. Thank You, God, for being Three; thank You for being One. I desire nothing but to please You. Come, make Your dwelling place in my heart, and I will try to keep it a peaceful cool retreat, full of love and quiet."

My heart sings a love song all day long. This is God's gift.

But the interior life is His free gift and the Spirit moves where He will.

And I am so little worthy of all this goodness. I am full of worms. Scraps of self love, useless and ugly. And yet I hang on to them tenaciously. I will not let the "old man" die. I have *none* of this virtue that such an interior life would presuppose. How can this be?

A few lines popped into my head one day that sum it up.

> If one could skid the id
> And shy the I
> He'd find the Three
> in Thee.
> (But I'm a stinker
> Not a thinker;
> I'll probably die
> In love with I.)

Let us hope God's grace will be enough and I will not *really* die in love with I.

I am *not* discouraged and I will keep right on trying and climbing (with God's grace) no matter how many times I fall down the mountain. I am even glad I am weak and little because it teaches me humility and God knows best how to prune stubborn pride, even if by showing it how very little it accomplishes.

Thank you again for your book. It is indeed stimulating. I shall pray for all its readers that the Holy Ghost inspires them on to the way of perfection and that they do not give up no matter how rugged the way. Needless to say, I shall pray for you and your work.

I would be deeply grateful to you if you would pray for me that one day, in God's due time, I will make "that last surrender and will leap out of self to be ready for union with God." You could not know how very much I desire to be lost in Christ, that our Heavenly Father would see in me only His Beloved Son, that all my ugliness would be hidden by the brightness of the Light that came into the world.

As a matter of fact I'd appreciate a prayer for all mothers. I do not know a harder (or more wonderful) job than being a mother (unless it is being a priest). We must also be co-creators with God, bringing forth Christ in our children and helping our husbands so that they too will find it easier to have union with God.

It is a big deal and I am glad it is mine. I even dare to hope that one day I will be a saint. Thanks to such direction as your splendid book *Perfection Is for You.*

It may be too much to say that here is "some mute inglorious Milton." If, however, the lady who wrote this letter had time and opportunity she would write a more attractive spiritual book than ever I can. But at least she can go on reading. She and thousands more whose chance discovery shows that choice blooms of sanctity flourish in hidden un-expected places. May God be glorified by their increase!

Loyola College, Baltimore   THOMAS J. HIGGINS, S.J.

Contents

HELPS AND HINDRANCES TO PERFECTION

1. Faith

"I believe; help my unbelief" (Mk. 9:23).

It is cold enough comfort to say that heresy must accomplish some good, that otherwise God would not allow it. The big heresy of our day is materialism. True, it has swept away many old superstitions; yet it has blighted the faith of many and produced the new paganism. For it erases the line between the visible and invisible, dogmatically asserting that the invisible cannot exist.

A little boy was excited by the experience of coming to Mass for the first time. He brimmed with solemn delight and looked around the church with devouring interest. "Is this God's house?" he demanded of his mother. "Yes," his mother whispered. "Does God live here?" "Yes." He gave another big look around and loudly exclaimed, "I don't see God."

Many a university professor has made the same observation and then concluded to the nonexistence of God. The little boy, however, was willing to go along with what Mother said. If she said God was here he should be able to find Him. As he came to Mass Sunday after Sunday, his attention was caught by the most important person present: the man in strange fascinating clothes who stood at the altar and said strange things, who also read the names of people out of a book, people who wanted Masses said, people who ran card parties or made donations to them. After five or six weeks the little boy felt he had solved his problem and confronted his mother with his findings. "Mother, God does not know you." "Why not, Jackie?" "Because God never reads your name from the altar."

God had to be someone he could put his finger on. He

1

never dreamed that God is invisible. So in his attempt to
pin-point God, he had succeeded merely in confusing Him
with His representative. Imagination can play such tricks
on us all since desire for sense images is the penalty, or at
least the shortcoming, of the spiritual soul which is immersed
in matter.

The little boy, however, had been given a divine gift at
baptism, the infused virtue of faith, the power to believe
in God as He is and to enter into the world of divine mysteries.
Given time and suitable preparation he will make a proper
act of that power and rise above the limitations of imagination and natural reason. First he learns something about
God on the say-so of his mother. Then he acquires more
knowledge upon the say-so of the nun who teaches him
and yet more upon the word of his priest. Although it would
be idle to try to fix the exact time, he comes to accept the
truths of his religion, not upon the say-so of any human
being, but solely upon the word of God. When he does
this, his habit of faith issues in an act of faith, one of the
most familiar but mysterious acts of a Christian.

THE ACT OF FAITH

St. Thomas[1] says that no one has improved upon St. Paul's
definition of faith: the substance of things to be hoped for,
the argument of things which appear not.[2]

Substance here means two things: first, the basis which
supports a thing. Faith is the foundation upon which the
hope of man rests. I hope when I tend toward something
which I have not but which I see is realizable and expect
to get. Man's supreme hope is that he will be made completely happy in the vision of God as He is. But God as
He is is both unseen and unseeable by any natural power.
How then can "we hope for that which we see not"?[3] How
can anything unseen exist? How can an unseeable God be
seen and make us perfectly happy? The only way of knowing that we shall be perfectly happy in the vision of God
is by believing God who assures us that such indeed is the

---

[1] Cf. *Sum. Theol.*, II–II, 4, 1.
[2] Cf. Hebr. 11:1.
[3] Rom. 8:25.

case. Believing in God is the act of faith. Where then does the thing hoped for exist? In the act of faith! But does it also exist in the world of reality? The word of God is the unshakable link which binds our faith to the firm ground of reality. Therefore, since faith alone can tell us what will make us happy, the object of our hope exists in faith, as the objects of knowledge exist in the principles of knowledge. We can say even more about faith. We possess truth by seeing it. Although we cannot possess the First Truth which is God until we see Him, yet faith is an anticipatory possession of this promised blessing. Faith is our first hold on God as He is. For to believe what one does not see is to deserve to see what one believes.

Second, substance, according to St. Thomas,[4] is that which comes first. He means that faith precedes hope and is the first of all the virtues. Since the theological virtues are concerned with the last end, and since end is the principle of action, the theological virtues precede the moral virtues. Among the theological virtues faith is first because the last end must be present to the intellect before it can be sought by the will. Since the last end is present in the will by hope and present in the intellect by faith, faith must be the first of all the virtues. Faith then is the real commencement within us of eternal life. "For this is eternal life, that they may know Thee, the one true God."[5] No act of natural knowledge could discover God as the object of heavenly bliss. By making the act of faith one takes the first step toward the beatific vision.

Faith is also the means of knowing the things which appear not. We know visible things when they are evident to us, directly or indirectly. The cause of our knowledge is their evidence which forces the intellect to conclude to their reality. But what evidence have the unseen things of God? None whatever, says the materialist; the nonexistent can be evident to no one. The believer says that although these things have no evidence of themselves for us in our present state, yet something supplies for this lack, the revealing word

---

[4] Cf. *Sum. Theol.*, II–II, 4, 7.
[5] Jn. 17:3.

of God, an argument more valid than any natural evidence. It is the utterance of the First Truth!

Out of the void which surrounds our little world and limited knowledge leaps the word of God. It illumines some of the hidden things of God and tells us that the important world is as yet unseen, that neither eye hath seen nor ear heard the truly enduring realities. Emphatically it commands acceptance and submission on the part of the created intellect. For two reasons, then, we are to be believers, accepting the meaning of life and the great secret of the universe upon the word of an unseen God.

First, since man's final destiny consists in a supernatural vision of God, man cannot reach it unless God tells him about it. Christ says: "They shall all be taught of God."[6] This kind of teaching necessarily demands faith on the part of the taught. For, says St. Thomas, "man acquires a share of this learning, not indeed all at once, but little by little . . . and everyone who learns in this manner must believe . . . as also the Philosopher remarks that it behooves a learner to believe. Hence, in order that man arrive at the perfect vision of heavenly happiness, he must first of all believe God as a pupil believes the teacher who is instructing him."[7]

Second, the vision of God is given as a reward after a test. The trial endured ought to be proportioned to the reward given. And the reward is the perfection of human nature. Therefore, to secure it, a man must observe the law of human nature, that is, keep the moral virtues. The reward, however, is also and especially a share in the divine life, a knowing and a loving of God in the divine manner. In order therefore to deserve the brightness of the vision man must walk in the obscurity of faith where the things of God are unseen, where he must accept the existence of these things upon the sole word of God, where he must choose the unseen God in preference to fascinating visible things. God could flood the minds of all men with such illuminations of divine truth that the most stupid and vicious could see at a glance that God is the only thing worth having. God has not chosen

---

[6] Jn. 6:45.
[7] *Sum. Theol.*, II–II, 2, 3.

to do this, for to take away the darkness of faith is to destroy the great test.

While the act of faith is mysterious it is no denial of human dignity or repudiation of natural powers. Let us see it as proceeding from the total man whose specific human powers have been happily elevated to a divine level. Since it is a supernatural act of the intellect placed at the inspired command of the will, it is related to the object of the will, which is the good, and to the object of the intellect, which is the true. To understand that in neither of these relations is there contradiction, let us see, first, the good which the will has in view in commanding the act of faith, and, second, the reasonable motive which enables the intellect to obey without abdicating its own claim to be the judge of truth, a function inherent in its nature.

As for the first, the good sought by the will is the supreme good, God, our last end. The beatific vision is natural to no creature, but God can allure man to a destiny beyond his capacities by giving him new powers, a divine impetus. Far from bemeaning man, his call to divine life is his greatest glory. Hence, when the act of faith is made, the will, by divine impulse, flies directly to God and the force which drives it is yearning for the fulfillment of God's loving designs upon us, the attainment of the last end, the completion of our being in union and likeness with God. "We shall be like to Him because we shall see Him as He is."[8] Here are the things we hope for — eternal happiness, the vision of God, loving union with God — and apart from them nothing is important. Under the inspiration of grace the will makes for these things as the homing pigeon, on release, unerringly wheels toward its distant cote. Hence the will demands of the intellect an assertion of these things' reality — an act of belief in them. And for these reasons. First, he who hopes for heaven must be assured that, while he makes an act *above* his nature, he is not acting foolishly and *against* nature. The act of faith is assurance of the reasonableness of his hope. Second, the will commands the adherence of the intellect precisely because in that adherence man's su-

---

[8] 1 Jn. 3:2.

preme good consists; not of course as it will exist in the glory of the vision, but as best it can now, in promise and in germ. For the act of faith is the obscure but real beginning of our union with God as He is. Here is mystery but not contradiction. Contradiction is the assertion of the unreal and impossible. Mystery is the adumbration of the real which is too big to fit in human minds.

In examining the motive which induces the intellect to obey and accept as true something it does not see, remember that the will cannot make us believe unless the intellect sees the reasonableness of assenting. However much we may want to, we cannot believe in that which is clearly non-existent. What is believed must be the truth or at least have the appearance of truth. Materialism says that the unseen things of God cannot be true because they cannot exist. Agnosticism says they may bear some appearance of truth but one cannot get at their reality. Truth is reality manifest: what cannot be manifested cannot be known; what cannot be known is nothing. How can that which does not manifest itself be real and knowable?

This is the perennial objection of the arrogant mind which imagines that the human mind is the measure of all reality, that whatever does not fall within its compass simply cannot be. The unseen, however, can be manifest in a fashion and therefore be real and true. How? If we ourselves cannot see something its reality may nevertheless be conveyed to us by one who does see it. If we can trust the accuracy and veracity of his report, then his testimony becomes our reason for accepting it. The unseen things of God do not manifest themselves to us by their own evidence, but God, to whom they are always present, tells us of them. In His report is their evidence and reality because He is the First Truth who can neither deceive nor be deceived.

Assuredly, the inquiring intellect by a laborious but natural process of reasoning can form the certain conclusion that God has spoken. The assent of faith, however, is neither elicited by, nor founded upon, such natural reasons. These serve as a ladder which brings the human intellect into contact with the word of God. But once contact is made, the ladder can be thrust away, and the intellect, assisted by the special help of God, can assent for the sole reason that God has spoken. In the presence of God's word the believing mind leaps away from reason's support, out blindly into the dark, not to fall in confused ruin as the materialists say, but to find itself sustained by the First Truth. It is really a leap into God's proper light which to our dull mortal minds is darkness. Here again is mystery without contradiction.

In the act of faith, then, it is God Himself who directly moves both intellect and will. As the Supreme Good in which alone the created will can rest He allures the will As the First Truth He induces the assent of the intellect.

Materialism reduces man to an animal whose knowledge ranges only as far as the hand can reach or the eye see. By contracting being to within the sights of a microscope or telescope, it expunges Infinite Being from the realm of the real. While unbelief contracts, faith expands by making man fellow to the Infinite, affording him access to the area of reality which has no horizons, and giving him the freedom of the region where Divinity dwells.

THE OBJECT OF FAITH

The object of belief is God as He is in Himself and whatever He has thought fit to reveal that man may attain the beatific vision.

Man's instruction in divine things — the most important in the universe — has been provided by Him, "who at sundry times and in diverse manners spoke in times past to the fathers by the prophets, last of all in these days has spoken to us by his Son."[9] Of old the prophet prayed: "O that thou wouldst rend the heavens and come down!"[10] The heavens were rent and the Word of God was made flesh. The God-Man appeared as the great spokesman of divinity, the Prophet who illumines every man that comes into this world. He said to Pilate: "For this cause came I into the world that I should give testimony to the truth. Every one that is of the truth, heareth my voice."[11] Since some will never accept the unseen, He is a sign of contradiction set for the rise and

---

[9] Hebr. 1:1–2.
[10] Isa. 64:1.
[11] Jn. 18:37.

fall of many; acceptance of His revelation is the first requirement for life eternal. "Amen, amen, I say unto you, that he
that heareth my word, and believeth him that sent me, hath
everlasting life; and cometh not into judgment, but is passed
from death to life."[12] For "what," asks St. Hilary, "is more
dangerous for the world than rejection of Christ?"[13] No one
will live the life of God in glory who has not begun to live
that life now in faith.

The God-Man invites all to partake of His doctrine which
He aptly describes by the metaphors of light and water. "I
am come a light into the world; that whosoever believeth in
me, may not remain in darkness. . . . Yet a little while the
light is among you. Walk whilst you have the light, that
the darkness overtake you not. . . . Whilst you have the
light, believe in the light that you may be the children of
light."[14] Reference to simple familiar things gives us some
notion of the unknown and mysterious. Ignorance is darkness and what dispels darkness is light, blessed light. How
lost in darkness is the mind of man with regard to divine
things until God speaks! The revealing word is truly a light
shining in a dark place until the daystar arise in our hearts.[15]
Without the revealing word men sit in the shadow of death.
They who oppose the revealed word are the powers of
darkness.

In the semi-arid Orient on the edge of the desert where
Jesus spoke, water is the life-bearer; for all men its absence
spells death. So truth is the water of the mind. Teresa of
Ávila compares the instruction of the soul to the watering
of a garden. Pius XII prays the Mother of God: "O crystal
fountain of Faith, bathe our minds with the eternal truths!"
Jesus told the Samaritan woman: "He that shall drink of the
water which I will give him shall not thirst forever: but
the water that I will give him shall become in him a fountain of water, springing up into life everlasting."[16] The mind
thirsts for reality manifest and only divine truth will quench

12 Jn. 5:24.
13 *Comment. in Matt.*, c. 18, 2; *PL* 9, 1019.
14 Jn. 12:46, 35–36.
15 Cf. 2 Pet. 1:19.
16 Jn. 4:13–14.

this longing because it alone is full and enduring reality. Without the water of divine truth the soul is frustrate and wastes away without hope of a happy eternity; with it, the soul is the garden whose fountain never runs dry.

On the last day of the festivity Jesus stood and cried: "If any man thirst, let him come to me and drink. He that believeth in me, as the scriptures say, Out of his bosom shall flow rivers of living water."[17] It is difficult to sound the full depths of this promise. The least that is offered is that the believing mind shall drink and be nourished by the rivers of living water. What does this living water contain?

First, the simple homely truths necessary for daily living which man will come to ignore unless he be reminded by God: trust in Divine Providence, love of God above all things, forgiveness of injuries, reverence for womanhood and childhood, the fellowship of man transcending the bounds of nation and class, the need of humility and self-denial, the obligation of ministering to human needs, the subordination of all earthly concerns to the one end of life. Jesus, the Way and the Truth, indicated in language which the rude and ignorant could understand how every man should live in order to arrive at life eternal. In the Gospel He etched in simple words the grandeur of human conduct.

Men of good will might discover these high precepts of conduct for themselves. The rivers of living water, however, contain not only human but divine truths, glimpses of reality utterly beyond the reach of all finite minds. For to the believing mind is revealed "the wisdom of God in a mystery, a wisdom which was hidden, which God ordained before the world, unto our glory: which none of the princes of this world knew . . . But to us God hath revealed them, by his Spirit. For the Spirit searcheth all things, yea, the deep things of God."[18] Here are the proper objects of faith — little insights into the mysterious triune life of God.

These truths, moral and dogmatic, are entrusted for preservation and diffusion to the infallible teaching of the Catholic Church. Apart from her there are no wellsprings of divine

---

[17] Jn. 7:37–38.
[18] 1 Cor. 2:7–10.

truth; only broken cisterns and ditches of muddied water.

The little boy is soon taught that he must believe and adhere to what the Church teaches him; otherwise he cannot please God. For these truths are the foundation of salvation. How docilely he receives the teaching, unaware, however, that it is not merely a priest or religious woman who is instructing him. Only when he is older and has penetrated further into the hidden things of God will he know that his teacher is also the Holy Ghost. That he accept the teachings of the Church with an assent worthy of eternal life, it is not enough for him to be convinced of their divine authorship; he must learn them also from God. Here is a truth to which some Catholics seldom advert; yet "the things that are of God no man knoweth but the Spirit of God. Now we have received the spirit not of this world but the spirit that is of God, that we may know the things that are given us from God."[19] Christ Himself promised this instruction: "The Holy Ghost, whom the Father will send in my name, he will teach you all things, and bring to your minds, whatever I have said to you."[20] The promise is given not merely to the Mystical Body as a whole but also to each of His little ones, the members of His Body. The little boy acquired a right to this instruction when he was incorporated into the Body at baptism, when the charity of God was poured into his heart by the Holy Ghost who was given him.[21] In due time the Spirit of God assures him that it is the heavenly Father whom he believes. The same Divine Spirit testifies to his spirit that he is a son of God and it is only in the Spirit that he can cry Abba, "Father."[22] "For the God, who commanded light to shine out of darkness, has shone in our hearts, to give enlightenment concerning the knowledge of the glory of God."[23]

The reverse is true of unbelief: the light of God has been repelled. St. Paul says in awe: "If our gospel also is hid, it is hid only to those who are perishing. In their case the

---

[19] 1 Cor. 2:11–12.
[20] Jn. 14:26.
[21] Cf. Rom. 5:5.
[22] Cf. Rom. 8:15.
[23] 2 Cor. 4:6.

god of this world has blinded their unbelieving minds, that they should not see the light of the gospel."[24] Divine light humbly received in the believing mind and human darkness proudly clung to by the unbelieving mind are the seeds of the General Judgment when the human race will be irrevocably cleft in twain, into the just and the unjust. The line of demarcation is even now apparent: the unjust accept only what is seen and temporal, but the just "look not at the things that are seen but at the things that are not seen. For the things that are seen are temporal, but the things that are not seen are eternal."[25]

Taught of God and docile to the promptings of the Spirit, the boy grows up and as a young man serenely walks the way of salvation heeding the advice of the Apostle: "As the anointing [of the Spirit] teaches you concerning all things, and is true and is no lie, even as it has taught you, abide in him."[26] By abiding in Him he little by little enters the narrow way which leads to Christian perfection. The youth is fortunate. He never had, as St. Augustine and so many have had, the problem of recognizing and crossing the line between the visible and the invisible. As a lisping child he distinguished one from the other. His problem now is this: how shall he so completely master visible things and subordinate them to the invisible things of God as to attain the plenitude of their promises, not merely in the next life but *now?* This is faith's most difficult undertaking.

He has come to this point of his mortal journey through faith quickened by charity. He will continue with success accordingly as he keeps in mind that the signposts along the new way are written also in symbols of faith. If ever he thinks he is in a psychic world whose laws are not the laws of faith, he will go astray. To answer his new problems he must keep going to the Gospel. Should he ever, relying on past experiences and natural powers, imagine he can be his own guide, he will be mistaken. The more he advances along the way of perfection, the more he will realize that the wayfarer walks by faith and not by sight, that the dark-

---

[24] 2 Cor. 4:3–4.
[25] 2 Cor. 4:18.
[26] 1 Jn. 2:27.

ness which is faith does not recede but grows apace, that
the only way to tread the darkness is with his hand blindly
clasped in the hand of a God he never sees.

There is danger that his clasp of that hand may relax with
the passing years. Even in so high a venture familiarity may
breed, if not contempt, certainly carelessness. One may grow
so accustomed to the truths of faith that they cease to have
their proper impact. One can grow weary of listening to
spiritual exhortations and reading ascetical books. One may,
without being fully aware of what is happening, allow
worldly maxims, half true and half false, to mingle in his
mind with the counsels of the Gospel. Should then the
aspirant wonder if he is drifting or losing headway, let him
examine his beginnings and inquire how he stands with regard to faith. Have his powers of faith expanded in proportion to the time he has put in and the distance he had hoped
to traverse? For faith, like any faculty, sharpens with use
and dulls with disuse. Faith is just as much the foundation
of the spiritual life and perfection as it is of salvation. All
supernatural results in the soul of man are wrought through
faith.

THE INCREASE OF FAITH

The working of supernatural effects through faith and the
proper attitude of the man of good will with regard to faith
are set forth by St. Mark in the story of the possessed boy.

When the disciples of Jesus are unable to cure the boy
possessed by a dumb spirit, the father pleads his case before
Jesus who makes this strange reply: "O unbelieving generation, how long shall I bear with you? How long shall I put
up with you? Bring him unto me."[27] When the boy is brought
the evil spirit casts him into convulsions and the father says
this has been happening to him since infancy. "But if thou
canst do anything, have compassion on us and help us." Jesus
replies: "If thou canst believe, all things are possible to him
who believes." And the father cries out: "I do believe; help
my unbelief." Here it is. The power of faith is expressed by
Jesus: "All things are possible to him who believes"; and

---

[27] Mk. 9:18.

the attitude of good men is summed up in the humble admission of the father: "I believe; help my unbelief."

All things are possible to him who believes. Jesus says: If you can believe, I will mercifully help you because genuine faith deserves to obtain everything which it asks for salvation.[28] The cure of the boy is a help to the father's salvation: Jesus cures the boy both because the father has some faith and because He wishes to stimulate in him more faith unto salvation. Can faith then do all things? Certainly the seemingly impossible is done for the implanting of faith and the impossible springs from faith.

To see the power of faith, let us distinguish between faith, the virtue given a man for his own supernatural good, and the charism of faith, given a few for the benefit of others. The charism is distinct from the virtue and adds to it a certain confidence of having even its impossible requests granted when the glory of God is at issue. This, the faith which moves mountains, is explained by our Lord Himself. For when the disciples asked Him why they could not cure the boy, He said: "Because of your little faith; for amen, I say unto you, if you have faith like a mustard seed, you will say to this mountain, 'Remove from here,' and it will remove."[29] The charism works miracles to build up the faith among unbelievers.

These miracles, however, bear no comparison to the wonders produced in the soul by the virtue. It is said that Gregory the Wonder-Worker made a mountain move into the sea. If that be true, it was a trifle in comparison with the effects wrought in the soul of the Good Thief by his acceptance of faith. Unless he had believed, Christ could not have said to him: "This day thou shalt be with me in paradise."[30] Not only can nothing worthy of eternal life spring from a soul destitute of faith but all the wonders of charity and union which God produces in the soul are proportioned to the depths of faith and the continuing petition of faith.

Sanctity is a noble tree whose health and beauty are

---

[28] Cf. Venerable Bede, *In Marci Evangelium Expositio,* III, 8; PL 92, 222.

[29] Mt. 17:19.

[30] Lk. 23:43.

measured by the condition of its roots, and its roots are
faith supplying it with the nourishment of divine truth. The
charity of Francis of Assisi, rewarded by the stigmata, did
not outrun his faith. With what vividness and constancy
then do we live in the unseen world of faith? Our union
with God depends finally upon charity but basically upon the
height and depth of our faith. Whatever is possible in the
realm of sanctity — and by divine promise all things are
possible — will be achieved through the medium of faith.

Is such great faith possible? At the thought of power so
divine everyone must admit his insufficiency and confess
with the father of the possessed boy: *I believe; help my unbelief.* We are all like him. Venerable Bede includes us when
he says: "At one and the same time he who had not as
yet perfectly believed both believed and was unbelieving."[31]

Yet perfect faith is possible. We must look for it from
God, admitting that we can no more advance in faith by
our natural power than we can make the first act of belief.
The beginning, increase, and glorious climax of faith ever
requires the grace of God. It is not enough to say that "by
grace you are saved through faith, and that not of yourselves
. . . that no man may glory . . . for it is the gift of God."[32]
Only the God who began in us this noble work will bring
it to perfection for "the God of all grace, who hath called us
unto his eternal glory . . . will himself perfect you, and con-
firm you, and establish you."[33] Indeed when the soul comes
to the upper reaches of faith and sanctity, the initiative of
its advance passes to the Holy Spirit. Although it does not
become inactive, it finds itself, as it were, carried in the arms
of the Spirit.

Growth in faith, as in any virtue, requires our co-operation.
The first thing demanded of us is prayer. Let us pray with
the Apostles: "Increase our faith."[34] Since we can never have
too much faith our prayer should be unremitting. It must
also be full of confidence for "you shall ask whatever you

---

[31] Venerable Bede, *op. cit.*, III, 8; *PL* 92, 222.
[32] Eph. 2:8–9.
[33] 1 Pet. 5:10.
[34] Lk. 17:5.

will, and it shall be done unto you."[35] Fulfillment, however, of the request for faith depends on how much we humble ourselves. For Jesus said: "I praise thee, Father, Lord of heaven and earth, that thou didst hide these things from the wise and prudent, and didst reveal them to little ones."[36] Jesus is here approving no arbitrary choice but the very nature of things. For the mysteries of God are fit only for them who are little in their own esteem. Since they are not filled with self and worldly wisdom, they have room for the lofty things.

How shall we become a little one to whom divine secrets may be revealed? What is necessary is not mere ignorance or lowly station but, first, a life already based on faith. "For he called them little ones," says St. Hilary, "who believe through the faith of hearing."[37] Our sincere humble petition for enlightenment will show we are convinced of our supernatural helplessness. To be apt pupils of the Holy Ghost we need simplicity and docility of mind. Simplicity is the single-mindedness which sets knowledge of divine things above all human learning. Learning follows interest and liking. Some teen-age boys have a marvelous acquaintance with the mechanics of an automobile. Girls of all ages have a knowledge of clothes, materials, styles, and the like which a male expects only in a department-store buyer. Only the lover wishes to know all about the beloved. So also, only they hunger to know the hidden things of God who love Him very much. For where the treasure is, there also is heart and interest.

Faith increases in extent and in intensity. It increases in extent when we learn more about the deposit of faith. Here is an inexhaustible treasure, and theology, in some form, is a pursuit which one should never put aside. It is for all, lay and cleric, learned and unlearned. It is rewarding and consoling. It keeps pace with our development in years and grace. Loose ends of knowledge are brought together; questions asked long ago and forgotten are answered; the golden

---

[35] Jn. 15:7.
[36] Lk. 10:21.
[37] *Comment. in Matt.*, XVIII, 1; *PL* 9, 1018.

threads which run through the whole pattern of revelation
are traceable; the unity of revelation takes shape for us.

Faith, however, is not any kind of knowledge nor is its
increase the result of mere study. A scriptural critic may
have at his finger tips all the sayings of Jesus, a scholar may
have thoroughly mastered the *Summa Theologica* of St.
Thomas, and neither of them have a scintilla of faith. They
may indeed pass from a state of unbelief to one of natural
conviction of the truth of our Lord's mission and of the
teaching office of the Church without any inclination to submit to the word of God and say, "I believe." For without the
grace of the Holy Spirit, freely accepted, no one can have
that special and interior knowledge which is faith. Faith is
a prayerful knowledge of the whole man proceeding from both
heart and mind and acquired in submission. The easy practical way of growing in it is by loving meditation upon the
official prayers of the Church; for the formulae of the sacraments, the hymns of the divine office, the contents of the
missal are teaching addressed to the heart, dogmatic utterances of the Church praying. This, however, is supplementary
to reading the Gospels with loving care, pondering the inci-
dents of Christ's life, penetrating the meaning of His sayings,
resolving to imitate His example. We must do as Mary did.
After the visit of the shepherds to Bethlehem, "Mary kept
all these words, pondering them in her heart."[38] After the
three days' loss "his mother kept all these words in her
heart."[39] Her long and loving reflection on these mysteries
shows us, first, that the mind alone is quite useless; one must
use both heart and mind to grow in faith. Second, it is only
little by little that the Light which is Eternal Truth is ac-
commodated to the dark confines of the human spirit.

We can believe with greater intensity when, first, we adhere to the faith with greater force of emotion. This may
be the result of personal experiences which impress on us
the value of this or that doctrine or of living in a place where
the faith is bitterly assailed. Increase of intensity, however,
more properly refers to a deeper penetration of the meaning

[38] Lk. 2:19.
[39] Lk. 2:51.

of revealed doctrines on the part of the intellect and a more loving savor of them on the part of the will. To achieve this deeper penetration we are given the gift of understanding. St. Thomas says: "Man needs a supernatural light in order to penetrate yet farther so as to know what it cannot know by its natural light: and this supernatural light is called the gift of understanding which denotes a certain excellence of knowledge which penetrates into the heart of things."[40]

Understanding operates, first, by separating the wheat from the chaff, by purging our faith, by rejecting, for the pure unadulterated truth of God, that which we had imagined to be faith. Let us not be surprised that commingling with our acts of faith are things like natural reasonings, imagination, emotional promptings, worldly maxims, even superstitions. Since it can safely be said of the natural knowledge of most of us that "he knows a lot of things which are not so," we ought not to be chagrined that the same lament can be made about our faith. If then we would know the true nature of divine faith and carefully distinguish it from the confused elements with which it is often entangled in men's souls, we should study it in a perfect specimen, in the life of a great saint. There we see how great a purification was necessary before faith could reign supreme and unchallenged. It should be carefully noted, however, that the purification of a saint includes not merely his doing but his knowing. Not only must his senses be tamed and emotion submitted to reason, but his faculty of reason must be utterly rectified and aligned with divine truth. This is the most difficult part of his purification. Mental fixations and prejudices are deeply ingrained and when one is stripped of them he finds himself cold and naked in a strange world. But in the faith of a saint there can be no flaw.

Many good people, unfortunately, do not realize the importance of the mind's total submission to the word of God. They do not fully appreciate that, since will must follow intellect, their conduct will not be wholly pleasing to God until their faith is cleansed of its flaws. They are either unaware of the flaws or they cling to small errors which have

---

[40] Sum. Theol., II–II, 8, 1.

become so ingrained as to be a kind of second nature, and they say that nothing can be done to eradicate them. True, no ordinary effort will touch them; only the deepest and most far-reaching purgation.

St. Thomas explains purgation of faith when he connects the beatitude, "Blessed are the clean of heart," with the gift of understanding: "The sixth work of the Holy Ghost which is understanding is applicable to the clean of heart, they, whose eye being purified, can see what eye hath not seen. . . . The cleanness is twofold. One is a preamble and disposition for seeing God and consists in the heart being purified of inordinate affections. . . . The other cleanness of heart is a kind of complement to the sight of God. Such is the cleanness of mind which is purged of errors and phantasms so as to receive the truths which are proposed to it about God, no longer by way of corporeal phantasms, nor infected with heretical misrepresentations: and this cleanness is the result of the gift of understanding."[41]

The principles of an art are often learned in the exercise of the art. This is eminently true of the art of human living. The aspirant for perfection attains purity of faith by doing the truth in charity. Just as we acquire knowledge of the moral virtues by subduing passion and acting justly and temperately, so we grow in faith and shed erroneous notions by living the precepts and counsels of the Gospel. We are all inclined to believe in what we do. Actual conduct tends to become its own justification and the norm of future conduct. "For every one that doth evil hateth the light, and cometh not to the light, that his works may not be reproved. But he that doth the truth, cometh to the light, that his works may be made manifest, that they are done in God."[42] Faith and charity must go hand in hand. Doing the truth in charity leads to perfection of faith. Perfection of faith assures consummate charity in action. Therefore the goal toward which the saint daily strives is that his every act be illumined by pure faith and motivated by the love of God.

It is, however, the part of practical wisdom for the soul

---

[41] *Sum. Theol.*, II–II, 8, 7.
[42] Jn. 3:20–21.

ambitioning sanctity that he humbly seek more faith in his
intellect before expecting the perfection of charity in his
conduct. Perfect charity is the crown of a Christian's work
but the crown will not sit well upon an insecure foundation.
We must ever await the action of God upon our souls and
it is more likely that He will purify our thinking before He
perfects our conduct.

Taking as a text the words of St. Peter, "Purifying their
hearts by faith," St. Thomas profoundly remarks: "The impurity of a thing consists in its being mixed with baser
things. . . . Since man is more excellent than transient and
corporeal things, he becomes impure by subjecting himself
to transient things through love of them. He is cleansed
from this impurity by the contrary movement of tending to
that which is above him — God. The first beginning of this
movement is faith; and if this be perfected by being quickened by charity, the heart will be perfectly purified thereby."[43]

Out of the bosom of him whose heart is purified shall flow
a river of living water. It is a pure crystal stream unmuddied
by misleading phantasm or taint of error. The snares and
deceits of life are evaluated. The big puzzles are ended.
Things visible and invisible have fallen into their rightful
places. For him the heavens have been rent and there has
come the day of messianic plenty when "the mountains shall
drop down sweetness, and the hills shall flow with milk, and
water shall flow through all the rivers of Juda."[44] How many
saints, like Ignatius, have declared that if all Scripture disappeared they would still be fully cognizant of God's revelation from what they learned from God Himself.

Is this abundance a personal treasure? It is clear in many
cases that God gives it that it may be shared. The great
teachers and doctors were purified and illumined precisely
that they might enrich the whole Church with their doctrine.
Augustine thought there was no other reason for the river
of living water. He says: "He who drinks will have a fountain:
he will even be the fountain. What is the fountain and what
is the river which flows from the bosom of the interior man?

---

[43] *Sum. Theol.*, II–II, 7, 2.
[44] Joel 3:18.

Good will, whereby one wishes to profit the neighbor. For if he thinks that what he drinks should be for himself alone, no living water flows from him. If however he hastens to help the neighbor, the flow of his stream never runs dry."[45] For them, however, whose ability or opportunity of self-expression is negligible or nonexistent, this divine abundance can only be a personal treasure.

The river of living water has its happy issue; for faith, purified by understanding, terminates in that fruit of the Holy Ghost called *faith* — certitude about the unseen. Now the fruits of the Spirit are so called because they are something ultimate and delightful produced in us by the operation of the Holy Ghost. Since the act of faith proceeds from the intellect at the command of the will, there is one fruit in the intellect and another in the will. The fruit in the intellect is unswerving certitude about the things of God. First is the virtue or the power to believe in God. The virtue is perfected by the gift of understanding and the perfection of understanding ripens into the certainty of faith. And in whom is the certitude of faith more conspicuous than in the poor of this world who are rich in faith?[46] The fruit in the will is joy for "you shall draw waters with joy out of the Saviour's fountains."[47] Even faith which is not purified is a source of great comfort in tribulation, especially in the presence of death. The bereaved Christian does not mourn as those who have no hope. Supported by his faith he looks on death as sleep in Jesus until the resurrection. Joy is a genuine mark of Christianity. The England which was Mary's dower was also Merrie England!

But what is the joy which flows from faith purified! The Psalmist revels in the theme: "Thou hast made known to me the ways of life, thou shalt fill me with joy with thy countenance, at thy right hand are delights even to the end."[48] Isaias cries: "I will rejoice greatly in the Lord, and my soul shall be joyful in my God. For he hath clothed me with the garments of salvation, and with the robe of justice he

---

[45] *In Joannis Evangelium Tract.* XXXII, Cap. VII, 4; *PL* 35, 1643.
[46] Cf. James 2:5.
[47] Isa. 12:3.
[48] Ps. 15:11.

hath covered me, as a bridegroom decked with a crown, and a bride adorned with her jewels."[49] Here are the authentic grounds of joy in this life, the garment of salvation and the robe of justice. It remained, however, for St. Peter to describe the joy of Christian faith: "[You], by the power of God, are kept by faith unto salvation . . . wherein you shall greatly rejoice, if now you must be for a little while made sorrowful in divers temptations: that the trial of your faith may be found unto praise and glory and honor at the appearing of Jesus Christ. Whom not having seen, you love; in whom also now, though you see him not, you believe; and believing shall rejoice with joy unspeakable and glorified."[50]

[49] Isa. 61:10.
[50] 1 Pet. 1:5–8.

2. Time

"Now is the acceptable time" (2 Cor. 6:2).

THE person who makes a New Year's resolution is not necessarily a victim of the mass suggestion which newspapers foster in the same way that they keep alive the faintly superstitious connotation of St. Swithin's Day or Ground-Hog Day. By a salutary instinct a person often makes a New Year's resolution because a particular New Year has become for him a great reminder. Usually time steals by unnoticed on noiseless feet but occasionally it is like the overweary reveler who, stealing up to bed on tiptoe, steps upon a noisy stairway tread and we sit up in bed and say, "Who's that?" Some trifle, like the hanging of a new calendar or the erasure of the wrong date from a letter written in early January, may remind us with unusual force that another year has come and gone, and the thought of that departed year may vividly cast our life before us, and make us ask if we are making the wisest use of it.

The coming of a new year recalls to us the mystery of time. But time is no mystery, says the philosopher smugly. Time is the measure of accidental motion. Ah, but every other man says it is a mystery. It is nothing you can lay hold of, for what substance have minutes, hours, and years? Yet Pindar[1] calls time sire of all things. Time is here and it is not here. The English poet[2] asks:

> Time goes, you say? Ah no!
> Alas, Time stays; we go.

---

[1] *Olympian Odes*, 2, 31.

[2] Henry Austin Dobson, *The Paradox of Time. The Complete Poetical Works of Austin Dobson* (Oxford University Press, 1923), p. 116.

But Horace said: "Even while we are speaking, envious time will have fled."[3] Time is the cormorant devouring all beauty, yet time is the beautifier of the dead.[4] The slowest poison is time, yet time heals all. Time will not abide, yet time will run back and fetch the age of gold. What a foolish thing is time, said Swift,[5] yet time is the great corrector, the rider who breaks in youth.

We shall understand this paradox better when we know more of the greater paradox which is ourselves. It is not time which flies: it is we who run through the joyous hour. It is not time which creeps: it is boredom which holds us prisoner. It is not the times which are bad, but men. What is time? Time is the witness of the mystery which is me. I am nothing and without warning I become something. I suddenly emerge from eternity and into time. I waver for a moment in time and I lapse back into eternity. Time is the recorder of my birth and my death, the surveyor of the little space that lies between. My moments are few indeed. They say that falling stars are meteorites, bodies whirling through space, which for a moment or two rush into the igneous warmth of our solar system and are thereby lighted up and made visible. In the very moment of their illumination they speed beyond that influence and their light is quenched with their passing. Of similar duration is my appearance in time. Scripture says that our days have passed more swiftly than the web is cut by the weaver.[6] Our days have passed as an eagle flying to its prey.[7] Our life is but wind[8] and our days a shadow. A tiny segment of time is broken off and given to me — an infinitesimal parenthesis in eternity. It is only a breath, a candle flame, a flash across the sky. Thoughtful men will pause to look at it and ask themselves what is the meaning of this thing.

Alas, more and more men are convincing themselves that

---

[3] *Odes*, 1, 11, 7.

[4] Byron, *Childe Harold*, Canto 4, stanza 130.

[5] Jonathan Swift, *To Miss Vanhomrigh* (Vanessa), August 7, 1722; see *The Works of Jonathan Swift*, ed. Thomas Roscoe (New York: Derby and Jackson, 1859), Vol. VI, p. 349.

[6] Job 7:6.

[7] Job 9:26.

[8] Job 7:7.

this brief candle flame is the whole of human existence. Time is all: eternity is only a fiction to gull the believer and frighten the superstitious. When death beats out the last spark, all is over, completely over. Therefore man, who was made for happiness, must grasp it now, quickly, unerringly, rudely, if necessary, for if he misses it now, he has missed it forever. Time is the season for happiness. Gather ye rosebuds while ye may. Whatever will make you happy, seize it before death seizes you. "Time is money," said Benjamin Franklin,[9] and Protestant America has been re-echoing that statement ever after him. Your happiness is commensurate with having money, so the success of your time is measured by the size of your bank account. Happiness is love which changes with the changing lover. Happiness is eating and drinking. So let us fill up our time with eating and drinking and carnal love. Happiness is power. So let us, by bluster or ability, by guile or merit, by favor or industry, win power. We shall be happy if we are looked up to, feared, flattered; if our opinions are sought and our wishes anticipated; if we associate with the great of the land and our picture often appears in print; if hundreds, thousands, millions depend on us for their mite of happiness.

This is an ancient view of time. Long ago, the Book of Wisdom described it. "The time of our life is short and tedious . . . For we are born of nothing, and after this we shall be as if we had not been; for the breath in our nostrils is smoke. . . . Which being put out our body shall be ashes, and our spirit shall be poured abroad as soft air, and our life shall pass away as the trace of a cloud, and shall be dispersed as a mist. . . . And our name in time shall be forgotten, and no man shall have any remembrance of our works. For our time is as the passing of a shadow, and our end has no return: for it is fast sealed and no man returneth. Come, therefore, and let us enjoy the good things which are present, and let us speedily use the creatures as in youth. Let us fill ourselves with costly wine, and ointments: and let not the flower of spring pass us by. Let us crown ourselves with roses, before they be withered: let no meadow

---

[9] *Advice to a Young Tradesman*, 1748.

escape our riot. Let none of us go without his part in luxury: let us everywhere leave tokens of joy: for this is our portion and this is our lot."[10]

The same Book of Wisdom goes on to declare how false this view is. "We have erred from the way of truth, and the light of justice hath not shined upon us, and the sun hath not risen upon us. We wearied ourselves in the way of iniquity and destruction, and have walked through hard ways, but the way of the Lord we have not known. What hath pride profited us? or what advantages hath boasting of riches brought us? All these things are passed away like a shadow . . . as a ship that passeth through the waves: whereof when it is gone by, no trace can be found. Or as when a bird flieth through the air, of the passage of which no mark can be found, but only the sound of the wings beating the light air. So we also being born, forthwith ceased to be: and have been able to shew no mark of virtue: but we are consumed in our wickedness."[11]

What is time? It cannot be the whole of existence. It is only a tiny fragment of our total living, but it is the most important part because it is the decisive part. This fragment is put at our complete disposal and upon our wise or unwise use of it depends our spending of eternity. It is the brief market hour wherein we are to trade with the Master's substance until He return for us. It is our chance to buy the pearl of great price or to squander the coin of eternity upon some creature, some love, our own sweet will. It is that crucial game of winner-take-all in which all men must play, the one game that can never end in a tie.

Time is testing for eternity. God tries man. He slacks the reins and gives him his head. What will he do with this freedom? Will he use it to kick over the traces or to find the narrow road that leads to life? Like the meteorite, he whirls through time and in his passage he must become illumined by the very light of God and marked by the mark of God. As he whirls out of time, he must bear upon him the stamp of the Most Blessed Trinity or he will wander through the

[10] Wisd. 2:1-9.
[11] Wisd. 5:6-14.

endless void forever. God puts time into his hands, a period of duration between birth and death — which in reality is the opportunity to make so many choices. Upon the number and quality of those human acts is determined a man's activity for eternity. The whole of his eternity depends on time. Time buys eternity. What a responsibility to lay on feckless men whose minds are darkened to the truth and whose choice is so prone to evil! Left to himself, no man could make the proper choice, but God makes it with him.

All men's names are inscribed on the roll of the divine Schoolmaster. But some of the pupils are truant and never come to His school. Some come to class, but are noisy and distracted and never hear the lesson. Some hear the lesson, but pay little heed to it and fail the great examination. Some are the honor students, they who are eager to be taught of God. Since they master well the essential lessons of the relation of time to eternity, little by little they learn more profound lessons which the less wise never have time to hear. They penetrate beneath the exhortation to work out one's salvation and they find the sweet invitation to perfection. As we lift off one by one, the petals of a rose and lay bare its fragrant interior, so they, under the guidance of the Holy Ghost, pierce the surface of the Gospel teaching and find there the fuller secret of time. The secret is this. Man is not a slave but a son.[12] As a son, he ought not to be a land-grubbing peasant or a hired workman, but an artist, a sculptor, and his task in time is to achieve a mighty masterpiece.

The Great Master, the Infinite Creator, makes upon crude, unformed substance the rough outlines yet a true image of His own Son, and then hands the tools to the honor pupil, and bids him finish the work and, with the divine assistance, execute a "memorial more enduring than bronze."[13] The crude substance is the pupil's own soul and the tools are the instruments of perfection. The tools are well constructed. None are missing. They are all in proper place: prayer, self-denial, the sacraments, the teaching and laws of the

---

[12] Cf. Gal. 4:7.
[13] Horace, *Odes*, 3, 30, 1.

Church. Each tool can be put to instant use, powered with the current of divine grace. For the honor pupil, then, every human act of every day ought to be a stroke upon the masterpiece, a cutting or a polishing, a refining of the divine image in his soul. To this St. Paul exhorts him: "All whatsoever you do in word or work, do all in the name of the Lord Jesus Christ."[14] Whatever act retards the great work or blurs the image is a lost act; whatever act does not develop the image is a wasted act. What, then, is time? Time is the golden opportunity which comes but once to every man to remake his soul in the image of Jesus Christ.

What sort of masterpiece are the honor pupils producing? When the Master returns, what kind of reproduction of His Son will He find in the souls of His chosen ones? Are they making intelligent use of their opportunities? Are they more single-minded, more energetic in the pursuit of their one professed aim than are unbelievers in seeking what they think will satisfy them? Do the children of darkness show more shrewdness and diligence in their pursuit of money, pleasure, and power than do the children of light in transforming themselves into Jesus Christ?

The tools of perfection are put into a person's hands when he gives himself to loving God with all his heart and dedicates himself to heroic sanctity. In the beginning he is all on fire to use them. Perhaps in his inexperience he uses them injudiciously and cuts himself. He may indulge in extravagant practices which injure health. He may have to endure scruples or discouragement. Difficulties can dampen the strongest ardor. What now is his present attitude? Is he as enthusiastic as ever to employ all the tools of perfection, or do some of them lie rusting on the workbench? From time to time he must stand back to take an unprejudiced look at his masterpiece and appraise his progress on it. How far has he come with it during the past year? If the Master should come tonight and he had to stop work on it forever, what kind of reproduction of Jesus Christ would he be through all eternity?

We can all look back upon the time of our service of God and sigh at the loss of precious days. "Alas for the days that

---

[14] Col. 3:17.

are lost to me, Postume, Postume."[15] The years are slipping
on. Have we been making the most profitable use of them?
The little candle flame will soon be sputtering out. We cannot
go back and remake or better the past: irretrievable time
marches on.[16] Instead of becoming disheartened at past negligence let us remember the remark of St. Paul: "I forget what
is behind, and strain forward to what is before."[17] Suppose
we are not now all that the grace of God might have made
us: suppose we have let slip through our fingers many golden
opportunities. Yet something — even much remains. The
poet reminds us that some deed of noble note may yet be
done.[18] It is not the nearness of death which matters, but the
sincerity and intensity of our desire to use well whatever
time remains. Whether we have a month or a year or forty
years, let us remember that youths like St. Aloysius and St.
Stanislaus accomplished much in a short time. "For venerable
old age is not that of a long time, nor counted by the number
of years; but the understanding of a man is grey hairs and a
spotless life is old age."[19] St. Stanislaus lived in religion less
than two years; at the age of seventeen, when he died, he
had attained consummate sanctity. What may we not hope
for if we are as faithful as he to the inspirations of grace?
We must heed the advice of St. Paul: "See, therefore, brethren
how you walk circumspectly: not as unwise, but as wise,
redeeming the time."[20]

What is it to redeem the time? St. Augustine likens it to
the purchase of necessities. To get food and clothing we give
up money, the price. So we must lose this or that temporal
thing to acquire God, the greatest necessity. The temporal
things thus lost are the price of time and the time so redeemed
becomes our opportunity of getting God. Augustine was quite
disturbed over the loss of time and charity resulting from
lawsuits indulged in by members of his flock.[21] Twice in a
sermon he makes particular application of "redeeming the

---

[15] Horace, *Odes*, 2, 14, 1.
[16] Cf. Vergil, *Georgics*, 3, 284.
[17] Phil. 3:13, Westminster version.
[18] Cf. Tennyson, *Ulysses*.
[19] Wisd. 4:8–9.
[20] Eph. 5:15–16.
[21] Cf. footnote 22; also *Sermo* 16, 2; *PL* 38, 122.

time" to these lawsuits and exhorts his hearers to refrain from them even at the risk of losing what was justly theirs. They should rather use the time, energy, and emotion saved for the improvement of their souls. When some of the congregation laughed at the simplicity of so Christian a suggestion, he sadly but sternly concludes: "Laugh, laugh and deride: I may be only entreating but there will come One who will demand."[22]

How, then, does a man redeem his time? By surrendering the person, thing, place, or advantage which is keeping him from his opportunity of getting what God wishes him to have. For a long time the Emperor Charles V weighed the cares and glory of his royal life against his chance of having God; finally, in 1558, he gave up the rule of half the civilized world to retire to the monastery of Yuste to make his soul. Christian soldiers and busy men of affairs have imitated his example. They beheld the shadow which death casts before and they began intensive preparations against its coming. Death impressed them with the value of time. Death is a wise counselor but no Christian need fear it. Nor is it always possible, or even necessary, to enter a monastery in order to make one's soul. Without changing residence or occupation, any man can do it through the grace offered him. This grace can make him vividly aware of how precious is the time God has left to him and suggest the means of redeeming it. Men think of time as composed of past, present, and future. Any man of good will can begin at once to do that which will heal the past, sanctify the present, and secure, as best he may, the future.

To heal the past, a person must destroy sin in himself, because unforgiven and unexpiated sin is the only thing which will keep him from God. For the destruction of sin, he requires, first, sorrow; not merely an *ad hoc* sorrow in the sacrament of penance for the forgiveness of particular sins, but especially an abiding, even a lifelong penitential spirit. Let it not be said that a penitential spirit is necessary only for beginners in the spiritual life. It should accompany one all through life. For no man can ever be sorry enough for his

---

[22] *Sermo* 167, 3; *PL* 38, 911.

iniquities. Continuing regret for the past is a preventative of future falls. What a lesson we can learn from the greatest saints! Holy David said: "Every night I will wash my bed: I will water my couch with my tears,"[23] because "my sin is always before me."[24] St. Peter never ceased to bewail with real tears his denial of the Lord. Such penance, however, does not mean that we keep recalling our sins in detail, for this could excite the imagination and lead to new temptations; but we are never to forget that we are fugitives from hell or purgatory, that it is only the mercy of God which now saves us from the deserved consequences of our sins. This spirit is no obstacle to advancement in the later stages of perfection; a contemplative soul can draw very close to God by perfect acts of sorrow.

The second requirement for the destruction of sin is the wiping out of the debt of temporal punishment incurred by sin. The best method is voluntary satisfaction. Of our own accord, we assume the deeds of penance and spontaneously offer God atonement. Thereby we both satisfy the justice of God and increase our merits. Another means is the use of indulgences. Let us develop this thought at some length by saying something of the history of indulgences.

In the ancient Church, which was still literally "the little flock," Christians, filled with gratitude for the great gift of membership in the Body of Christ, looked with amazement upon one who denied his faith or led an un-Christian life. Such an evildoer was unworthy of the corporate benefits of the Spouse of Christ, and, accordingly, these were denied him. The Church was willing to receive the fallen one again, but only after he had given substantial proof of amendment. Desirous of helping the sinner pay his debts to God, and wishing to impress upon the Christian community a horror of being separated from the Ark of Salvation, she insisted that the sinner who had given public offense should be pub- licly corrected. It was not enough for him to say that he was sorry and to ask for reconciliation; he had to wear a distinc- tive garb and, according to the gravity of his faults, pass

---

[23] Ps. 6:7.
[24] Ps. 50:5.

through various stages of penance. In the lowest grade were the "weepers," who knelt outside the church and asked the prayers of the brethren; next were "the hearers," who were allowed in the vestibule behind the catechumens and were dismissed with the catechumens after the sermon; next were "the kneelers," who were a little farther forward but behind the congregation; finally were "the co-standers," who mingled with the congregation but were excluded from Holy Communion. Ash Wednesday marked the beginning of the solemn performance of penances and on Holy Thursday the penitents, whose dispositions were judged satisfactory by the bishop, were reconciled to the Church.

The disintegration of the Roman Empire in the West saw the passing of the discipline of public penance, but the Irish monks who re-evangelized the continent brought with them a detailed system of penances for use in the administration of the sacrament of Penance. These penances were long and rigorous. *The Penitential of St. Cummean* prescribes a year of penance for stealing, two years for a repetition of the offense.[25] *The Irish Canons* prescribe seven years' penance for idolatrous practices, homicide, and adultery.[26] *The Penitential of Theodore*, Archbishop of Canterbury (668–690), demands five years of penance for divination, twelve years for apostasy, eleven years for sacrilegious perjury.[27] In *The Burgundian Penitential* the penalty for hurtful magical practices is seven years, for breaking and entry seven years, for self-mutilation three years, for failure to receive the Holy Eucharist one year.[28] Doing penance automatically meant strict fasting — usually on bread and water. If rigorous fast was impossible, there were the daily singing or recitation of psalms, going without sleep and keeping vigil, distribution of alms, self-scourging, reverential postures like standing with arms outstretched in the form of a cross, or with hands uplifted in supplication. Exile, long pilgrimages, and entering a monastery were also enjoined.

---

[25] McNeil-Gamer, *Medieval Handbooks of Penance* (New York: Columbia University Press, 1938), p. 105.

[26] *Ibid.*, pp. 118–119.

[27] *Ibid.*, pp. 189, 190, 198.

[28] *Ibid.*, p. 274 ff.

Besides, in a community whose public life was governed by the precepts of the Gospel, the Church acted as the guardian of *public* morals. Not only did popes depose unworthy kings, but by law the bishops kept watch over the morals of their flocks. Upon the occasion of episcopal visitation the bishop or the archdeacon inquired about the prevalence of certain sins. Persons accused of these sins were summoned before the bishop and, if they were guilty, suitable penance was imposed. Laws of fast and abstinence common to all the faithful were much more rigorous then. So for various reasons, a man might have to work off a considerable amount of personal penance.

There was wisdom in such penitential rigor. Men used to violence see nothing unusual in punishing their bodies severely for their sins. Since the faith was operative among these barbarized peoples, few influences were more efficacious than this penitential system in softening their habits. As manners, however, grew more civilized, man began to look for relief from the harshness of the system; and so, a parallel system of indulgences was gradually introduced. In the old Roman law an *indulgentia* was the merciful mitigation of a penalty due. In the days of solemn public penance an *indulgentia* meant that a sinner was restored to communion before he had completed his penance: what remained undone "was indulged to him."

Under the discipline of the penitentials an indulgence came to mean a substitution. Although the penitentials contained standard commutations to be invoked if it was impossible for the priest to demand the usual penance, an indulgence was the remission in whole or in part of penitential exercises already canonically imposed, by substitution of some action not mentioned in the penitential. This action was something extraordinary like a pilgrimage to Rome or Jerusalem. Greatest of all substitutes was taking part in a crusade. The Council of Clermont declared: "Whoever, out of pure devotion and not for the purpose of gaining honor or money, shall go to Jerusalem to liberate the Church of God, let that journey be counted in lieu of all penance." Sometimes indulgences were granted on rare occasions, like the canonization of a saint, the consecration of a church, or the incidence of the centennial jubilee year. In the later Middle Ages the proclamation of an indulgence was often the practical means chosen for building a road or bridge or erecting some socially useful building.

The medieval man was anxious to gain indulgences. Perhaps the ordinary soul desired them as relief from canonical penance, but the more faithful soul appreciated them for what they truly are — a more speedy approach to God. St. Louis of France inserted in his will this fatherly advice to his son and heir, Philip III: "Be eager to gain for thy own profit the indulgences of our holy Mother the Church." When St. Bridget of Sweden was seventy she went to Jerusalem with her daughter St. Catherine. On her first visit to the Holy Sepulcher, it was revealed to her that she and her companions were as completely purified from their sins as if they had been just baptized; furthermore, by their devotion several of them had delivered their parents' souls from purgatory.

Custom demanded of the medieval man many dour acts of penance. The same social pressure to make atonement is not exerted today, but the same fundamental need of satisfying the justice of God exists. The Church has mitigated the severity of fasts, austerities, and canonical penances but she insists all the more, perhaps, upon the efficacy of indulgences as substitution for the pains of purgatory. Since a man must answer for every idle word he cannot but accumulate a debt of punishment, the extent of which is known to God alone. Like a merciful mother, the Church puts at our disposal most copious means of paying that debt. It takes but an instant to make an ejaculation, but, if it is said with a contrite heart, it has as much efficacy to appease the justice of God as had forty or sixty or one hundred days of the old canonical penance. The gaining of indulgences is the prudent way of redeeming the past. Whoever has the faith, the industry, and the proper dispositions to gain enough indulgences will come to his judgment cleansed of the folly of his past.

Zeal for gaining indulgences has a beneficial effect upon one's present actions. It increases laudable concern for the state of one's soul, first, because one must be in the state of grace to gain an indulgence; second, one is inclined to be more careful to avoid whatever may stain the soul again.

A word of caution is necessary. Two extreme attitudes are

to be avoided. On the one hand, we are to esteem indulgences highly, as the Church counsels. It would be a mistake to regard indulgences as a pious but unnecessary bookkeeping of the spirit. They are a means of union with God. When the Church grants an indulgence she exercises her power of binding and loosing on earth and in heaven. Whenever a person exactly fulfills the conditions necessary for an indulgence, he wins release from punishment and gains more speedy access to God. This no one may make light of. In this liberation, however, there is no derogation from the demands of divine justice. For the debt of punishment is not condoned. "He who gains an indulgence is not, strictly speaking, absolved from the debt of punishment, but is given the means of paying it."[29] The punishment already undergone by one member of Christ is now imputed to another member. On the other hand, desire for indulgences ought not to make us neglect penance, for indulgences are no substitute for personal penance. This is always necessary for the healing of the wounds of sin which indulgences cannot effect. Of themselves indulgences have no medicinal value. Side by side with esteem for indulgences must go the faithful practice of penance.

Let us not speak of redeeming the present but rather of converting present opportunity into increase of merit and glory. Once he has amended the past by satisfying the justice of God, the prudent man concentrates his efforts upon the one thing which he truly controls — the present. The only thing we really have is the *now*. So fruitful is this thought that we do well to meditate upon St. Augustine's reflections concerning it.

Taking the verse of Psalm 76, *I thought upon the days of old: and I had in mind the eternal years*, he asks: "What are the eternal years? An overwhelming thought! See if this thought means nothing but a great silence. From every outward noise, from all the tumult of human affairs let him quietly refrain who wishes to contemplate the eternal years. Are they the eternal years, these in which we live, or our ancestors have lived, or our posterity will live? Let no one think them the eternal years. For what remains of these

---

[29] St. Thomas, *Supplement,* 25, 1, ad 2.

years? In our speech we say, This year; and what have we of this year but the one day in which we are? For the past days of the year have already gone and its future days have not arrived. We are in *one* day and we say, This year: rather say, Today, if you wish to indicate something present. For of the whole year what have you now? Whatever part of the year has elapsed, no longer exists: whatever part of it is to come, does not exist as yet: how [then do you say,] This year? Correct your expression: say, Today. All right, you say: I shall say, Today. Ah, but note that the morning hours of today are passed, its future hours have not come. And so correct this too: say, This hour. And of this hour what have you? Certain moments of it are already gone: its future moments have not come. Say, This moment. What moment? While I utter sylla-bles, if I shall speak in two syllables, the second is not uttered until the first is finished. What, therefore, have we of those years?"[30]

We have only the indivisible *now* — less than a pin point of time. When someone asked Will Rogers: "If you found out you had only forty-eight hours to live, how would you spend them?" he replied, "One at a time." There is no other way in which our moments can come to us. The past is fled and the future may not be for us. Seize your opportunity,[31] says Horace. Instead of wasting time by brooding over the past or worrying about difficulties which may never eventuate, a man should calmly concentrate upon the present. If we always made a virtuous use of the present, there would be no need of regretting the past or fearing the future. *Age quod agis* — do what you are doing the best you can. Hence we should perform each duty as it falls due, exactly and thoroughly. When we say vocal prayers, we give them all the attention and devotion we are capable of. When we examine our conscience, we avoid as best we can all distraction. When we speak, our words are worthy of us, our hearers, and the occasion. If the occasion demands meekness of us, we do not yield to irascibility; if compassion, we do not shrug off the claims of mercy. When we recreate, reason continues to guide

---

[30] *Enarratio in Ps.* 76, 8; *PL* 36, 976.
[31] Cf. *Odes,* 1, 11, 8.

our thoughts, words, and acts. Whether we are alone or in company, whether we stand or sit or walk, or talk or act or remain silent, each action measures up to the golden mean of virtue, that is, it is aptly right for this agent in these circumstances of time, place, health, and the like.

Not only should the act be the best act possible — unto that goal the pagan philosopher strove — but it should flow from the best motive, the love of God. "Therefore, whether you eat or drink, whatever else you do, do all to the glory of God."[32] And what is so apt to incite us to love God in all things as constant remembrance of His benefits? He who ponders upon the marks of God's affection for him will try to respond to such an outpouring of beneficence. "Acknowledge," says St. Gregory Nazianzen, "the source of your being, your breath, your intelligence — and what is greatest of all — your power to know God, to hope in the heavenly kingdom, to become the equal of the angels, to contemplate the glory which is now only in images and figures but which then will be more full and pure. The fact that you have become the son of God, co-heir with Christ, and to speak boldly, God Himself, whence is this to you and from whom? Or, to speak of less important things which are readily perceived, who gave you [the power] to behold the beauty of heaven, the course of the sun, the cycle of the moon, the multitude of the stars, the harmony and order which in these things, as in a lyre, exists ever the same, the succession of the years, the changes of the seasons, the prescribed course of the ages, the eventual evenness of darkness and daylight, the products of the earth, the profusion of the air, the vastness of the sea which ever changes and ever remains the same, the depth of the rivers, the flow of the winds? Who gave you the rains, tillage, food, the arts, dwellings, laws, the State, civilization, urbanity toward your own? . . . Who has set you as lord and king of all things upon the earth? Not to mention each thing singly, who has given all the things wherein man is superior to all other beings?"[33]

Can a person be ever mindful of the divine blessings? Can

---

[32] 1 Cor. 10:31.
[33] *Orationes*, 14, 23; *PG* 35, 888.

he always be so alert as never to permit any imperfection to spoil what he is doing? Certainly no man should do violence to himself by attempting what is beyond his strength. If a man develops scruples or a neurosis from pursuit of this ideal, he shows that, either he is lacking in prudence, or he is the victim of unwise guidance. No spiritual ambition is realizable without prudence. Two things must here be kept in mind. First, that to which God invites men cannot be impossible. Whoever is perfect in his acts as he performs them is the perfect man. If God sweetly draws men to perfection, He makes perfection possible with His grace. Second, perfection sought in a particular act is not an absolute perfection, that is, the greatest possible perfection by which this act can be performed, but a perfection relative to the agent's present capacity. The question is not, what is here the best possible act? or, what would St. Francis de Sales or the Little Flower have done in this case? but we should ask, is this the best which John Doe can do in these circumstances?

The story is told of a number of saints in a variety of ways. This time it is about St. Francis of Assisi who was asked, while he was hoeing his garden, what he would do if it were revealed to him that he would die at sunset. The Little Poor Man said he would go on hoeing. Since he was sanctifying the passing moment by accomplishing God's will in the hoeing of his garden, he would continue — until God's will bade him pass on to some other thing. God's will brings us the holy thing to do each moment: it sanctifies us, it sanctifies the moment. We need not be ever choosing between prayer or work, reading or writing, speech or silence, reflection or cessation of thought: the one necessary thing is that which God wills me to be doing *now*. It is the momentary but authentic manifestation of God's eternal order.

Whoever always demands the best of himself will sometimes be disappointed, because human weakness will defeat his resolve, but if he persistently clings to this ideal, he is truly living. He gets the maximum return from life. He redeems the time.

Christ Himself tells how to secure the future. "I say to you: Make unto you friends of the mammon of iniquity; that, when you shall fail, they may receive you into everlasting dwellings."[34] Mammon is lucre or wealth. Christ calls it the mammon of iniquity because it lures men into so many sins. In itself it is not evil. Hence it can be used. The wise man uses mammon well by giving alms and doing the works of charity. When he comes to die, the recipients of his charity will welcome him into everlasting dwellings. The reason is that, in loving and succoring the needy, the man has been loving and succoring Christ. "Amen I say to you, as long as you did it to one of these my least brethren, you did it to me."[35]

"Let us," says St. Gregory Nazianzen, "as long as there is opportunity, visit Christ, heal Christ, nourish Christ, clothe Christ, gather in Christ, honor Christ; not only by dining Him as some have done, nor by anointing Him as Mary did, nor merely by giving Him a tomb like Joseph of Arimathea, nor by seeing to his burial like Nicodemus (who only half loved Him), nor by giving Him gold, frankincense and myrrh as did the Magi before all these; but, since the Lord of all desires mercy and not sacrifice, and compassion surpasses holocaust of unnumbered victims, let us offer Him this mercy in the persons of the needy and of those who this very day are in dire straits, in order that, when we depart hence, they may receive us into everlasting dwellings."[36]

If eternal life is promised to those who feed the hungry, clothe the naked, and minister to the imprisoned, what may we not expect, if we minister to the needs of intellect and will. A man can own absolutely nothing, and yet daily give a thousand spiritual alms. By removing ignorance of God's revelation, by persuading men to abandon sin, by reconciling the sick and the distressed to God's good pleasure, by repaying evil with good, the wise man sends so many messengers of mercy before him into eternity. By prayer for the living he makes stronger the bonds which unite the faithful in the Body of Christ. By prayers, indulgences, and suffrages offered for the souls in purgatory he can release them from pain. They indeed will be his friends and receive him into everlasting dwellings.

Perhaps the past is strewn with broken resolutions and

---

[34] Lk. 16:9.
[35] Mt. 25:40.
[36] *Orationes,* 14, 40; *PG* 35, 909.

apathy. We can always begin again. Each day we can start afresh as though we had accomplished nothing heretofore. God will strengthen our weakness and steady our vacillation. He knows our levity of mind. He makes allowances for our inconstancy of purpose and He will buoy up our good will with the gifts of the Holy Spirit. He will infuse understanding and breathe fortitude upon us, if we only imitate the Apostle and "press on toward the goal, to gain the reward of God's heavenly call in Christ Jesus."[37]

Now is the acceptable time, now is the day of salvation.[38] Not tomorrow, for tomorrow never comes. God says "Today" but the devil says "Tomorrow." Whoever says, "I will start one of these days," never starts. "Tell me, Postumus," asks Martial,[39] "when does that tomorrow of yours come?" Now is the acceptable time, now is the time to redeem the time.

---

[37] Phil. 3:14, Westminster version.
[38] Cf. 2 Cor. 6:2.
[39] *Epigrams,* 5, 58.

3. Fear

"Fears shall terrify him on every side,
and shall entangle his feet" (Job 18:11).

FEAR is a devastating thing, one of the major burdens of our flesh. It lies uneasily upon the soul and robs it of peace. It prevents us from making proper decisions. It dissolves many a noble and resolute determination into cowardly inaction. Fear has always played a lamentably effective role in human affairs. The epic poet depicts his hero, the great-souled Odysseus, adrift in the deep and consumed with fear of a watery grave. Fear was the constant companion of our hero-aces cruising the war skies. Everyone has experience of abiding fears. A growing boy hates to be seen in that silly outfit which a doting, but deluded, mother insists on his wearing; he is afraid the boys will muss him up, or worse, that the girls will laugh at him. An employee fears the ill will of his supervisor; a husband, his wife's shrewish tongue.

Fear, together with joy, sadness, and hope, is a major passion or movement of the sensitive appetite. Since we have an animal nature, our rational soul must experience the rise and fall of animal desire. To appreciate fear let us see it against the background of all the passions. The primary passion upon which all the others rest is *love*, the first movement of approval or complacence wrought in the appetite by some desirable object. Love begets *desire*, the movement toward the pleasurable desirable object. When the object is secured, *joy* results, the satisfaction of appetite in possession of the desired object. The motion opposite to love is *hatred*, the recoil of appetite from what seems to be hurtful or distasteful. Hatred begets *aversion*, the flight of appetite from the evil object. When the agent is burdened with an evil unwanted object, *sadness* results. When the desired object is difficult but possible of attainment, desire of it is *hope*. From hope arises *daring*, appetite assailing the evil which makes the desired object hard to get. If the desired good is seen as impossible of attainment, appetite withdraws, and its withdrawal is *despair*. From hope and sadness arises *anger,* or the motion of appetite against a present evil with the intent to destroy it. *Fear* is the shrinking of appetite from a future evil difficult to avoid.

If every man were master of himself and an integrated personality he would not be concerned with his passions any more than he worries about his fingernails or little toes. All are part of his lower nature and as such they are good. However, since the passions so easily get out of hand and slip the control of reason, they present serious problems.

The problem of fear is psychic and moral. The psychic problem is one of mental hygiene; that is, continuing fears are a real obstacle to a man's control of his soul and to the happiness which should proceed therefrom. With anxiety constantly gnawing at him, efficiency in thinking and willing is considerably impaired. He views things in a dark abnormal light. He makes a decision only to unmake it or he fretfully vacillates, unable to make any choice. Whoever is ridden by fear lives an unenviable life. Indeed, any protracted loss of emotional poise is detrimental to physical health and may well bring on a neurosis. There is a proved connection between the constant upset of anxiety and mental disorder. Eliminate abnormal fear and anger and psychiatrists would have to close up shop.

The problem is not solved by determining to root all fear from the soul. Such a determination reminds us of the naïve prayer of some good souls who ask to be relieved of all pride, sloth, anger, and the rest of the capital sins. As we cannot, generally speaking, be completely healed of the disorder existing in our appetites as the result of original sin, so *a fortiori* we cannot get rid of the appetites themselves. We can no more rid ourselves of fear than we can lose the instinct of self-preservation. A group of men will crawl into the battle line and fear of death will tense the nerves of all of them. The good soldier goes ahead and does his duty. The coward listens to his fears and, if he can, hides in some convenient spot. The difference between the coward and the brave man is not that the former has fears and the latter has none. Both fear, but the brave man has the virtue to act reasonably despite his fears. Without fear he would be inhuman.

The solution to the psychic problem lies in learning how to live with and control one's fears. To accomplish this one should first see fear as a moral problem and master the difficulty upon this higher level.

It is a dictate of morality to which no exception is possible that a man should always shun moral evil, and if this cannot be done without endurance of physical evil, then physical evil, no matter how fearful, must be accepted.

The rule is simple but men always experience difficulty in observing it. First, they may fear certain physical evils more than moral guilt. Second, they may have an inordinate bias toward physical good which can be had only at the expense of moral good. As sin can wear the guise of good, so a moral good, like resistance to temptation, can be identified with what the lower nature finds repulsive. Children lie to avoid a father's anger. Young men yield to incontinency because they are afraid of being called sissies. Faith and reason urge a man to give up a dangerous intimacy but he suffers acute distress at the thought of the surrender. We can never be wholly rid of this spontaneous reaction of recoil from temporal disadvantage. Granted the excitory cause, fear will arise, but — and this is the moral problem of fear — it must never induce us to omit a duty or to act against the law of God.

The evils which may occasion sin through fear range from trifling embarrassment to death. The moral law can make some truly awesome demands. To win the kingdom of God people must sometimes overcome their most elemental fears. In the Decian perscution a Roman Christian had to conquer his terror of brutal torments and death or forfeit the name and destiny of a Christian. Before the turn of the century no Pole or Hungarian ever dreamed that he would face the same grim choice. Nor is it impossible that before another century turns English-speaking Catholics will find themselves in the same dilemma.

How a man will meet the big crises depends on his mastery of fear. If he has schooled himself gradually to overcome fear from motives of moral uprightness, he can face the most trying situation. If he disdains to lie, even when speaking the truth would bring down on him his employer's wrath, he is preparing himself to avoid the perjury which saves from imprisonment. If he accepts loss of employment and ration cards rather than forego the religious instruction of his children, he is ready to face violent death undisturbed.

What a comfort to see a man like Thomas à Becket face the certain prospect of bloody death with complete tranquillity! Although he knew death was hourly imminent, he went about the routine of his last day as if nothing were amiss. At midnight he recited matins in his room with several of his monks and clerics. He assisted at Mass in Canterbury Cathedral. According to his custom he visited the shrines of the saints there. He went to confession. He received callers and conducted his usual business. At three o'clock he dined with good appetite. At the end of the meal one of the clerics said: "Thank God, I see you dine more heartily and cheerfully than usual." Thomas answered: "A man must be cheerful who is going to his master." This was the only sign he gave that he had been warned by letter the day before that he was about to be killed. By evening his brains were scattered on the cathedral floor but as he awaited his ordeal he was composed and cheerful.

While the problem of fear interests all men, its solution is of special importance to the seeker for perfection. He must master all the motions of passion. Total mastery of passion is a truly awesome undertaking. First, as in carpentry, the mastery of rudiments lies within ordinary capacity but the finest skills require minute instruction and infinite pains, so in the art of human living, the attainment of perfection demands exquisite skill and patience. Second, precisely because he ambitions perfection, a person must expect the constant opposition of the evil spirit. Satan does not bother the man who is happy in his sins: he attacks the man who tries to do better. St. Ignatius says: "Concerning those who go from good to better, the good angel touches such a soul sweetly, lightly, suavely, like a drop of water entering a sponge; and the devil touches it sharply and with noise and disquietude, like water splashing on a rock. . . . The reason is because it belongs to God and His angels to drive out of the soul all that darkness and melancholy with which the enemy has filled it, and to pour into it true spiritual joy. While, on the contrary, the devil by false and specious reasoning seeks always to destroy the peace which he finds there." The evil spirit works upon the imagination, deludes a man, if he can, into substituting phantasms for acts of reasoning, excites images of imaginary danger, plays upon the fears of the soul. If then, any man must, the aspirant to perfection must come to realistic grips with his fears. He does so, first, by separating his imaginary from his real fears.

People who should know better sometimes fear things which are entirely creatures of the imagination. Even the best of men may once in a while be disturbed by these things of shadow and semidarkness hidden in obscure corners of the soul. But it is especially persons of lively imagination and timorous disposition who are most often prevented from substantial progress toward perfection by tricks of their imagination. How often does such a person allow his imagination to make a mountain out of a molehill. He has a persistent little cough and he feels too hot after he has got to bed, so he diagnoses for himself a case of tuberculosis. He chooses the sanatorium for his cure and tortures himself with visions of five years of helplessness. He gets pains in the arm and, because he read in the *Reader's Digest* that arm pains are the prelude to heart attacks, he reads up on heart disease. His back aches and at once he thinks of kidney disease.

What time, energy, and good emotion are wasted by unreasonable fear of what is yet to be experienced. New teachers dread the first hours of class; new administrators, the first decisions they must make. Suppose a person, unused to public speaking, is selected for an executive post which requires public appearances. If he is sensible he takes lessons and practices under competent direction; if he cannot do this, he plucks up his courage and learns as he goes. If he is timorous, he grinds the gears of his nerves worrying that his voice will not be strong enough, that his memory will fail him, that he will not make a good impression. Unfortunately, some people carry this fear with them into every new situation in life.

Some people unreasonably fear the opinions and reactions of others. A good man may hold back from receiving Holy

Communion daily because the neighbors might think he is becoming too pious. A penitent, in need of careful direction, fears to open her soul to the confessor. Persons capable of writing books never get to the point of publication because they are afraid of criticism. A parishioner may hit upon an excellent project of Catholic Action and fear to broach it to the pastor.

All of us at times are afraid to make good resolutions. Give up some pet failing! Practice some new virtue! We fear that, deprived of the comfort of the old familiar defect, we shall shiver like shorn lambs in the winter of our discontent. We fear we shall fail. We exaggerate the difficulties involved. We telescope all future and possible obstacles into one present and invincible force of difficulty, imagining that this grim totality has to be met at each instant that we try to keep the resolution. Fear keeps us from seeing that, if we break up the difficulty into its true components, separating the parts into their proper place in time, space, and reality, they are all quite vincible.

The first remedy for imaginary difficulties is to purge the pessimistic imagination which continually borrows trouble. It has not learned that sufficient for the day is the evil thereof.[1] It converts trouble that is only possible into certain woe. Imagination should follow after reason and never run on before it, uncontrolled. A person should always be a realist, seeing his world as it actually is, and not as his fears terrify him into believing it to be. Insubstantial fears thrive because the light of reason is too seldom shed on them. Let them be driven into the open and they are seen for what they are, the moths of the souls which are killed by the sunlight of common sense. Let the objects of fear be faced and boldly handled. There was a woman who had a deadly fear of snakes. She cured herself by going on a snake-hunting expedition and handling every snake that was caught. Concerning all such fears, we can honestly say, "Fear is ignorance."

Next, one should consider the causes of fear. The first is love. When her children go off on a picnic, a mother is fearful that some accident will happen to them. Her fear

---

[1] Mt. 6:34.

arises from her love; and it is hard to find fault with it. If, however, a person finds himself constantly enmeshed in fears, he does well to seek the cause in disordered love of self. He is fearful that some unpleasant thing will happen to him or that he will lose something he likes. Suppose he dreads the onset of chronic disability and gloomily contemplates the discomforts which the years will bring. No amount of self-hypnotism will persuade him that pain and loss of activity will be pleasant. He frets and sometimes rebels, thinking how his efficiency will be cut in half and he be excluded from work he loves. Now if his appetites were in order and he loved these things only in God, that is, for their ability to unite him to God, he would never fear the loss of any created thing.

The difficulty is that we love many things, not for God's sake, but for their own sakes. We love our own will more than God's will. We are not indifferent to all created things nor do we seek union with God in our every choice. In theory we recognize that close union with God demands separation from love of created things, a demand entailing physical or psychic suffering. Practically, however, our love of these things is so great that we dread to pay the price. We shrink from the pain of separation from our various created loves. In close union with God we are offered the pearl of great price but all that our weak eyes can see is the rough casing which covers it. To extract the pearl we must cast away things loved for their own sakes. At that prospect a foolish paralysis comes over our courage. But as we grow in love of God we see that the price is really small and our courage grows. When we finally cleanse desire of all things loved for their own sakes and seek them only in God, we have no fear of losing them. We don't care. Love of things is subjection: love of God is the only freedom.

The second cause of fear is defect of power. Hence we should fear only what we cannot control. Without his brother's protection a small boy flies from the fists of the neighborhood bully. All men fear horrendous acts of nature like hurricanes, floods, and earthquakes. With no weapon of defense, a man will run from a vicious dog; with a stout stick in his hand, he will drive it back and laugh. The greater a man's power the smaller is the number of things he fears.

People fear overmuch because they underrate the extent of their power. Dread of failure is a case in point. As we love to be known as skilled and competent so we hate to be accounted blundering and inefficient. If we are given a difficult or delicate task we ought never to fear that we will be unsuccessful and be shamed by the assignment of the task to another. We have a hidden source of strength to rely on — our partnership with God. If we seek God's will and do what we can, failure is impossible. For the only real failure is failure to do God's will. Doing the will of God is always under our control: for this we have the divine promise. And even if we do not produce what men expect of us, we can, nevertheless, from that kind of failure achieve a peculiar success. For failure to measure up to men's expectations of us may be a bitter pill to swallow but under its nauseous coating is a specific for pride. By teaching us our true nothingness the failure leads us toward humility. Nothing can more effectively engrave on our minds the words of the Psalmist: "Not to us, O Lord, not to us; but to thy name give glory."[2]

Not all the pangs of life are mere figments of the imagination. Only Christian scientists and fatuous Pollyannas can persuade themselves that the sky is always serene and no storms lurk upon the horizon. What then are the valid objects of fear and how should we evaluate them?

Franklin Roosevelt gave currency to the phrase that the only thing to be feared is fear. Is it possible to fear fear? Just as one may love his love or sorrow for his sorrow so he may dread the onset of fear. St. Thomas says: "A man may fear lest he should be threatened by the necessity of fearing through being assailed by great evil."[3] The counsel not to fear fear means that one ought not to borrow needless trouble and become anxious about merely possible evils. This is accomplished, not by a mistaken effort to root out all fear, but by rigorous exercise of the will.

All men fear the coming of outstanding physical evils like war, intractable pain, corporal incapacity, loss of fortune, es-

---

[2] Ps. 113:9.   [3] *Sum. Theol.*, I–II, 42, 4.

trangement of dear ones, death. The proper attitude toward
these evils was indicated above when we said that all created
goods whose loss we may understandably fear should be loved
only in God and for God. Firm trust in the providence of
God is the sure bulwark against fear of temporal physical
evil.

What about moral evils like temptation and sin? Sin —
the deliberate choice of what God's law forbids — ought not
to be feared because it always lies within our control to
avoid sin. But the consequences of sin — separation from God
— are a principal object of fear. Temptation is partly within
and partly beyond our control. It is always within our power
to resist temptation and that is the important thing. We
cannot always check the onset of temptation but we have the
assurance that "God is faithful and will not suffer you to be
tempted above that which you are able: but will make also
with temptation issue that you may be able to bear it."[4] Unfortunately people who undergo prolonged temptation can
bring on a fresh attack of their trouble precisely by fearing
they will be tempted. Their recourse is the rigorous suppression of the first qualms of such fears.

What then remains to be feared? Christ answers: "And I
say to you, my friends, be not afraid of them who kill the
body, and after that have no more that they can do. But I
will show you whom you shall fear: fear ye him, who after
he has killed, hath power to cast into hell."[5] *The Shepherd*
of Hermas says to the early Christians: "Fear the Lord and
keep his commands; therefore keeping the commands of God
you will be able for anything, and your work will be beyond
compare. For he who fears the Lord does everything well.
This is the fear you should cultivate and you will be saved.
But do not fear the devil. For whoever fears God has dominion
over the devil since power is not in him."[6]

It is fitting that a discussion of fear terminate with the
fear of God, for this is the only sure remedy for the ills of a
very sick society. International sickness will not be remedied
by coexistence, peace conferences, or such like palliatives. Nor

---

[4] 1 Cor. 10:13.
[5] Lk. 12:4–5.
[6] *Mandatum*, 7, 1; *PG* 2, 929.

will juvenile delinquency, broken homes, and rampant sex yield to surface remedies. The cause of all these ills is lack of the fear of God. Only when people and society begin again to fear God will we be able to breathe again.

What is the fear of God? In one way we cannot fear God because He is all good. We can fear only evil. But we can, and must, fear to offend God because offense separates us from God. We must fear His punishments because they deprive us of Him, our only good. Sin and its punishments are the only evil; all other so-called evils are inconveniences of passing duration. Since God is the author or, to speak more accurately, the administrator of these punishments, He is to be feared above all things else.

There is, however, a fear of divine punishment which is wrong. After stating that conversion from sin involves complete turning from evil, St Gregory speaks of one "who does not wholly withdraw from evil; because he sins by the very fact that he would be willing to sin if he could do so without being punished."[7] He does not abandon his will to sin: he wishes there were no hell so that he might do what he pleases. As Gregory says: "Whoever does good precisely because he fears the evil of punishment, wishes that the object of his fear did not exist, so that he might do boldly what is forbidden."[8] In other words, the man's motive of fear is utterly disordered and contrary to the love of God. It evinces no love of God; only a monstrous love of self. For he considers the greatest possible evil to be his own loss of heaven and not the offense against God in sin. Hence, he places his last end and greatest good not in God but in himself. The love which begets such fear is completely selfish and blameworthy.

So the sinner who makes a mission and confesses his sins out of fear of hell does wrong? He would if his sentiments were those which are described above. But this is hardly the case with a Catholic who repents. Since the ordinary sinner believes God is his last end, and since he now turns back to God through His supernatural gift of repentance, he

---

[7] *Moralium Lib.* I, 26, 37; *PL* 75, 544.
[8] *Regulae Pastorum*, III, c. 13; *PL* 77, 70.

has a servile fear of God and His punishments which is salutary. But he lacks filial fear of God which reveres God as a Father and dreads to be separated from Him. Both are from the Holy Ghost and constitute that fear of God which is the beginning of wisdom.

In his incomparable way St. Thomas explains this fear. "A thing may be called the beginning of wisdom in two ways: in one way because it is the beginning of wisdom itself as to its essence; in another way, as to its effect. Thus the beginning of an art as to its essence consists in the principles from which that art proceeds, while the beginning of an art as to its effect is that wherefrom it begins to operate: for example, we might say that the beginning of the art of construction is the foundation, since that is where the builder begins his work. Now, since wisdom is the knowledge of divine things . . . it is considered in one way by us, and in another by philosophers. For, since our life is ordained to the enjoyment of God, and is directed thereto according to a participation of the divine nature conferred on us through grace, wisdom, as we look at it, is considered not only as knowledge of God, as it is with the philosophers, but also as directive of human conduct . . . Accordingly the beginning of wisdom as to its essence consists in the first principles of wisdom, i.e., the articles of faith, and in this sense faith is said to be the beginning of wisdom. But as regards the effect, the beginning of wisdom is the point where wisdom begins to work, and in this way, fear is the beginning, yet servile fear in one way, and filial fear in another. For servile fear is like a principle disposing a person from without, in so far as he refrains from sin through fear of punishment, and is thus fashioned for the effect of wisdom, according to Eccu., I, 27, *The fear of the Lord driveth out sin.* On the other hand, chaste or filial fear is the beginning of wisdom, as being the first effect of wisdom. For, since the regulation of human conduct by divine law belongs to wisdom, in order to make a beginning, a man must first of all fear God and submit himself to Him: for the result will be that in all things he will be ruled by God."[9]

---

[9] *Sum. Theol.*, II–II, 19, 7.

Filial fear is the necessary foundation of the interior life. St. Gregory says: "Since it is written: *The fear of the Lord is the beginning of wisdom* (Prov. IX, 10), it undoubtedly follows that one rises from fear to wisdom but one does not descend from wisdom to fear. For it is written: *Perfect charity casteth out fear* (1 Jn. IV, 18). Since, therefore, the words of the prophet were from heavenly to earthly things, he began with wisdom and ended with fear. But we who tend to heavenly from earthly things designate the same stages by ascent so that from fear we may arrive at wisdom. For the first stage of the ascent of the soul is fear of the Lord."[10]

The fear of God is the first of the gifts of the Holy Ghost. To walk in the way of God a man must first embrace the divine law in its entirety and avoid all deliberate sin. Just as you cannot call a man a good Catholic who is chained by habits of mortal sin, so neither may we say that a man has really entered the way of perfection who is shackled by habits of deliberate venial sin. A constant upward movement of the soul toward God is impossible, if the soul is the willing prisoner of sin. It is supreme delusion to concentrate attention upon the higher steps of the way of perfection, if one has not as yet secured the lower, which is freedom from habitual venial sin. Since sin is rooted in pride, the Holy Ghost offers as the antidote to sin His gift of fear whose first fruit is humility. For fear moves one to contemplation of the judgment of God which imparts to the soul the clearest picture of its true standing before God. He who knows what he is in God's sight cannot but be humbled. Humility then preserves him from sin.

This was the constant teaching of the ancient fathers of the desert whose forthrightness and virile hardihood we cannot but admire. When they perceived a desirable end, they did not hesitate to choose the necessary means, rugged though these might be. St. Dorotheus sets forth the stern but practical means of attaining the fear of God. "The fathers said," he writes, "that a man possesses the fear of God by keeping mindful of death and hell; by examining himself at evening

---

[10] *Hom. in Ezech.*, II, VII, 7; *PL* 76, 1016.

as to how he spent the day, and again in the morning as to how he spent the night; by not presuming upon oneself; by attaching oneself to a man who fears God. We read about a brother who asked one of the older monks: 'What shall I do, father, in order to fear God?' The old man replied: 'Go and attach yourself to a man who fears God and from his fear of God he will teach you to fear God.' We drive away the fear of God from us when we do the opposite of these things, that is, when we are unmindful of death and hell, when we do not examine our progress but live indifferently and consort with the indifferent, when we presume upon ourselves. This is the worst of all, this is the height of destruction. For what so drives the fear of God from the soul as overcomplacency in self?"[11]

Since fear is the first stage of perfection it corresponds to the first beatitude, "Blessed are the poor in spirit." Fear aims at producing reverence and perfect submission to God. He who truly fears God no longer seeks greatness in himself, in another, in external goods, but solely in God. "Some trust in chariots, and some in horses; but we will call upon the name of the Lord our God."[12] To act otherwise would deny perfect submission to God. Perfect submission can spring only from poverty of spirit. Since a man seeks no greatness in himself, he has no inflated spirit of pride. Since he seeks no greatness in another nor in riches and honors, he has renounced the love of these things. Absence of pride and renunciation of the love of created things is poverty of spirit.

As charity increases does fear disappear? The servile element in it certainly does. For the more a person loves God, the less he cares about himself and his being punished by God: the faster he clings to God, the more confident he becomes of his reward. Although fear becomes purified of every unworthy element, it nevertheless grows with the growth of charity. As charity increases so do the gifts of the Holy Ghost. Hence the more a man loves his heavenly Father, the more he fears to offend Him and the more he appreciates how awful a calamity would be separation from Him. The

---

[11] *Doctrinae*, 4, 5; *PG* 88, 1664-1665.
[12] Ps. 19:8.

closer he is drawn to Him, the more he reverences Him and stands in awe of His infinite perfections. As the gift of fear is perfected, he is able to elicit most lively sorrow for the slightest fault and to avoid the least stain with assiduous care. The gift of fear prevents undue familiarity with God. Surely a person may ambition intimacy with God, but it is for God to make the initial advances.

Taking the word of the Psalmist, "The fear of the Lord is holy, enduring forever and forever,"[13] St. Thomas concludes that fear will exist even in heaven.[14] His argument, however, is unconvincing. He admits that St. Augustine doubted the fact. Modern commentators on the Psalms say that the text mentioned by St. Thomas should read: "The *worship* of God is holy, remaining forever and forever." It would seem, then, that since hope cannot exist in heaven, neither can its contrary, fear. If no evil is possible in heaven, no object of fear can be found there. The fear of God will be replaced by awe and wonder at His supereminence and incomprehensibility.

As often happens, they who need fear most usually have too little or none. What do great sinners care about death and hell? What qualms does the thought of God's judgment arouse in Communist leaders? Yet gentle souls of a naturally timorous or indecisive temperament are sometimes tormented by excessive fear of God. Too much fear is almost as bad as too little. The moral virtues are to temper one another. As prudence is to temper rashness into bravery, so hope is to counterbalance fear.

Now the scrupulous person is he who either fears too much or hopes too little. Scruples of short duration are usually good for a person. At least, they are a healthy sign of earnestness in the service of God. Prolonged scruples, however, are a dire affliction and a seriously potential danger. The scrupulous person is fear-ridden and guilt-haunted. He sees mortal sin at every turn. His practical notions of God have become distorted. Without explicitly adverting to his false notions, he imagines that God is overrigorous and almost impossible to please, that He catches people off guard and delights

---

[13] Ps. 18:10.   [14] *Sum. Theol.*, II–II, 19, 11.

therein, that He blames people for committing sin even when they tried their best to avoid it. Hence the scrupulous person fears to do many innocent things lest he be trapped into sin against his will.

His first serious mistake is to fear sin. He should hate it and detest it, but never fear it, as we said before. The poor man wastes time which should be devoted to other duties by examining and re-examining his conscience, now declaring himself free of guilt, now accusing himself of sinful consent. He keeps repeating matter already told in confession. His panacea is a general confession. He thinks that just one more general confession will free him from his troubles once and for all. He will not be convinced that by yielding to his inclination he only whets his appetite for more and more general confessions. His conduct is outstanding proof of the assertion that fear is ignorance. For his second great mistake is that he allows fear to obsess his imagination and his imagination to rule his moral judgments. While his intellect acts sensibly enough in other matters, once it attempts a moral judgment it wavers and fluctuates like a compass needle in a magnetic field. For he converts anything which may bear the most doubtful tinge of obligation into an absolutely certain obligation, the possibility of sin into certitude of sin. He constructs for himself a fantastic burden of contradictory duties. Then he reverses himself, declares himself free of obligation. The toils of doubt tighten around him and in the hopeless tangle he knows not what to do.

This person is suffering from a dangerous malady. For, first, his intellectual function, at least in moral matters, is not operating efficiently. Second, in an atmosphere of darkness and tension the supernatural functions of hope and love can be impaired. Although God allows the trial in order that the soul may expand in hope and love, nevertheless the soul can easily miss the opportunity. Heroic souls have responded nobly with an increase of hope and love; others, however, hugging their fears to themselves, contract their hope and dry up their love. Third, and this is the very great danger, to rid itself of this torment, the scrupulous soul may go to the opposite extreme of carelessness and laxity. From fearing too much it may come to fear not at all.

Martin Luther is the classic example. He was an imagina-
tive man whose conscience was ridden by fear. He entered
religion because of a vow made amid the terrors of a lightning
storm. He honestly set out upon the way of perfection, but
scruples kept his soul in torment. For example, he was so
terrified of our Lord in the Holy Eucharist and so fearful of
committing a sacrilege unknowingly that he would have fled
from the altar of his first Mass, if his novice master had not
bodily restrained him. He tried to flee from the anxieties of
the interior life by plunging into external activity that was
enough to occupy half a dozen men. Unwilling to accept the
scriptural injunction, "Work out your salvation in fear and
trembling,"[15] in its traditional meaning, he wanted absolute
certitude that he was going to save his soul. He was so afraid
of his inability to master his lower desires that he formulated
the heresy that good works are not necessary for salvation. But
what would give him certitude of salvation and freedom from
doubt? Another heresy — faith alone avails to salvation. Since,
then, he had fiducial trust that his sins were covered by the
merits of Christ, he had saving faith and was among the
number of the elect. So he boldly emerged from his doubts
to exclaim: "Sin bravely and believe more firmly."

In order to master the fears of conscience, the scrupulous
person must recognize that he is suffering an abnormality.
Since he is temporarily incapable of judging for himself in
moral matters, he must entrust his conscience to a prudent
guide who, as far as possible, will judge for him. Then he
must blindly do what he is told. As long as he disobeys his
director, he may not hope for a cure. Without enough hope,
his spiritual development has been lopsided; he must take
his courage in his fist and go ahead blindly, hoping in the
goodness of God. He must look on God as a loving Father
who, although He may impose a grievous burden, is always
faithful to His promises. Meantime let him act as other good
people act, convincing himself that what is right for them
is also right for him.

The director who endeavors to cure him requires sympathy
and compassion for a sick soul: harshness or brusqueness will

---

[15] Phil. 2:12.

only drive the tormented soul deeper into its own dark self. He needs humility because the scrupulous person will often question his competence. He will keep asking, "Do you understand what I am telling you?" The person will not be satisfied with the advice given and will go to three or four others, only to receive from them the same solution. Above all things the director needs great patience. He will have to listen to needless details and tedious repetitions. He will be subjected to constant and often importunate demands upon his time. He will feel irritation, because the person does not see what is perfectly obvious, and he will be tempted to say, "Use your common sense," when the person is bereft of common sense. Like a nurse teaching a disabled veteran how to walk again, he must show the person how gradually he is to make his own decisions and resume his moral responsibility.

Sometimes an appeal to the ludicrous helps in the regaining of common sense. A person once came to a priest and explained how he raised fine roses as a hobby. Unfortunately the neighborhood was infested with rats which often ate the roses. So he ingeniously strung his rose garden with wires charged with an electric current strong enough to kill a rat but not a man. He turned the current off when he went to bed but one night he forgot. Waking at two o'clock he remembered and came down in panic to turn off the current. He wished to know from the priest if he were obliged under pain of mortal sin to turn off the current every night. The priest asked: "Who would be prowling around your back yard at two in the morning who might be injured by your charged wires?" The answer came: "A burglar with a weak heart." Scrupulous persons all have their burglars with weak hearts, dozens of them. The great point is to make them recognize them.

The soul afflicted with scruples must make strenuous efforts to shake off the malady. His effort, however, should never consist in shaking his head or gritting his teeth at temptation, in furious acts of the will, but in a quieter but all-inclusive activity, namely, the utter abnegation of his judgment and will before the judgment and will of his director, the steadfast refusal to depart from the instructions given him. If he

is stubborn and self-opinionated, he will remain in his scruples
and so doom himself to the way of fear. But God intends
that he rise from fear to love, as the saints so often testify.
For example, St. Augustine says: "Fear is a slave, charity is
free; and, if we may so speak, fear is the slave of charity.
Lest the devil possess your heart, let the slave go first into
your heart and keep the place for the mistress who is to
follow. Act, act at least from fear of penalty, if as yet you
cannot do so from love of justice. The mistress will come
and the slave depart; because perfect charity casteth out
fear."[16]

---

[16] *Sermo* 156, 13; *PL* 38, 857.

4. Renunciation

"In him, too, you have been circumcised with a circumcision not wrought by hand, but through putting off the body of the flesh, a circumcision which is of Christ" (Col. 2:11).

RATIONALIST historians like to say that the feasts of the Church are only pagan festivals baptized. If they refer to Epiphany, Easter, or Pentecost, their charge is absurd. If they refer to New Year's Day, they may be talking facts. It is not fair, however, to say that New Year's Day is merely a pagan festival made over. It is a natural holiday which men always have and always will celebrate. If the Church injected a flavor of religion into an existing secular holiday in order to tone down excess and to direct men's minds to God, the element of religion was not far to seek. Thanks to St. John Chrysostom, the area of Antioch accepted the twenty-fifth of December as the rightful day on which to celebrate the birth of our Lord. The western half of the Roman world quickly followed suit. Now the eighth day after the twenty-fifth of December was in the calendar of Rome the beginning of the new year. Hence on the first day of the new year the Church could commemorate the events recorded by St. Luke: "And after eight days were accomplished, that the child should be circumcised, his name was called Jesus, which was called by the angel, before he was conceived in the womb."[1]

In considering this mystery let us fix our attention upon the idea of renunciation which is contained both in the central action of the ceremony and in the name given the Child.

The original facts are few and simple. The law did not

---

[1] Lk. 2:21.

command that the child be taken to the Temple or even to the synagogue for the ceremony: the home was the place of circumcision. We may reasonably conjecture that the Holy Family no longer lived in the stable but that Joseph had secured a dwelling house for them. After the example of Abraham and Isaac, the head of the family was the usual ministrant. The office of professional *mohel* had not then developed. To Joseph, then, was accorded the honor of marking the Child's body with the distinguishing sign of the people of God.

As Joseph used the knife he repeated the liturgical prayer: "Blessed be God, the Lord. He has sanctified his beloved in his mother's womb and he has written his law in our flesh. He marks his sons with the sign of the covenant, to give them the blessings of Abraham our father." The witnesses answered: "May he live whom thou hast taken for thy child." The function of the witnesses was to attest to the incorporation of the child into the civic and religious life of the chosen people. The chief of these witnesses was the invisible Elias for whom the seat of honor was reserved. Immediately after the child received the name he was to bear through life, he was placed upon the seat to receive the blessing of the greatest of the prophets. If this detail of ceremony actually was carried out in the circumcising of Mary's Son, and if it really was the mission of Elias to see to it that the patriarchial sign of circumcision should seal the sons of Abraham until the Messias should come, Elias could relax his vigilance. The Son of the Promise was born. The need for circumcision was about to cease.

Among the ancient Jews circumcision was a most sacred rite. As an act of religion it had been ordained by God who said to Abraham: "The male, the flesh of whose foreskin shall not be circumcised, that soul shall be destroyed out of his people: because he hath broken my covenant."[2] Until the Gospel was sufficiently promulgated, circumcision remained the outward sign of God's choice of Abraham and his children of the promise as His peculiar people. It separated a chosen race from the unbelieving heathen, for it was a

---

[2] Gen. 17:14.

profession of faith in a future Redeemer. It was a true
type and forerunner of Christian baptism: it admitted the
recipient into the body of true believers; it remitted original
sin and afforded a remedy against concupiscence, not however as in the case of Baptism, in virtue of the rite itself,
but on account of the faith of the person or his parents. Like
every means of salvation, its value derived from the Passion
of Christ. Even he who was not of the blood of Abraham,
Isaac, and Jacob could, by circumcision, be assimilated to
the chosen people as one of God's elect and an heir of the
messianic blessings. As St. Paul has pointed out, the children
of Abraham are to be reckoned not so much by carnal descent
as by faith. As a protestation of faith it was the first step
toward the vision of God. It imposed the burden of the
Mosaic law as long as that law was in force. There is a
shame-imparting symbolism to such a sign as circumcision:
God deliberately chose it as appropriate for a fallen race. It
is a sign of original sin which is contracted through the act
of generation.

The cutting in the ceremony signifies the need to circumcise the heart — to cut from it all affection for sin. It is
significant that Abraham, in whose person the rite was
made sacramental, was commanded to cut himself off from
the society of unbelievers according to the word of God:
"Go forth out of thy country, and from thy kindred."[3] This
was a painful command to fulfill. In those days the de-
pendence of a man upon his family was absolute. Nothing
was more abject than the man without land or kindred. So
great was the idolatry and corruption of his race that God
took Abraham from it and set him in a strange land that
from him the body of believers might issue. Whoever is
aggregated to this body of believers by circumcision must
renounce the ways of sin according to the command of God:
"Circumcise the foreskin of your heart, and stiffen your
neck no more."[4] Circumcision was no empty formality: it
inducted a man into the life of faith, but no one can live
the life of faith who does not cut away his sinful tendencies.

---

[3] Gen. 12:1.
[4] Deut. 10:16.

Only if he cut them away were the promises fulfilled to him. "The Lord thy God will circumcise thy heart . . . that thou mayest love the Lord thy God with all thy heart and with all thy soul, that thou mayest live."[5]

How absolutely were the words verified in the case of Abraham! Since he was chosen to be the father of all believers, he had to give proof that he loved God above everything else. He had to choose between God commanding him to slay Isaac and Isaac whom he loved the best in the world. When Abraham "put forth his hand and took the sword to sacrifice his son,"[6] he was surely circumcising his heart. For Abraham, God did come before Isaac. How aptly God calls the place of Abraham's sacrifice "the land of vision."[7] As Abraham climbed the mountain, he had nought to go by but faith which is the beginning of the vision of God. His natural reason must have told him that the promise that he would become a great and mighty nation was dashed in the death of Isaac. But he beheld the word of God which endures unto the ages: to that he could hold fast. So, too, our great circumcisions take place in the land of vision which is faith. We are stripped of a love, and it leaves us breathless and bleeding. We have no natural light to go by — only faith which is convinced that to them that love God all things work together unto good.[8]

The Child is the Lord and Lawgiver, the Holy One unblemished. Why, then, must He submit to the sign of sin? St. Bernard asks: "What is circumcision but the sign of something superfluous and of sin? What is superfluous in Thee, Lord Jesus, that may be circumcised? Art thou not true God of God the Father, true man without sin of the Virgin Mary? What do you do circumcising Him? Do you think that on Him can fall the sentence: 'The male, the flesh of whose foreskin shall not be circumcised, that soul shall be destroyed out of his people'? Can the Father forget the Son of His womb? Or fail to recognize Him without the sign of circumcision? If indeed He could possibly fail to know

---

[5] Deut. 30:6.
[6] Gen. 22:10.
[7] Gen. 22:2.
[8] Cf. Rom. 8:28.

the Son in whom He was well pleased, the ignorance would proceed from the fact that He finds in Him circumcision, which He Himself had provided for sinners for the cleansing of their sins. But why wonder if our Head undergoes for His members a cure which He needs not for Himself? Does it not happen even in our members that a cure is applied to one member on behalf of another? The head aches and a poultice is put on the arm. The thighs are sore and the poultice goes on the shin: so today for the corruption of the whole Body the hot iron is applied to the Head."[9]

He is circumcised because he wishes to show from the very beginning the reality of the human nature He had assumed. If He is to be a man like unto us in all things, sin alone excepted, He must assume human nature not merely in the abstract. He must take to Himself a country, a nationality, a family descent, a definite form of religious worship, a name, a standing among a people. Again, messianic reasons urge His circumcision, for without it He could never be accepted by any Jew as the Son of David and the promised Redeemer. Above all, He wishes to demonstrate to a self-willed, rebellious humanity the sanctity of the law of God. Although the Mosaic law was imperfect, and the shadow of a future and more perfect dispensation, nevertheless, it was established and ordained by God as the way to, and the preparation for, the Messias. The child has come to do the will of the Father, and the Father has willed that the Child keep the prescriptions of the Mosaic law, for that law will be valid until the Gospel will have been sufficiently promulgated. Too often men set at nought the will of God. The Child then will show by His every act that the will of God, whether manifest in the Old Law or in the New Law, must be obeyed. There is greater reason now for such example because, although the Old Law was intended for the Jews alone, the New Law, like the law of nature, is meant for all men.

The principal action of this mystery is that in the shedding of His blood the Child received His proper and peculiar name. Joseph declares that His name shall be Jesus. It is

---

[9] *In Circumcisione Domini Sermo* III; *PL* 183, 138.

the name of Saviour, chosen for the Incarnate Word by God
from eternity. There is no other name under heaven whereby
men may be saved:[10] the Child alone will save His people
from their sins. On the cross of Calvary He will shed all His
blood to effect that saving. It is fitting, then, that the name
of Saviour should be given Him on the occasion of the first
shedding of His blood. He is only eight days old and His
blood begins to flow. The knife of circumcision foreshadows
the scourge, thorns, nails, and lance which will complete the
shedding of that blood.

As were the Jews of old, so we today are the chosen of
God. The individual Jew renounced heathendom and was
admitted into the body of the faithful by the rite of circumcision. We were engrafted into that same body, which is
now the Body of Christ, by the sacrament of Baptism. We
do not remember the solemn occasion when the minister of
the sacrament of Baptism put to us the question, "Dost thou
renounce Satan?" Through the mouth of our sponsors we
answered, "I do renounce him." "And all his works?" "I do
renounce them." "And all his pomps?" "I do renounce them."
The life of Christian faith is a greater renunciation than was
the life of premessianic faith. The law of the Gospel cuts
cleanly and thoroughly to all the roots of human wrong-
doing. It involves a fiercer struggle with Satan and with the
great concupiscences. The observance of our baptismal vows
is the overthrow of Satan. The historian Livy writes: "When
Hannibal, then about nine years old, was childishly coaxing
his father Hamilcar to take him with him to Spain, his
father, who had finished the African War and was sacrificing
before crossing over with his army, led the boy up to the
altar and made him touch the offerings and bind himself
by oath that, as soon as he was able, he would be the declared enemy of the Roman people."[11] By keeping that oath
Hannibal brought Rome to the verge of destruction and
deflected the course of history. By like fidelity to their
baptismal vows Catholics could renew the face of the earth.
Europe would be a very different place if Napoleon, Cavour,

---

[10] Cf. Acts 4:12.
[11] XXI, I.

Hitler, and Mussolini had attended to their baptismal obligations. If all lax and worldly Catholics were to seek the death
of their concupiscences with the same pertinacity that Hannibal sought the overthrow of Rome, the words of the
prophet might soon be fulfilled: "The calf and the lion, and
the sheep shall abide together, and a little child shall lead
them."[12]

Perhaps we do not appreciate, as did the ancient Christian,
the full potential of sanctity contained in Baptism. He saw
in it total opposition to Satan and the world, the summons
to an exalted life and to a renunciation which might easily
include his life and all his goods. For the baptismal promise
is to abjure, not merely some, but all the pomps of Satan; not
merely big sins, but little sins and imperfections — anything
unbecoming a son of God. Avoidance of mortal sin satisfies
the minimum requirement of the Gospel law; it does not
come close to fulfilling its injunction of love. As God asks
us to love Him with all our hearts, so He bids us renounce,
not partially but totally, whatever may interfere with that
love. So absolute is the opposition between God and Mammon that God is to have everything we have, Mammon
nothing. Blessed are the earnest souls who see in total renunciation a living law of life.

Some souls discover this law early. With God's help they
live an upright innocent youth and, since they can honestly
say of God's commandments, "All these have I kept from
my youth,"[13] they are invited to observe the counsels. These
are like the laborers who were called into the vineyard at
the first or third hour. To others the great awakening may
come at the sixth or ninth hour; after they have spent, like
Matt Talbot, years in sin; after their children are raised;
after they have tasted the hollow successes and bitter de-
feats of life. It came to the good thief at the last moment
of the eleventh hour. With three hours to live he makes a
renunciation which atones for his past and sends him to
his judgment ready for the beatific vision. They tell of a
missionary to Japan in the seventeenth century who was

[12] Isa. 11:6.
[13] Mt. 19:20.

arrested. He apostatized and gained great influence and wealth. For forty years his brother missionaries in the East offered their lives to God begging for his conversion. He finally proclaimed himself a Christian and at the age of eighty made the supreme sacrifice for Christ which at forty he had not the courage to make.

It is not the time so much as the completeness of the renunciation which is our present interest. Nor does it matter essentially whether it be done by a public act at the altar of God or without benefit of ceremony or manifest action — the point is that one choose the Lord as the portion of his inheritance,[14] totally, irrevocably. He takes on the full yoke of Christ. He spells out to the last logical syllable every conclusion deducible from his baptismal promises and says: "This is the bond to which I subscribe." Everyone who so elects may then say with the prophet: "[The Lord] hath made me as a chosen arrow: in his quiver he hath hidden me."[15] Here we find some light upon the Gospel phrase: "Many are called but few are chosen."[16] For although God calls everyone to perfection, yet He chooses only the few whom He foresees will co-operate and actually renounce themselves.

To be a chosen arrow of the Lord requires, as it did of John the Baptist, a manifold circumcision. Not everyone must wear rough garments and live on locusts and wild honey but each is to practice whatever bodily mortification his present advance in perfection demands. Its kind and quantity will vary according to circumstances of person, situation, age, and the like. For instance, St. Bernard said to the monks of Clairvaux: "What, therefore, is our moral circumcision but that which the same apostle commends, saying: *Having food and clothing with these let us be content.* This voluntary poverty, penitential labor, and observance of regular discipline quite thoroughly circumcise us and cut away every superfluous thing."[17] Cistercian austerities would not help a soldier. The privations of the Poor Clares are not for the mother of small children. Since, however, this circumcision aims at making the body

---

[14] Cf. Ps. 15:5.
[15] Isa. 49:2.
[16] Mt. 22:14.
[17] *In Circumcisione Domini Sermo* I, 4; *PL* 183, 134.

the servant of the soul, it includes for everyone that prudent guard of the senses which excludes from the soul every avoidable blandishment; the refusal to be soft and indulge in unbecoming bodily comfort; the cheerful endurance of cold, heat, fatigue, pain; the acquisition of that Christian modesty which is the outward splendor of a pure soul.

The flesh is a stubborn enemy, but it will yield in the face of persistent effort. Origen assures us: "The patience of the spirit extinguishes the impatience of the flesh, and goodness overcomes malice, mildness destroys harshness, self-restraint intemperance, chastity lasciviousness. . . . And we ought to know this too, that the mortification of the acts of the flesh is accomplished through patience, not suddenly but gradually."[18]

The death of the flesh is the liberation of the spirit. "By this death," says St. Ambrose, "the soul is set free . . . Wherefore, while we are in the body, let us, imitating the action of death, raise on high our body from the chamber of this flesh and, as it were, let us rise out of this sepulchre . . . Therefore like an eagle let our soul seek the heights, let it fly above the clouds, let it shine in new garments, let it wing its way to the heavens where it can fall into no traps. For the bird which comes down from on high, or cannot leave the ground, is often caught in traps, or deceived by bird lime, or enmeshed in some kind of snare. So also our soul must beware of descending to earthly things."[19]

A person circumcises the intellect by not confusing fancy with fact or mistaking prejudice for evidence, by suppressing useless daydreams, by stern pursuit of truth. By cutting it loose from the sources of error, he liberates his intellect for its sole function of contact with reality. He uses modern means of information, not, however, to burden himself with knowledge of useless things, like passing fads or the doings of the glamorous people who fill the public eye. He cultivates serious tastes and his first thought is of undying realities — the word of God, the truths of faith, the means of perfection. If he is a religious he sees in his institute and rules the one way which leads him to God. Every aspirant to perfec-

---

[18] *Comment. in Romanos*, 6, 14; *PG* 14, 1102.
[19] *De Bono Mortis*, 5, 16; *PL* 14, 575.

tion will circumcise his affections, forbidding himself useless friendships, frivolous ties, and any merely carnal love. His one and only love is Jesus Christ the Lord and whatever tends to lessen that love he is willing to part from. A person must give exceedingly great care to cultivating this love because the mephitic air of this world, which can seep within the walls of the holiest house, can poison and kill this love.

The supreme circumcision is of the will. This truly fulfills the prescription of St. Paul: "Circumcision is that of the heart, in the spirit, not in the letter."[20] According to St. John of the Cross, human perfection is "the total transformation of the will into the will of God, in such a way that every movement of the will shall always be the movement of the will of God only. This is the reason why, in this state, two wills are said to be one — my will and God's will — so that the will of God is also that of the soul. But if the soul then cleaves to any imperfection, contrary to the will of God, His will is not done, for the soul wills that which God wills not . . . If the soul is to be united in love and will with God, every desire of the will must first be cast away, however slight it may be; that is, we must not deliberately and knowingly assent to any imperfection, and we must have such power over it, and such liberty, as to reject every such desire the moment we are aware of it."[21] Perfection consists in always willing the right thing, that is, what God wills for us — our own good. The will achieves union with God's will by circumcising its worldly desires. These are voluntary acts of the will, not those natural urges and indeliberate motions of the lower appetite which no one can empty from his heart. They are worldly, part of that world of temporal happiness which ever opposes Christ, the gauds which are the easy substitutes for God. We should remember that it is not the things of the world which injure the soul, for they enter not into it; but rather the wish for these things, which abides with us. Besides being able to deprive the soul of the Spirit of God, these desires weary and fatigue it. They are like restless difficult children, impossible to satisfy. They are like stinging bees tormenting and

---

[20] Rom. 2:29.
[21] *Ascent of Mount Carmel,* Book I, Chap. XI.

afflicting the soul. They enfeeble the soul, distracting it from its one rightful object and scattering its strength over many unworthy things. They steal away its simplicity. Ridden by its desires, the soul is like the moth whose eyes avail it little, since the attraction of the gleam of the light leads it to be consumed in the flame.

It is one thing to make a promise in the fire of youth and quite another to fulfill it in the maturity of experience. It is easy enough to say at the age of twenty-five that one will circumcise all worldly desires, and quite another at the age of fifty to look back on the years of slack fulfillment. Whoever takes on self-assumed obligations needs to be a realist. He cannot afford to let pious wishes run ahead of his intellect. He must know both the ideal and the actuality. He should realize that counsels of perfection rest upon a solid basis in reason and be aware of how men measure up to them. It is no denial of the beauty of the ideal, nor should it be an inducement to relinquish the ideal, to know that some men pledge themselves to it and fail to keep their promise. All begin the way of perfection with the same attitude — the crusader aflame to make himself and the world over for Christ. This attitude will be sternly tested: by the ups and downs, the shocks and disappointments of daily living; by the disillusionments and heartaches attendant upon the realization of a high ideal; perhaps by the rebirth of passions once subdued or by opportunities for self-indulgence which gradually and unnoticed can crowd around a man. He will have moments of regret and ask himself: "Why did I start this? This is more than I can do." He will find quite a gap between the original intention and the final execution. So the crusader will in time assume one of three attitudes.

First, he may become a drifter who releases himself from much of what he promised. Once he asked to stand close to the cross of Christ: now he has edged himself little by little away. He permits the keen edge of will to grow blunt from disuse. He fails to will the better things he should will. So he assumes an attitude of permanent pretense. He goes through external motions and maintains some outward form of his renunciation. If he is a lay person, he still reads spiritual books, attends an occasional retreat, fills in some measure of devotion. If he is a cleric or a religious he retains an academic interest in perfection and can glibly talk the technical language of asceticism. Lay or cleric, his inner spirit of renunciation has been quite thoroughly eviscerated and he is blithely unaware of the catastrophe. He imagines he is doing well, keeping his part of a lofty bargain, but he is leading a more or less natural life. He has drawn the teeth out of his original promises. Instead of the law circumcising his unruly appetites, he circumcises the law. He drops this, that, or the other demand of virtue or point of observance, arbitrarily deciding that he is free of obligations he wishes to be free of. He has stopped the generous giving of self.

Sigrid Undset wrote of Protestantism that as it "goes cutting away more and more dogmas, it becomes more and more emasculated. Because dogmas in the body social are like the ductless glands in the human body . . . Without them the power of acting and contending goes to the winds. Take something away, and metabolism is disturbed. Take away some more, and the body becomes swollen with pale, dead fat . . . till one is reminded of Constantine the Second's court eunuchs, who may be able to quarrel and intrigue, but are no use for fighting — at any rate, for fighting to the death against heathendom."[22] As the drifter cuts away more and more of the obligations he assumed, he becomes less able to contend with the principle of corruption within him. At what point will he stop? He may personally be willing to stop far short of serious sin, but circumstances over which he has no control can compel him to choose between an easy life and absolute defection. The bishops of Henry VIII must have been drifters, because, when the great crisis came, with the exception of the martyr, St. John Fisher, they all apostatized. Bossuet tells us that "of the sixteen thousand ecclesiastics who made up the body of the English clergy . . . three-fourths renounced their celibacy in Edward's time."[23] Who knows when Mammon may not again stand astride our world like a huge colossus and demand absolute conformity of all men under penalty of death? The drifter is ill prepared to make the right choice.

---

[22] Sigrid Undset, *The Wild Orchid,* p. 372.

[23] *History of the Variations of the Protestant Churches* (New York: Sadlier, 1845), Vol. I, Book VII, no. 96., p. 265.

Heroicity is the second attitude. The hero is first a person of high purpose. When Theodosius II died, his sister Pulcheria became empress of the Eastern Empire in A.D. 450. Theodosius II had been a weakling from whom Attila, the scourge of God, had extorted much tribute. When the barbarian attempted to mulct her, he got the uncompromising reply: "I have gold for my friends, but iron for my enemies!" Living such a principle, it is no wonder, that, although she could command every Byzantine luxury, she died in the odor of heroic sanctity. The hero is a cool logician who sees the inevitable consequences of desiring lofty purposes and does not boggle at them. He who wishes greatness must be willing to pay the price of greatness. They tell the story of Foch that one of his generals came to him to say that the troops under him would have to retire. Foch said: "They must not retire." The general expostulated: "That means that we all must die." Foch replied: "Exactly. You have hit it."

But, above all, the hero is the enduring man. Many persons enter like a hero upon the way of perfection, but only he is deserving of the hero's crown who maintains that attitude to the end. The hero does that which without qualification is humanly difficult. To make large surrenders of self for a time is hard enough: the thing is to continue making them for the remainder of one's life. The Norwegians say that a hero is one who knows how to hang on one minute longer. When it was clear that God did not wish him to be a priest or a religious, Benedict Joseph Labre chose to be an exile and a vagabond, not for a summer's vacation, but for always. Having nothing but the clothes on his back, eating whatever charity extended, sleeping where chance directed, he unpretentiously challenged the Age of Reason and gave eighteenth-century Europe thirteen years of proof that the only wisdom is laying up treasure where no thieves break through and steal.[24]

It is praiseworthy to make grand resolutions by the tabernacle light in the seclusion of a good retreat but what counts is keeping them on the street, on buses, in the living room, at work, at play. To seek close union with God in a protected life is one thing, but actually to realize that union when the

---

[24] Cf. Mt. 6:20.

hot breath of passion blows and when crosses, contradictions, and humiliations pile up — that proclaims the substantial hero. If a person generously dedicates himself to God, and ever after that dedication continues to pour himself out in self-immolation, yielding whatever God may ask, he is deserving of canonization on his deathbed.

Between extremes of pretense and heroicity is the third attitude of resigned and somewhat complacent mediocrity, that of persons who, having once made a bid for high perfection, now say that the heights are too much for their plodding gifts. They draw two lines: one below, indicating practices they will not give up and faults they will not commit; another above, which emphatically bars them from the perfection which brooks no limit. Between these boundaries they move at their own comfortable gait, confident that the same God who began in them this good work will perfect it unto the day of Christ Jesus.[25] They excuse themselves from a more exacting pace, saying that their limitation allows of nothing swifter. Heroicity can kill, and it is better to be a live jackass than a dead lion. They are grateful to the Church for giving them more than a very laborious life can repay. They tend their modest garden of virtues and fill in their little round of duties done, prayers said, and small faults deliberately committed.

Does nothing more remain? Must they say good-by to heroism forever? Having once been heroes, can they not again abandon themselves to God's designs for them, asking love of Him to take complete possession and bear them where it will? They do well to remember who they are and the name they bear. For they share the name which the Child received in the shedding of His blood. By baptism every Christian has been made a participant of that name. "Know ye not, that as many of us as were baptized unto Christ Jesus, we were baptized unto his death? We are buried therefore with him through this baptism into death."[26] Is not every Christian called to be another Jesus? How much more so are they who once were taught, and generously tried, to imitate

---

[25] Cf. Phil. 1:6.
[26] Rom. 6:3, Westminster version.

Him? If, then, a man's courage droops at the thought of return to great sacrifice, he should ponder again the power of that Name. He should reread the heart-warming words of St. Bernard: "One of you is sad? Let Jesus come into his heart, and thence leap into his mouth; and, lo, at the light begotten of that name, every cloud disappears and serenity returns. Someone commits a grave sin, and even runs in desperation to the snare of death? Who will not at once breathe life if he invokes the name of Life? Whose hardness of heart, as they call it, cowardly tepidity, rancor of soul, or slothful apathy has ever held out against that saving name? Whose dried-up fountain of tears did not at once burst forth more abundantly and flow more sweetly when Jesus was invoked? To whom in dangers' toils did not the invocation of that powerful name bring confidence and dispel fear? To whom, I ask, in the turmoil of doubt, did not certainty suddenly shine forth when that illustrious name was mentioned? Even though he were afraid and on the point of giving up, to whom was courage ever lacking, if only he mentioned that helping name?"[27]

To accept a plan of complete circumcision and put it into execution seems a rugged, dismal prospect — but only to those who are afraid to hope enough. To the man who is willing to risk it, it will become the joy and sweetness of the promised hundredfold. No man has ever generously put on the livery of Jesus Christ and failed to find the yoke sweet and the burden light. But even if this inner circumcision condemns a man to a chill and lonely existence, he knows that, if he shares in the suffering inevitable in the bearing of the name of Jesus, he will likewise share in its glory. To the fullest extent Christ fulfilled the bloody foreshadowing of His circumcision. The chalice which His Father gave Him He drank to the dregs. And now His name is exalted. At the name of Jesus hell trembles; a rejuvenated earth will one day cry: "Sing ye a psalm to his name,"[28] and the heavens will answer: "Glory ye in his holy name."[29]

---

[27] *Sermones in Cantica*, Sermo XV; *PL* 183, 847.

[28] Ps. 65:2.

[29] Ps. 104:3.

Our circumcision will also find its suitable reward. While the life of man is now a warfare, the warfare is not forever. The longest life is like the arrow which is shot from the bow and speedily falls to the ground. The endurance of sorrow and the need of self-sacrifice come quickly to an end. In His Father's house are many mansions, and He has gone there to prepare a place for us, but what sort of place it will be, and the glory of it, depends on the generosity whereby we here and now circumcise from our lives everything which is not of God.

While evangelizing Gaul for twenty years, St. Columbanus had enjoyed the favor of Burgundian royalty until he crossed Brunehault, the grandmother of the king. Columbanus refused to recognize and bless the four illegitimate children of her son Thierry as royal heirs. With the single-minded vindictiveness of a hating woman, she drove him from place to place, subjecting him to every manner of vexation, until she had him exiled from Burgundy. After painful journeyings he arrived at Nantes. It was his last night on the soil of the land he had glorified. Sadly his thoughts reverted to the monks he had left at Luxeuil and, in a long letter, he poured out his heart to them. He said in part: "What has happened to us is nothing new: we daily predicted it . . . The Gospels are full of this and were written for this purpose . . . to teach the true disciples of Christ to follow Him, bearing their cross . . . We must, therefore, walk the royal road unto the city of the living God, through afflictions of the flesh and contrition of heart, through labor of the body and humiliation of the spirit . . . In the flesh are many perils. Remember the reason why you struggle and the magnitude of the reward . . . Without adversaries no conflict; and without conflict, no crown. Where the struggle is, there is courage, vigilance, fervor, patience, fidelity, wisdom, firmness, prudence. Where there is no fight, misery and disaster. Thus, then, without war, no crown! And I may add, without freedom, no honor."[30]

But hope is not enough. There must be love. What does a good mother think of all the inconveniences and even hard-

---

[30] S. Columbani Abbatis, *Epis. IV ad discipulos et monachos suos;* PL 80, 272, 273.

ship she may endure for the sake of her children? Love makes all things easy. "For while we cling to His love," says Origen, "we are not conscious of pain. For the charity, wherewith He loved us and drew our affection to Himself, makes us insensible to pain of body and to sorrow. Therefore, *in all things we overcome*. The Bride in the Canticle said the same thing to the Word, namely, *I am wounded by love*. In like manner also the soul receives from Christ the wound of charity, and although it may deliver its body to the sword, it does not feel the wound of the flesh on account of the wound of charity."[31]

---

[31] *Comment. in Romanos*, 7, 11; *PG* 14, 1132.

5. Humility and Dedication

"I will be little in my own eyes" (2 Kings 6:22).

ON THE second of February the Church commemorates the events recorded in the second chapter of St. Luke, verses 22–40. The outstanding facts are the purification of the Mother and the presentation of the Son. These are liturgical actions done in fulfillment of two precepts of the Mosaic Law.

THE PURIFICATION OF THE HUMBLE

According to Leviticus,[1] a woman, by giving birth to a son, contracts certain legal disabilities. For forty days she may not touch any holy thing nor enter the sanctuary. Like a dutiful daughter of the Law, she should not leave her home until she goes to the Temple for her rite of purification. She is to bring a lamb for holocaust and a young pigeon for sin. This is not moral sin, as though childbirth involved moral guilt. The sin is legal, prohibiting the person from religious contacts and activities. If the woman is too poor to afford a lamb, she may substitute another pigeon for the holocaust. The priest then prays for her and her disability is remitted.

The Fathers who treat this subject and the vast majority of commentators[2] say that, in complying with this law, Mary was performing an act of supererogation. Certainly the reason for legal uncleanness was not present in Mary's case. One author,[3] however, argues that as the Son was "made under the law,"[4] the Mother of the Son was subject to the Law. His argument falls because the Son explicitly says that

---

[1] Chapter 12.
[2] Cornelius a Lapide, *Commentarii in Sacram Scripturam*, VIII, p. 679.
[3] J. Knabenbauer, *Comment. in Quatuor S. Evangel.*, In Luc. 2, p. 131.
[4] Gal. 4:4.

He is not subject to the Law.[5] The author does make this point, however, that, since the mystery of Mary's conception was unknown, she was obliged for the sake of example to do as other women did. Be this as it may, it is surely inconceivable that Mary should assert, even to herself, that she was not as the rest of Jewish mothers, or that she should make any claim for exemption for the reason that He who is mighty had done great things to her.[6] In her compliance with this law, as in any other act of her life, she is the handmaid of the Lord. She could act in this manner only because of the serene and boundless humility whence all her virtue sprang.

Since our souls grow weary of their failures and discouraged when the process of self-refinement becomes distasteful; since we seek ourselves and then find ourselves incredibly empty, vain, and wanting, we need a quiet hour away from our petty striving, our discontents, and the brawling clamor of daily living that we may sit and contemplate the ordered peace of Mary's humility. It is vast, serene, and all-encompassing; more fair than the heavens and the earth on the first morning of creation. Yet with all its flawless perfection it never repels. Despite the exactions which its imitation demands of us, we bless it and find it appealing. For, in the presence of her virtue, tranquillity possesses the beholder. Discontent subsides, because one is in the presence of the fair and gracious and unperturbed which rouses no competitive envy. Here is human virtue that is beauty, loveliness, and unmixed delight. The heroic proportions of her virtue are deftly concealed in the graciousness which exhales from it.

There are compelling reasons for Mary's humility. The first is God's esteem of the virtue. Bossuet says: "God cannot win greater glory than when He abases and humbles Himself. Here is indeed a strange novelty . . . but the proof of my assertion is in the fact that, notwithstanding the infinite extent of His power, God could do nothing greater than bestow on the world a God-man — *Domine, opus tuum*. Lord, that is your greatest work; and consequently it is His greatest glory, since God's glory consists in His works . . . Let us then say

---

[5] Cf. Mt. 12:8; 17:23–26.
[6] Cf. Lk. 1:49.

with the prophet: God hath wrought a new work. He has chosen to reach the very peak of greatness; for that purpose He abased Himself. He has willed to reveal His glory in greatest splendor; for that purpose He clothed Himself in our weakness. Do not imagine I am preaching this novelty to amuse your minds . . . but to make you love humility by showing how God loved it. He cannot find it in Himself; for His sovereign greatness cannot allow Him to humble Himself whilst in His own nature . . . But what he cannot meet with in Himself, He seeks in another nature. He, infinitely rich, goes borrowing. Why? That He may be enriched by humility. That is what the Son of God sought on earth, that is why He is made man — that His Father may behold in His Person a submissive and obedient God."[7]

The second reason is Mary's own greatness. St. Augustine says: "Each one's humility is measured according to his greatness."[8] Since Mary is raise above all creation, her moral splendor must rest upon a base of humility wider and deeper than that of any creature. The loftier the building the deeper the foundation. "When we compare Mary's destiny with that of the apostate angel she was to overcome, with that of Eve whom she was to reclaim; when we consider that she was raised from a condition infinitely lower to a rank infinitely higher than those grand victims of pride, that she was elevated from the condition of a poor obscure maiden of Judea . . . to the incommensurable grandeur of the Mother of God . . . a dizziness comes over the imagination; and we can easily understand that it was far more necessary for such greatness to be tempered by humiliations than to be exalted by praise . . . We learn from Tertullian that the illustrious conquerors of ancient Rome marched to the Capitol surrounded by glory so great, that for fear of being dazzled by so much splendor, and then believing themselves to be more than mortal, a slave was appointed to follow behind them and warn them that they were but men, in the words: *Look behind you, remember you are a man.* And so it was with Mary, preceded, as she had been, by the

---

[7] *Sermo III Sur le Mystere de l'Incarnation du Verbe,* premier point, Oeuvres Completes, ed. by Migne, Vol. 6, pp. 1028–1029.

[8] *De Sancta Virginitate,* c. 31; PL 40, 413.

prophets of the Old Law, who had foreseen her as well as her Son, followed by all future generations who until our day and to the end of time were to proclaim her Blessed; leading captive and in chains, by her virginal maternity, the enemy of the human race, hell, and its powers, celebrating in her own wonderful hymn their defeat and her triumph and advancing thus, in the footsteps of her Son, to receive as Mother, Spouse, and beloved Daughter of the Most High, upon the throne next to that of the deity, the crown predestined for her from all eternity; so it was that Mary needed in so prodigious a triumph the voice, not of a slave, but of that God to whom so much glory seemed to equal her, to remind her of her extraction and say to her: 'Woman, what is there between me and thee? Glance below, look behind you, be mindful of your condition and remember you are a woman.' Salutary humiliation for the holiness of Mary, but a humiliation nonetheless glorious, since, as Tertullian said of the Roman conquerors: 'The greatest subject of their joy consisted in seeing themselves surrounded by such glory as to inspire the fear lest they should forget they were mortals.' Mary did not forget it, she who considered herself not merely as a simple woman but a servant. But as her fearful elevation exposed her incessantly to the vertigo of pride, her soul could not be protected by too many precautions."[9]

Mary acquired her humility by the perfect acceptance of the humiliations which came to her because of the Divine Maternity. Indeed this was the only source whence humiliations could come to her. She was incapable of being humiliated by creatures. Aristotle says of his magnanimous man: "honor from casual people and on trifling grounds he will disdain, since it is not this that he deserves, and dishonor too, since in his case it cannot be just."[10] Mary's magnanimity was of a nobler order. Although she contemned no one's praise or censure, nevertheless she was too far above men and angels to be touched by created praise or insult. Hence her humiliations had to come from God and strike her in her exaltation.

They began with the fact of her Purification. She who had

---

[9] Auguste Nicolas, *La Vierge Marie d'Apres l'Evangile,* pp. 33–35 (Paris, 1857).

[10] *Ethics,* IV–3, 1124a.

brought Purification Itself into the world must herself undergo purification at the hands of men! She, who had wondered about becoming the mother of the Messias on the ground of the virginity she had vowed, must now appear despoiled of that glory! Soon she had to fly into Egypt because she was the mother of the Child whom Herod sought to kill. She had to endure the heartbreak of losing her Boy for three days, and the only explanation she ever got from Him was: "Did you not know that I must be about my Father's business?"[11] Her request for a miracle at Cana met with an initial rebuff: "Woman, what is that to me and to thee?"[12] The question meant: "You and I do not agree about this." Did He not test her as well as teach us in the incident of her attempt to speak with Him while He was preaching? The crowd within the room where He was speaking passed up the word: "Behold thy mother and thy brethren without seek for thee." And answering them, He said: "Who is my mother and my brethren?" And looking on them who sat around about Him, He said: "Behold my mother and my brethren. For whosoever shall do the will of God, he is my brother, and my sister, and my mother."[13] The mother of a convicted criminal, she had to keep the three-hour deathwatch for her Son.

Her humility is as vast as the depth of heaven. She realizes that however boundlessly she is exalted above mere man, nevertheless she is still infinitely removed from the sanctity of God. She knows she is queen of angels and of men, and yet a mere creature; the mother of the Infinite Son, and yet a contingent being. She is humble, because she appreciated to the last practical consequence her place before God, and acquiesced in it perfectly. In perfect contentment, therefore, she can accept every manifestation of His will, even though it may have involved a testing and a searching of her virtue. Humility is truth, the exact recognition of a lowly status. Mary could appreciate the sinlessness of her actions, the sublimity of her exaltation above all created intelligence but One, and still recognize that none of her excellence was rooted in herself, but in the prodigal giving of Divine Wisdom and

---

[11] Lk. 2:49.
[12] Jn. 2:4.
[13] Mk. 3:32–35.

Love. She is full of grace and entitled to a plenitude of glory, not because of her initial deserving, but because of the eternal decrees. Not to her, then, was the ultimate glory, but solely to Him who had devised and made all this possible. Adorned with the Divine Maternity as with the moon and the seven brightest stars of the firmament, effulgent with the untarnished splendor of her Immaculate Conception, radiant in her unmatched virginity as no samite or cloth of gold can make radiant, yet she does not make of herself what is incompatible with her creaturehood; she accepts with tranquillity the humiliations which prove her deserving. Above all men, she verified the statement of the Roman orator: "To him who has attained the summit of human grandeur, there remains one way of rising yet higher, which is to abase self without fearing any diminution of true grandeur. For of all the risks the great have to avoid, that of lowering themselves by voluntary humility is the smallest."[14]

How different from Mary's is the lowliness of our status. Her condition was sinlessness. No need in her of expiation, nor call to repair the inroads of concupiscence. In contrast, which of us can say, "Who will convict me of sin?"[15] All of us have many sins which one day we must account for, but how reluctant we are to face the sordidness of these follies. How grudgingly we accept the unpalatable truth that, if we do not manfully grapple with our concupiscences, they will surely overthrow us. If we are to be humble according to the pattern Mary has left us, we must appreciate who we are, and take the humbling tests which God has designed for us.

We are neither brute nor angel, but we should have no false delusion about the excellence of man — the lowest species of the intellectual creature. Without God we are simply nothing. The beginning, the middle, and the end of us is God — God creating, God conserving, God co-operating. Whatever is fine and noble in us is the pure gift of God. Whatever is mean, sordid, stained, or ungenerous results from our malice and stupidity. We belong to God absolutely and completely. No single thing of ours may be outside of Him or apart from

---

[14] Pliny the Younger, *Panegyric to Trajan*, c. 71.
[15] Jn. 8:46.

His will. Whatever we conceive of as existing outside of Him is pure nothingness — it is moral evil, self-destruction. The overlordship of God is so all-inclusive that we cannot exaggerate its practical consequences. Our glory is that He made us to His own image and likeness. Therefore, we should be not what we choose to be, but what God intends us to be — true reflections of His sanctity, of His love, of His reasonableness. But we are not fully what God from eternity has intended we should be. In many ways, times, and occasions we have fallen short of God's original idea of us. We have been false to the nature and grace given us. We have gone against the light of reason. We have set our hearts on things very different from God. We must confess that we are men who have sinned.

The first reason, therefore, for humbling self, which did not exist in Mary's case, is the conquest of sin. We must wipe out the past by due contrition and satisfaction. Of ourselves, none of us could have effaced the guilt of malice nor offered satisfaction equivalent to the requirements of sin's due punishment. The Son of God had to act in our place and do for us what we never could have done. "His own self bore our sins in his body on the tree: that we, being dead to sins, should live to justice."[16] We must join ourselves to Him and make our own the benefits of His atonement. We must also provide that the future is not a repetition of the past. This involves surrender of affection for the persons, places, and things which have been the immediate occasion of our deliberate lapses. Since both animal and spiritual appetites have been disordered by original sin, we must rectify them by wise restraint. We can do none of this without constant exercise of humility.

The greater reason is that we, like Mary, are to be tested in those things which God intends should be our future glory. God will give His gifts irrevocably to His free creatures only after He has tested their worthiness to possess them. If God gives eloquence of speech, facility in writing, warmth of affection, depth of understanding, ability to lead, efficiency in practical accomplishments, He will test a person's use of these

16 1 Pet. 2:24.

things. The man will be humbled precisely because he possesses these things in order that he may prove that he prizes them, not as adornments of self, but as means of union with God. If God calls one to the priesthood, or religious life, or high sanctity in the world, the call will bring its special heart-burning. God's greatest gift in this life is membership in His Church, the call to be a branch of the Vine. Herein lies the reason why God humbles all the faithful. For no one can be exalted unless he has first been humbled. This is the rudimentary pattern of Christianity. Mary's career in this respect is the exact counterpart of her Son's. He first descended and then He rose. "O foolish, and slow of heart to believe in all the things which the prophets have spoken. Ought not Christ to have suffered these things, and so to enter into His glory?"[17]

The vast majority of good people must live a life unknown and shorn of great deeds. If an obscure and commonplace life becomes a trial, let us remember the role of Mary. She brought forth the Word and thereafter she is the woman wrapped in silence. After the archangel addresses her as full of grace, and Elizabeth calls her blessed among women, and the angels hymn the birth of her Son, her life is total obscurity and utter humility. She never worked a miracle, she never wrote an inspired book or any other kind, she held no post of authority in the Church. Having given the Child to the world, she must so efface herself that men have eyes and ears only for the Child. By fulfilling this function perfectly she rises to be Queen of creation.

THE PRESENTATION OF THE DEDICATED

The second mystery to consider is the presentation and the buying back of the Child. According to the law of Moses every first-born child was the peculiar property of God. For "the Lord spoke to Moses, saying: Sanctify unto me every first born that opened the womb among the children of Israel, as well of men as of beasts: for they are all mine."[18] When the angel of death had passed through Egypt and had slain the first born of man and beast, God spared Israel. Hence, the

---

[17] Lk. 24:25–26.
[18] Exod. 13, 1–2.

first born of Israel were His. He set them aside as the liturgical agents by whom divine worship should be conducted. Later God took the tribe of Levi[19] to perform this sacerdotal function in place of the first born. In each case, however, the substitution could be effected only if the first born were offered in the Temple and redeemed by a ransom of five shekels. The parents offered the child to the priest who accepted it and, upon payment of the ransom by the parents, the priest handed the child back again, thus maintaining the rights of God and the duty of each family.

In His turn the Child Jesus was presented to the God of Israel. After receiving the ransom for Him, the priest gave Him back to Mary and Joseph. The action signified that the Child was now at liberty, that liturgically He no longer was God's exclusive property. Such action of course was meaningless in connection with this Child. He could not be other than the Lord's. What ransom price could substitute for Him who came as the substitute of all mankind? The tribe of Levi could not function for Him. He is the true High Priest, the Pontifex who builds the one bridge whereby man can get to God, and who offers the one sacrifice by which alone God is adequately worshiped. Thirty-three years later on Calvary it will be seen that no one has dispensed Him from immolating Himself to the glory of His Father. On that occasion He will deliver Himself for us, an oblation and a sacrifice to God for an odor of sweetness.[20] It is, therefore, impossible for the priest to give this Child back to ordinary uses. He cannot be returned to a profane life because He comes as the High Priest of the good things to come, to enter into the holy of holies, having offered Himself unspotted unto God, to cleanse our consciences from dead works.[21] This ceremony cannot release Him from divine service. The Child has a baptism wherewith He is to be baptized:[22] from before the daystar He has been consecrated unto it. In the head of the book it is written that He should do Thy will, O God.[23]

---

[19] Cf. Num. 3:12.
[20] Cf. Eph. 5:2.
[21] Cf. Hebr. 9:11, 14.
[22] Cf. Lk. 12:50.
[23] Cf. Hebr. 10:7.

Assuming the solemn accents, the lyric phrase, the original and enigmatic words of the ancient prophets, the holy old man Simeon proclaims the anointed character of this Child. He is the Salvation which God has prepared before the face of all peoples. He is the Light of revelation for the Gentiles. He is the Glory of Thy people Israel.[24] Salvation, light, and glory!

Can we find a parallel to the rite of presentation in Christian liturgy? In the sacraments of Baptism, Confirmation, and Holy Orders, wherein the minister anoints the recipient and the sacrament unites him to Christ the Priest, there is certainly dedication. Liturgically, anointing signifies consecration to sacred uses. Since Jesus is our High Priest and the perfect example of dedication, He is rightly called *Christos,* the *Anointed One.* By Baptism the soul is snatched from Satan, dedicated to God, and given the right to participate in the Eucharistic Sacrifice. By Confirmation a share in the prophetic office of Christ is bestowed. By Holy Orders the fullness of the priesthood of Christ is given. Each Christian ceremony is a dedication, but in none of them is there any giving back of the soul to profane uses. Rather is there increase of attachment and obligation.

Baptism is dedication to sublime ideals, to a life of faith in God as He is. They who think that Christian living is meant to be quite pedestrian for the great multitude of the faithful should carefully examine St. Paul's concept of the life of the baptized. Let them keep in mind also that the Apostle is addressing men who "were once darkness but [are] now light in the Lord."[25] He reveals with penetrating detail how dark was that darkness and how steeped in iniquity was the ancient world. A short while ago his converts were part and parcel of the darkness: "You yourselves were at one time estranged and enemies in mind through your evil works."[26] Many of them perhaps were but late "filled with all iniquity, malice, immorality, avarice, wickedness."[27] But thanks be to God,

---

[24] Cf. Lk. 2:30–32.

[25] Eph. 5:8.

[26] Col. 1:21. The Confraternity of Christian Doctrine version is used for the remainder of this chapter.

[27] Rom. 1:29.

who "predestined [them] to be adopted through Jesus Christ
as his sons,"[28] they have been rescued "from the power of
darkness and transferred into the kingdom of his beloved
son."[29] For Baptism made them sharers of the death and
resurrection of Christ. "Do you not know that all we who have
been baptized into Christ Jesus have been baptized into his
death? For we were buried with him by means of Baptism
into death, in order that, just as Christ has arisen from the
dead through the glory of the Father, so we also may walk
in newness of life."[30]

Newness of life involves a new goal and a new way of life.
To men who recently "were unwise, unbelieving, going astray,
slaves to various lusts and pleasures, living in malice and
envy,"[31] what goal does he propose? It is with awe we read his
various exhortations. He tells the Ephesians: "Be you, therefore, imitators of God, as very dear children and walk in
love, as Christ also loved us and delivered himself up for us."[32]
He says to the Romans: "I exhort you therefore, brethren, by
the mercy of God, to present your bodies as a sacrifice, living,
holy, pleasing to God — your spiritual service. And be not
conformed to this world, but be transformed in the newness
of your mind, that you may discern what is the good and
acceptable and perfect will of God."[33] He exhorts the Corinthians: "Let us cleanse ourselves from all defilement of the
flesh and of the spirit, perfecting holiness in the fear of
God."[34] These brands just saved from the burning are to
ambition a perfect life; they are to imitate God, discern the
perfect will of God and perfect themselves in holiness. These
are not random fitful exhortations; they characterize the
whole tenor of his pleading. He says that the desire of Christ
for the soul is "to present you holy and undefiled and irre-
proachable before him."[35] What sublime blessings he begs
for his charges when he prays: "I bend my knees to the

---

28 Eph. 1:5.
29 Col. 1:13.
30 Rom. 6:3–5.
31 Titus 3:3.
32 Eph. 5:1–2.
33 Rom. 12:1–2.
34 2 Cor. 7:1.
35 Col. 1:22.

Father . . . that he may grant you from his glorious riches to be strengthened with power through his Spirit unto progress of the inner man; and to have Christ dwelling by faith in your hearts: so that being rooted and grounded in love, you may be able to comprehend with all the saints what is the breadth and length and height and depth, and to know Christ's love which surpasses all knowledge, in order that you may be filled with all the fulness of God."[36]

The late votaries of Astarte and Diana of the Ephesians are to seek after the fullness of the living God — here indeed is revolution! And remember, the first readers of his epistles were the poor of this world, workingmen, slaves, the fathers and mothers of families. These he offers ideals worthy of today's most cloistered communities! Nor is the offer made to a few promising souls but to all. For "Him we preach, admonishing every man in all wisdom, that we may present every man perfect in Christ Jesus."[37]

What means are available for attaining the fulness of God? Of themselves they can do nothing; for all their sufficiency is from God. He it is "who of his good pleasure works in you both the will and the performance."[38] Their part is to co-operate with the Holy Spirit who has been poured into their hearts. That they may do so they must be properly instructed in becoming conduct. Hence we expect their father-in-Christ to teach them the natural and Christian virtues. But what great surprises his pupils must have experienced when the instruction leaves the ordinary and humdrum and rises to sublime heights. The Christian husband is to love his wife as Christ loves His Spouse, the Church. All are told: "Bless those who persecute you . . . Do not avenge yourselves . . . If thy enemy is hungry give him food."[39] Quite a surprise for the Jewish convert brought up on the doctrine of an eye for an eye and a tooth for a tooth! No less was the surprise of the Greek who was asked to accept the foolishness of the Gospel, "lest the doctrine of the cross be made void. For the doctrine of the cross is foolishness to those who perish, but

---

[36] Eph. 3: 14–19.
[37] Col. 1:28.
[38] Phil. 2:13.
[39] Rom. 12:14, 19, 20.

to those who are saved, that is, to us, it is the power of God.
. . . Has not God turned to foolishness the 'wisdom' of this
world? For since, in God's wisdom, the world did not come
to know God by 'wisdom,' it pleased God, by the foolishness
of our preaching to save those who believe."[40] The Christian
is called upon to become a fool. "If anyone of you thinks
himself wise in this world, let him become a fool, that he
may come to be wise. For the wisdom of this world is foolishness with God."[41] The man who passes by easy money,
easy pleasure, easy advancement on account of the Ten Commandments is a fool to this world. But what further follies
does the Apostle suggest in his invitation to perfect chastity
and in the portrait he paints of perfect charity! His children
are to give shining example of unity and disinterestedness,
"doing nothing out of contentiousness or out of vainglory, but
in humility let each one regard the others as his superiors,
each one looking not to his own interests but to those of
others."[42] What a standard of meekness he proposes. Do not
go to law with a fellow Christian: "Why not rather suffer
wrong?"[43] Put up with it "if a man enslaves you, if a man
devours you, if a man takes from you, if a man is arrogant,
if a man slaps your face."[44] Finally, he gently sums it all up:
"Do all things without murmuring and without questioning
so as to be blameless and guileless, children of God without
blemish in the midst of a depraved and perverse generation."[45]

That they may live up to the difficult expectations enter-
tained of them he offers this practical ideal: "Be imitators of
me, as I am of Christ."[46] Let them learn from him that Christian living is dedication to Christ, the effort to reproduce His
life in one's own life. He unbares to the Philippians the personal drives of his life: "The things that were gain to me,
these, for the sake of Christ, I have counted loss. Nay more,
I count everything loss because of the excelling knowledge of
Jesus Christ, my Lord. For his sake I have suffered the loss

[40] 1 Cor. 1:17, 19, 20, 21.
[41] 1 Cor. 3:18–19.
[42] Phil. 2:3.
[43] 1 Cor. 6:7.
[44] 2 Cor. 11:20.
[45] Phil. 2:14.
[46] 1 Cor. 4:16.

of all things, and I count them as dung that I may gain
Christ . . . so that I may know him and the power of his resurrection and the fellowship of his sufferings: become like to
him in death, in the hope that somehow I may attain to the
resurrection from the dead. Not that I have already obtained
this, or have already been made perfect, but I press on
hoping that I may lay hold of that for which Christ laid
hold of me. . . . One thing I do: forgetting what is behind
I strain forward to what is before, I press on to the goal, to
the prize of God's heavenly call in Christ Jesus."[47] He puts his
whole life in the simple statement: "To me to live is Christ."[48]

There was no shadow of pretense in this intense little man.
He meant what he said and he left nothing undone to realize
his ideal. Nothing but sincerity and truth rings in his claim:
"God forbid that I should glory save in the cross of our Lord
Jesus Christ, through whom the world is crucified to me and
I to the world."[49] It is not necessary to recite his exploits and
recall the dangers, stripes, shipwrecks, stonings, and suffering
he underwent for the attainment of his ideal. The single statement is eloquent: "With Christ I am nailed to the cross. It
is no longer I that live but Christ lives in me."[50] To live for
Christ, to become transformed into Christ, and to share Him
with others, that is his life. Indeed it is the central purpose
of all Christian living and so precious is the teaching that he
is willing to defer the consummation of his own personal union
with Christ in order to help his beloved children assimilate
the lesson: "For to me to live is Christ and to die is gain. But
if to live in the flesh is my lot, this means for me fruitful
labor, and I do not know which to choose. Indeed I am hard
pressed from both sides — desiring to depart and to be with
Christ, a lot by far the better; yet to stay on in the flesh is
necessary for your sakes."[51] As far as any mortal man may be
said to have it, he had his wish. He lived Christ. He breathed
Christ. He would allow no conscious act to fall short of the
norm he had set: his whole being must conform to the model

---

[47] Phil. 3:7–14.
[48] Phil. 1:21.
[49] Gal. 6:14.
[50] Gal. 2:20.
[51] Phil. 1:21–24.

of his Beloved. How logically then, how tenderly, how consolingly can he say: "None of us lives to himself, and none of us dies to himself; for if we live, we live to the Lord, or if we die, we die to the Lord. Therefore, whether we live or die, we are the Lord's."[52]

This was a Christian and from his lips with perfect propriety falls the counsel: "Put on the Lord Jesus Christ."[53] How does one put Him on? First, "you are to put off the old man which is being corrupted through its deceptive lusts."[54] For "we are debtors, not to the flesh, that we should live according to the flesh, for if you live according to the flesh you will die; but if by the spirit you put to death the deeds of the flesh you will live."[55] Putting off the old man is not accomplished by mere wishing and pious velleities; it requires hard grim work. "I so fight as not beating the air; but I chastise my body and bring it into subjection."[56] The renunciation of Satan which we promise in Baptism means dedication to the death of sin in us. Therefore we are "always bearing about in our body the dying of Jesus, so that the life also of Jesus may be made manifest in our bodily frame."[57] For Baptism is also union with the risen Christ. On the ruins of the old man of corruption there is to rise the "new man which has been created according to God in justice and holiness of truth,"[58] who does the truth in charity, and brings forth the fruits of the Spirit. One is not to put on the new man in some respects and cling to the old man of corruption in others. The transformation into Christ must be as complete and far reaching as the grace of God will allow. "Whether you eat or drink, or do anything else, do all for the glory of God."[59]

The fellowship with Christ, given by Baptism, is made strong and enduring by Confirmation. The soul, anointed by Baptism as the temple of the Holy Trinity, is now enriched by the plenitude of the gifts of the Holy Spirit so that even

---

[52] Rom. 14:7–9.
[53] Rom. 13:14.
[54] Eph. 4:22.
[55] Rom. 8:12–13.
[56] 1 Cor. 9:26.
[57] 2 Cor. 4:10.
[58] Eph. 4:24.
[59] 1 Cor. 10:31.

the greatest danger may be powerless to separate the soul from Christ. By Baptism we become the children of God and by Confirmation we come of mature spiritual age. Confirmation brings to perfection the new creature produced by Baptism; it especially enables one to persevere in the Christian ideal. If much is expected of the baptized, no limits of holiness may be set for those who are confirmed save only those determined by the Holy Spirit who breathes where He will.

Besides perfecting the spiritual gifts we receive by Baptism, Confirmation adds something which also includes a dedication. St. Thomas teaches that in Baptism man receives power to do whatever pertains to his own salvation: whereas in Confirmation he is empowered to engage in spiritual combat with the enemies of the faith. Therefore the Holy Spirit is given in this sacrament for strength just as He was given to the Apostles on Pentecost. Before the Apostles received the fullness of the Holy Spirit they were in the upper chamber persevering in prayer; afterward they went out and boldly confessed the faith. Hence he who is confirmed receives the power of confessing his faith by words, as it were, *ex officio*.[60] Obviously such power is a share in the prophetic office of Christ. Here is the sacramental foundation of our efforts to engage in Catholic Action. Neither is there in Confirmation any giving back of the soul to profane uses; the ties with Christ become stronger and more intimate.

The perfect replica, however, of the Child presented in the Temple is found in those who receive Holy Orders. As a consequence of their anointing they no longer belong to themselves but entirely to Christ and the people of God. Here is the supreme dedication.

They belong to Christ entirely because they were especially given Him by the Father. Predestined in the eternal decrees, "they were thine, and thou hast given them to me."[61] To them Christ manifests the name of His Father and the words of His Father. "The words which thou hast given me I have given to them. And they have received them and have known of a truth that I came forth from thee."[62] Christ guards them

---

[60] *Sum. Theol.*, III, 72, 5 ad 2.
[61] Jn. 17:6.
[62] Jn. 17:8.

as the apple of His eye, for "those whom thou hast given me I guarded; and not one of them perished,"[63] except he who chose to be lost. He makes them the living continuation of His own mission, for "as thou hast sent me into the world, so I also have sent them into the world."[64] Therefore He prays for them: "Holy Father, keep in thy name those whom thou hast given me, that they may be one even as we are one."[65]

They belong also to the members of Christ, the people of God. St. Isidore says: "The priesthood has been established midway between the divine nature and the human nature in order to worship the former and improve the latter. If anyone, then, esteems any work better than this, he does not seem to me to have any sense."[66] The faithful cannot be without these other Christs; they are indispensable. Their times and interests belong to the public life of the Church. Their talents and powers are no longer their own but are to be poured forth on behalf of others. They are visible shepherds taking the place of the Invisible Shepherd. Like Him, they are salvation, light, and glory!

They are salvation because, like the Child, they are "destined for the fall and for the rise of many in Israel."[67] They open or close the way of salvation. They can free their fellow man from the bonds of sin in the sacraments of Penance and Extreme Unction. Christ not only shares with them the power of binding and loosing the conscience but He appoints them healers of souls who pour the medicine of counsel into hearts that are sick and blind and weary. They are the father of the prodigal, welcoming the wanderer home. They are the heavenly Father who spoke by the prophet: "I will seek that which was lost: and that which was driven away, I will bring back again: and I will bind up that which was broken, and I will strengthen that which was weak."[68]

They are salvation because they alone can renew the One

---

[63] Jn. 17:12.
[64] Jn. 17:18.
[65] Jn. 17:12.
[66] St. Isidore Pelusiota, *Epistolae*, 3, 20; *PG* 78, 745.
[67] Lk. 2:34.
[68] Ezech. 34:16.

Sacrifice which saves. They make the living bread which comes down from heaven for the life of the world and enables him who eats It to walk to Horeb, the mount of God. They are the watchmen of the house of God and the dispensers of the eucharistic mystery. Around this mystery the whole life of the Mystical Body of Christ revolves. From the tabernacle, as from an infinite dynamo, radiate the sparks of divine life which keep the Spouse of Christ active and vigorous. It is the storehouse of heavenly food and drink which keeps divine life in the members of Christ. Destroy the priest and the eucharistic mystery will vanish! Most significantly is the cross of Christ engraved on the chasubles of priests. They guard the eucharistic heart of the Church, the source of its vitality. From Nero until Antichrist the enemies of Christ will try to pierce that eucharistic heart. Therefore priests have been crucified, sawed in half, hanged and disemboweled, cast into foul sewers, lined up against barracks walls and shot, legally declared the enemies of their people.

They are light, partakers of the Light which enlightens every man that comes into this world.[69] They stand to the Divine Word, the infinite source of our knowledge, in a relationship which no other men enjoy. They are masters in Israel commissioned to teach the wise and the unwise, those who do the truth and come to the light, and those who do evil and hate the light.[70] They are to approach men as a guide to the blind, a light to them who sit in darkness.[71] They are to call men out of darkness into His marvelous light. They are to be a light which shines in a dark place until the day dawns and the day star of Eternal Truth arises in men's hearts. Hence the faithful naturally turn to their priests for a knowledge of divine things. "For the lips of the priest shall keep knowledge and they shall seek the law at his lips."[72]

As Simeon called the Child the glory of Thy people Israel, so priests are the glory of the Mystical Body of Christ. They are the salt of the earth. As salt gives savor and preserves,

---

[69] Cf. Jn. 1:9.
[70] Cf. Jn. 3:19–20.
[71] Cf. Rom. 2:19.
[72] Mal. 2:7.

so priests give men their taste for God and preserve their souls for eternity. To fulfill this function they can never allow this world to corrupt them. They must be above the pleasures, habits, prejudices, and vain likes and dislikes of ordinary men. They must cultivate exalted sanctity. Indeed "priests must be holier and more spotless than they who have betaken themselves to the desert," says St. Isidore, "for the former have the care both of themselves and of the people, the latter only of themselves."[73] The priesthood, then, is the supreme dedication. Priests, however, should confidently expect to attain the high holiness required of them. For Christ prays on their behalf: "Sanctify them in truth."[74] That this prayer be efficacious He adds: "And for them I sanctify myself, that they also may be sanctified in truth."[75] St. Chrysostom asks: "What does it mean, I sanctify myself?" And replies: "I offer sacrifice to you. For all sacrifices are called holy, and properly so, which are offered to God . . . For I consecrate them to you and make them an oblation."[76] Jesus immolates Himself especially for priests that they may be truly sanctified, consecrated and separated from profane things.

As is the priest, so will be the people. No people will rise above the teaching and example they receive from their priests. Assuredly the priest is to "preach the word, be urgent in season, out of season; reprove, entreat, rebuke with all patience and teaching."[77] But above all, he himself is the living pattern of that dedication which is the core of Christianity.

As the Church rejoices in the triumph which the Head of the Body achieved by the virtues of His mortal life and the sufferings of the cross, so the faithful are warmed by the virtuous example of their priests and glory in it as in the shining badge of their champions. A regiment is capable of high things when it cherishes the heroic feats of those who bore its colors in former days. In the Body of Christ only holy deeds are the subject of legitimate rejoicing: any other

---

[73] St. Isidore Pelusiota, *Epistolae*, 2, 284; *PG* 78, 713.
[74] Jn. 17:17.
[75] Jn. 17:19.
[76] *In Joan. Homil.*, 82, 1; *PG* 59, 443.
[77] 2 Tim. 4:2.

kind of achievement is foreign to its purposes. For deeds of holiness which are to adorn the Church the faithful look first to their priests, the lieutenants of the regiment who lead every forward movement. It is good when people are edified remembering the virtue of dead priests; it is better when they are daily uplifted by the holy lives of living priests. For "just as a king who obeys the laws is a living law, so also the priest who observes the sacred canons is a silent canon."[78]

The Church is a temple intended to house sacrifices acceptable to God.[79] It is a spiritual edifice, constructed of living human stones, whose architect and first builder is Christ. Through all the ages from the Crucifixion to Gabriel's trumpet that temple is abuilding. And each member of Christ is also a chosen builder, officially designated, marked for a particular kind of service. The marking is done by the sacraments which impart the sacramental seal.

For the chrism of these sacraments deputes the souls of Christians to the worship of God, some more, some less — but for all, the dedication is everlasting, the seal is indelible. From priestly example of irrevocable dedication to the altar, the faithful learn that they too are marked for God's service, that God has full title to all their devotion, that anything of theirs — action, work, value — which is withheld from God becomes worthless. For truly the larger offering which is expected from, and rendered by, the few stimulates the many to pay their dues to God.

---

[78] St. Isidore Pelusiota, *Epistolae*, 3, 306; *PG* 78, 976.
[79] 1 Pet. 2:5.

6. Patience

"Humble thy heart, and endure: incline thy ear, and receive the words of understanding; and make not haste in the time of clouds. Wait on God with patience: join thyself to God, and endure, that thy life may be increased in the latter end. Take all that shall be brought upon thee: and in thy sorrow endure, and in thy humiliation keep patience. For gold and silver are tried in the fire, but acceptable men in the furnace of humiliation" (Ecclus. 2:2–5).

THE Wise Man gave this advice to men of all time. But, like the thoughtful Roman of the fifth century, the contemporary of St. Leo and St. Augustine, we feel these words have more than ordinary reference to us: like them, we are asking if the very ground of civilization is beginning to crumble. At the turn of the century, through its prophet, Herbert Spencer, optimistic materialism was saying that man's possibilities of betterment were infinite, that he was moving surely from present achievement to earthly beatitude. And now only the very young and the insane can be unaware of the calamities which have beset the world since 1914. What has happened seems but the beginning of evils.

Since the Potsdam Conference, our leaders have been making cheerful sounds with their mouths and pointing optimistically to indications of real peace or at least of possible compromise with the Kremlin. They know they are whistling to keep up their courage. Now they know that we know. They hoped they saw streaks of light in the sky, that the respite from actual combat was not a false dawn. Do portents of unimaginable evil stand upon the threshold? Is the night of atomic catastrophe about to descend? Reluctantly we suspect the worst. We know positively that atheistic Communism

plots our destruction and ambitions control of the world.
Either that ambition will be peacefully relinquished by God
working a moral miracle, or we must destroy it by force
and the endurance of unprecedented horrors. If the possibility
of atomic warfare is actualized, how shall we withstand its
impact? That will depend, first, upon how we have trained
ourselves to accept lesser and more commonplace trials.
No one stands up under major crises who has not in the
solution of minor troubles evolved a philosophy of coping
with evil.

Here is an inescapable fact — adversity in some form, large
or small, always confronts us. We all have something to
suffer, either from the stupidity or ill will of other men, or
from the mischances of nature, or from the disorder of our
own physical or psychic make-up. What amazing accidents
happen! Although there were only two automobiles registered
in Kansas City in 1904, yet they met in head-on collision before the year was out. Á Kempis says: "Dispose and order
all things according as thou wilt, and as seems best to thee
and thou wilt still find something to suffer, either willingly
or unwillingly; and so thou shalt always find the cross."[1]
How do men react to this fact? There is a Pollyanna attitude
which attempts to wish all trouble out of existence. A few
people use a form of self-hypnosis to persuade themselves
that everything is always right with them. Only a fool will
seriously deny that the life of man upon earth is a warfare.[2]

How do men interpret this stubborn fact? Is adversity
totally evil, something to be removed at any cost? And if it
cannot be removed, is it to be endured with grudging re-
bellion? Millions of our contemporaries consider adversity
the unjust withholding of happiness which a man ought to
have here and now. This view was expressed succinctly by a
man from the state of Washington, who, when asked if he
believed in an afterlife, replied: "Pie in the sky may be O.K.,
but I'll take mine down here. And make it huckleberry." He
and the rest of them want an earthly millennium. If this life
is their one and only chance at happiness, they cannot bear

---

[1] *Imitation of Christ*, Bk. II, C. 12.
[2] Job 7:1.

with equanimity to suffer now. They cannot afford to go searching for the silver lining in the cloud; there must not be any clouds.

An astonishing number of men and women, descendants of Christian forebears, have never heard, or if they have heard they have rejected, the Christian explanation of life's sorrows summarized by St. Peter: "God hath begotten us anew . . . unto a heritage imperishable and undefiled . . . Whereat ye exult, even though for a while . . . ye have been grieved somewhat by divers temptations."[3] Since so many learned men have been scoffing for a hundred years at an imperishable heritage, we need not wonder that so many psychiatrists tell their patients that chastity breeds nervous disorders, that patience is bad for them. Their argument against patience is that, by uncomplaining sufferance of many annoyances, people pile up within themselves a huge psychic potential, a thunderhead of inhibitions, which will work great psychological harm, unless they constantly release it by direct irascible action. So if a man is annoyed at the breakfast table because the toast is burned, let him pound the table a bit, if he dare. This is a wiser proceeding, they say, than that of the mousy little man who silently endured all wifely irritations, until one evening he went upstairs during a bridge game and got a pistol and shot his wife dead because she had trumped his ace.

Nietzsche went so far as to say that the patient Christian betrays a slave mentality and a slave morality which is to be despised by all strong souls who have the will to power. In the morality of the superman, adversity must not be taken meekly; it is to be resented, hated, trampled on. Only by ruthless domineering over persons and obstacles does one rise to the level of the superman.

It is pitiable to watch how people, who must have happiness now, meet serious adversity. Some commit suicide. Some seek oblivion in fantastic pleasures of sense. During the awful inflation of the 1920's Berlin blossomed with a dank lush growth of night clubs specializing in perversion. The stresses of World War II begot world-wide moral aberrations. If

---

[3] 1 Pet. 1:3, 4, 6, Westminster version.

we may believe the Anglican Bishop of Southwell, vast numbers of his countrymen sought relief from their war neuroses in the occult sciences. In December, 1941, he said: "In times of strain and calamity the old dark gods emerge from the jungle and crude, primitive religion comes back. We are today threatened with it in the prevailing cult of astrology."[4]

But the word of God is not confounded by the false wisdom of the learned of this world nor is the eternal law of human conduct made void by men's follies, no matter how much these are multiplied. Faith and reason tell us that through many tribulations we must enter the kingdom of God.[5] No psychologist has better advice to offer than the succinct words of Christ: "In your patience you shall possess your souls."[6] No newspaper psychiatrist has bettered the exhortation of St. James: "Be patient, brethren, until the coming of the Lord."[7]

St. Augustine says: "It is by patience that we bear evils with an equable mind lest with an inequable mind we abandon the good by which we may advance to better things."[8] St. Thomas says: "A person is said to be patient . . . because he acts in a praiseworthy manner by enduring things which hurt him here and now so that he may not be unduly saddened by them."[9] Patience, then, is the virtue inclining a man to act reasonably in the presence of sadness produced in him by adversity. If adversity evokes anger, a man requires meekness to master himself. When St. James says, "Patience hath a perfect work,"[10] he does not mean that patience is the greatest virtue bringing man the greatest good, but that it safeguards all the virtues by removing the obstacles to their practice. The patient man is rightly said by Christ to *possess* his soul; that is, he owns and controls it, because he has removed the disturbances which prevent his peaceful possession of it.

---

[4] *Time,* January 19, 1942, p. 43.

[5] Cf. Acts 14:21.

[6] Lk. 21:19.

[7] James 5:7.

[8] *De Patientia,* II, c. 2; *PL* 40, 611.

[9] *Sum. Theol.,* II–II, 136, 4, ad 2.

[10] James 1:4.

Instructed souls know well the particular answers which faith can render to the small and the great trials of life. They have perhaps used them for the guidance and consolation of others. They may have gone into a house of sudden death from which some younger member has been snatched before his years could fully ripen and have told the mourning parents that death is not the end but only the beginning of life, that the dear departed has gone before them to prepare a place for them. They may have written letters of condolence after the fashion of St. Jerome addressing Paula upon the death of her daughter, Blaesilla: "There come to your mind her conversation, her endearments, the tone of her voice, her companionship: and you cannot bear being bereft of them. We pardon the tears of a mother, but we look for restraint in sorrow. If I think of you as a parent, I do not blame you for grieving; if I think of you as a Christian and a Christian religious, the mother is excluded by these words. Your wound is recent, and this touch, wherewith I console you, does not so much heal as ruffle. Yet, the hurt which time must soften, why does not reason triumph over it? . . . Look at Job, how much he endured, and you will see that you are over-tender — that he, with eyes cast up to heaven, in the ruins of his home, endured with unshaken patience the pains of his ulcer, innumerable losses and finally the scheming of his wife. I know what you are going to answer: this happened to him as the testing of a just man. So do you choose whichever of two things you wish: either you are a saint, and are being tested; or a sinner, and unjustly complain while suffering less than you deserve."[11]

A priest may counsel newly-married couples that the success of their marriage depends not only on mutual understanding but especially on mutual forbearance. Or one may encourage a disconsolate friend or a scrupulous confidant to be patient with himself, reminding him that God is only trying him, exhorting him to "persevere under the discipline. God dealeth with you as with his sons; for what son is there, whom the father doth not correct?"[12]

---

[11] *Epistolae*, 39, 4; *PL* 22, 471.
[12] Hebr. 12:7.

Whenever, then, we tell others that the will of God is the law of life, that if the will of God imposes suffering it must be accepted at least with patience and resignation, we should be prepared to apply this truth to ourselves. Or must we sometimes say to ourselves: "Physician heal thyself"?[13] When we are about to advise others to be more patient, or after we have done so, it will help and humble our own souls to reflect upon the opening words of Tertullian's little treatise on Patience: "I confess to the Lord God that it is quite rash, not to say impudent, on my part to have dared to write about patience of which I am unable to offer an example — I, a man of no virtue — since it behooves those, who set out to teach and preach a virtue, to start by practicing it themselves and, by the authority of their example, to give solidity to their instruction, so that their defective deeds shame not their words."[14]

Each of us is intellectually convinced that annoyances and suffering are permitted to happen to us under divine providence in order to test our worth, to afford us opportunity of atoning for the past and of increasing in merit. These things are heaven-sent means of rubbing off the rough edges of character and of conforming ourselves to the image of Christ. We know, too, that God is not slow to grant these opportunities. Everyone has had his fair shares of hard knocks and bleak days. But have these things had their divinely desired effect upon us? Have we used these means of sanctification?

We usually react to the great troubles of life, to the huge slings and arrows of outrageous fortune, with virtue and fair composure of mind. Big trouble makes a call upon our hidden reserve of virtue. But what of the meaner, smaller irritants — the occasional headache, the snide remark which gets under the skin, the small rebuke, the rained-out holiday, the frustration of a little ambition? The right attitude toward petty annoyance is important because on it depend calm of mind and advance in virtue.

Some people fight annoyance with outspoken complaint. Whenever their good pleasure is crossed their spontaneous

---

[13] Lk. 4:23.
[14] *De Patientia*, C. I; *PL* 1, 1359–1361.

reaction is, "This will have to stop." "So and so must quit slamming that door." "The neighborhood buses ought to run on time." "The people across the street must keep their dog from barking at night." Complaint is the unlovely cry of wounded self-love. It contains a dart of ill will against the source of annoyance. As the quality of mercy is twice blessed, blessing him that gives and him that takes, so habitual complaint is twice wrong; it disgusts those who have to listen to it, and it embitters him who gives it off. The complainer is the pessimist who takes himself too seriously. He rates his own convenience too highly. He lacks the sovereign grace of being able to laugh at himself and his little mishaps and ironically enough he ends by being his own worst enemy. For persistent complaint engenders a bitterness which may in time destroy the savor of life.

Other persons react to annoyance with unspoken complaint. They grumble to themselves and allow resentment to keep simmering within. They may not be forthright enough to voice their sentiments because they fear to displease the persons who annoy them. Or they may be proud persons who meet adversity with sullen silence. They do not like what is happening to them, but they refuse to betray any signs of resentment. Their silence may issue from a natural stoicism, the angry refusal to let people see that anything can depress them. Or it may be a cloak of ambition. Complaint might be a black mark against them. Their superiors might think they had little virtue. Rather than hurt their chance of advancement or risk the loss of something nice which they have, they swallow their displeasure and say nothing.

It is a pity that from lack of sufficient reflection many people fail to grasp the value of patience. It has a natural fruit — calm of mind. This was the aim of so many pagan philosophers. Horace considered the acme of perfection to be a tranquil state of soul which could be shaken neither by prosperity nor adversity. Of his just man, firm of purpose, he says: "If the round sky should crack and fall upon him, the wreck would strike him fearless still."[15] Modern books on mental hygiene praise the same poise and tranquillity. This

---

[15] Odes, III, III, 7–8.

the patient man possesses. His soul is not at the mercy of every chance happening.

But the main consideration is that difficulties are the raw material of Christian sanctity. Sanctity, which is possible for every baptized soul, seldom consists in doing big things, but it always demands that a man do little things well. Hardship, accepted in the supernatural spirit of conformity to the will of God, increases sanctifying grace and makes the patient sufferer more like Jesus Christ. By constantly accepting annoyances and trials the earnest soul wisely uses the stuff out of which sanctity is made. The same opportunities are being offered to all Christians, but many of them have too little sanctity to show. Occasions of sanctity abound, but saints are few. The reason is not that most Christians are whiners, proud or ambitious, but they love self more than they love God. They lack all-out generosity with God which is shown in this way. When difficulty comes they are willing to accept it only on condition that it be accompanied by some natural consolation. They make a deal with God and creatures, and dull the excellence of their submission to the will of God by exacting some compensatory comfort from creatures at the same time.

For example, they humbly accept a reverse and later criticize the author of it. They accept an annoying situation with resignation, but they cannot refrain from all murmuring. They reluctantly admit that they should devote valuable time to some project of Catholic action and they cannot help using the occasion for the gaining of some personal prestige. Unexpected upsets happen and they must cushion the soul against them by relaxing self-vigilance, or by letting up a little in their work, or by seeking undue sympathy. Instead of taking their trouble to Christ in the Blessed Sacrament, their first thought is to find a sympathetic ear into which they can pour an exaggerated version of their woe. Instead of the solid comfort of prayer, they seek a human hand to massage the tensions of their soul. They do not make an outright refusal of the chalice offered, but before they say, "Not my will but thine be done," they want the cup sweetened with a little soothing syrup of their own choosing — like the castor oil of childhood disguised in ginger ale.

They act this way because they imagine that their capacity for accepting the will of God has definite limits to be fixed by themselves. They can do just so much work; they can pray to this extent; they can endure just so many annoyances. If, then, God obtrudes some added load of difficulty upon them, they can accept it only by curtailing some other duty or by seeking strength and solace outside His good pleasure. They are like a poorly made football bladder: if you blow more air into it, it will give at the seams. Unfortunately, these people underrate the power of grace to increase their supernatural capacity. God alone knows the extent of their power to endure, for He alone knows how much grace He wishes to give. It is for God, by the allotment of grace, to choose how great or how little will be their supernatural being. It is their business to unite their will to His will offering grace. The very fact that He offers the trial is clear proof that they are able to endure it. For "God is faithful and will not suffer you to be tempted beyond your strength, but will make with temptation an outlet that ye may be able to bear it."[16] In the mind of God there exists the real image of what they are capable of becoming as His adopted sons. Each refusal of grace, however, means that, to the extent of that lost grace, the divine plan for them will go unrealized.

Catherine of Braganza was reared in strict seclusion and admirable piety. At the age of twenty-four, she was married to Charles II of England. She was scarcely two months wedded when, in the presence of the whole court, Charles presented to her his notorious paramour, Lady Castlemaine. Catherine felt the insult all the more, since she had previously protested her disapproval of this creature, and had extracted a promise from the king that he would have nothing to do with her. Her struggles to repress her emotions of shame and indignation were so great that they nearly cost her her life. Blood gushed from her nostrils and she was carried from the hall in a fit. Her husband's neglect brought on a serious illness which resulted in a miscarriage and barrenness. During twenty-two years of married life Charles kept

---

[16] 1 Cor. 10:13, Westminster version.

a bevy of paramours and always insisted that the queen make them, even Nell Gwynne, ladies in waiting. On them he spent the thirty thousand pounds settled on Catherine by the articles of their marriage contract, while she had to eke out a parsimonious existence. She was forever hearing rumors that the king was going to divorce his barren wife. She was constantly pressed to retire into a convent. The infamous Titus Oates accused her of attempting to poison the king and several of her servants were executed.

Catherine's general reaction to a life of frustration and humiliation is expressed by a citizen of Norwich in a letter written upon the occasion of a royal visit to the Howards of Norwich: "I cannot, likewise, here forbear to let you know how infinitely gracious her majesty was to all our city, being pleased to condescend so far as to let almost all sorts of people, of what degree soever, kiss her hand, as she passed along the gallery with a most admirable and saint-like charity and patience: so as our whole inhabitants, within and without doors, ring and sing of nothing else but her praises, continual prayers and tears being offered up for her temporal and eternal blessings by us, who all conclude, that, if there be a saint on earth, it must be her majesty; since no eye alive did ever see, nor ear within the memory of man did ever hear of, so much goodness, charity, humility, sweetness, and virtue of all kinds, as are now lodged in her saint-like breast."[17]

When the king fell fatally ill, she sent to ask his pardon, if in anything she had offended him in their married life, and despite the five Anglican bishops and the twenty-five peers who crowded the death chamber, and despite the law of England which threatened death to anyone who reconciled an Englishman to the Romish Church, she saw to it that he died a Catholic.

Catherine could practice patience because she had great faith. Vivid faith not only gave her the general solution to the riddle of mortal existence, but it unraveled for her her personal problem of evil, enabling her to say with Judith:

---

[17] Agnes Strickland, *Lives of the Queens of England* (Philadelphia: Barrie, 1902), Vol. X, pp. 302–303.

"As for us therefore let us not revenge ourselves for these things which we suffer. But esteeming these very punishments to be less than our sins deserve, let us believe that these scourges of the Lord, with which like servants we are chastised, have happened for our amendment, and not for our destruction."[18]

The first Christian reaction to adversity is, "I believe in God." The very hairs of our head are numbered.[19] Therefore, no evil can vanquish us. We see behind every hardship God's loving care and providence. Nothing from the scorching of a breakfast omelet to the destruction of the Church in our country can happen without His express will or permissive nod. "Beloved, be not astonished at the fiery trial which hath come upon you, to put you to the proof, as though a strange thing had befallen you; but inasmuch as ye have fellowship in the sufferings of Christ, rejoice, that in the revelation of his glory also ye may rejoice and exult."[20]

Patience springs directly from hope. Without hope patience is inconceivable. The Wise Man says: "Give not up thy heart to sadness, but drive it from thee: and remember the latter end."[21] The Prophet consoles his people: "The Lord is good and giveth strength in the day of trouble: and knoweth them that hope in him."[22] Since we firmly hope that God will give us the means of life eternal, we are willing to endure contradictions and misunderstandings, the meanness of men, the thwartings of our will, all unpleasant odors, pain, and boredom. They are so many steppingstones to God. They are part of the cornucopia of means which God puts at the disposal of every soul: the sweet and the sour, the attractive and the unattractive, the pleasant and the nauseating; along with the grace to bear ourselves reasonably amid it all. Perhaps some persons do not appreciate that the sour, the unattractive, the nauseating are means no less than the sweet, the attractive, and the pleasant. It is enough that God know it. We must trust Him never to give us what is

---

[18] Judith 8:26–27.
[19] Cf. Mt. 10:30.
[20] 1 Pet. 4:12–13, Westminster version.
[21] Ecclus. 38:21.
[22] Nah. 1:7.

positively a hindrance. Every unpleasant means, virtuously accepted, spells increase of grace, and hence, is that much warrant of eternal glory. "No cross, no crown." In patient endurance our hope is perfected. We have the promise of God: "I, I myself will comfort you: who art thou, that thou shouldst be afraid of a mortal man, and of the son of man, who shall wither away like grass?"[23] We can only answer with the Psalmist: "In God I have put my trust: I will not fear what flesh can do against me."[24]

Faith and hope, however, are not enough for perfect patience. These keep the soul struggling grimly on: they do not lift it to the plane of serenity where adversity can roil it no longer. The true sweetness of patience must flower forth from love. Only he who loves much can endure much. We need the supreme kind of love of which the Canticle sings: "If a man should give all the substance of his house for love, he shall despise it as nothing."[25] How would children ever be reared, if mothers did not have such love as enabled them to ignore unnumbered annoyances which would be insupportable to others? So, too, if we love God very much we can scorn every tribulation. When St. Paul says, "Charity is patient,"[26] he means, not only that charitable people are also very patient, but that the real reason for being patient is love of God. An infallible measure of increase of the love of God is the deepening and widening of one's patience.

And, on the other hand, patience is essential to the exercise of true charity. St. Cyprian says: "Charity is the bond of the brotherhood, the foundation of peace, the cement and fixity of unity, it is greater than hope and faith, it precedes good works and martyrdom, it will remain with us eternally in the heavenly kingdom. Take from it patience, and it perishes miserably."[27]

The love of God makes us patient and sweet with others: to acquire the love of God we must be patient with ourselves. We make resolutions only to break them when the

---

[23] Isa. 51:12.
[24] Ps. 55:5.
[25] Cant. 8:7.
[26] 1 Cor. 13:4.
[27] *De Bono Patientiae*, 15; PL 4, 656.

opportunity occurs for putting them into practice. We aim high in prayer and fall short in action. We wake in the morning to find the big ambition of yesterday vanished. For days we are weighed down by apathy and are discontented because of our weakness. Sadness comes over us when we see the great gap between our holy resolves and our pitiful accomplishments. But patience! We are not supermen. Left to ourselves, we fail. We must wait for the love of God to uplift our weakness and smooth out our rough ways.

Love is an exchange of life; the giving of self to God and God's giving of Himself to us. Let us cling fast to His love. When discouragement tempts us to turn from the quest of perfection, let us, deploring our miseries, return to Him. His love will breathe fresh courage into us. He will teach us to trust in Him alone and be patient with our limitations.

If we stumble blindly on, accepting ourselves for what we are and humbly asking God to fill out our deficiencies, more and more God will fill our hearts. They who seek Him find Him. He has gone before us and given us the example of how to empty self of self. If we persevere in the attempt, we shall find sweetness where once we had only pain. And even if, to keep us humble, He leaves us burdened with certain defects to the very end, we can say with St. Paul: "Gladly will I glory in my infirmities, that the power of Christ may dwell in me."[28]

Let us face facts. A man may come to love God very much, and yet God may make his mortal burden no easier. He may make it harder. St. Gregory warns us of what might happen: "The higher each one advances, the more grievous burdens he finds in this world to endure; because, when the soul fails to find pleasure in the present world, the opposition of the world increases. Hence it is that we see many persons who lead a good life and yet sweat beneath a heavy load of tribulation. Earthly desires have fled and still they are wearied by heavier trials. But according to the word of the Lord they yield fruit through patience."[29] How will a man bear the trials of old age without abundant patience?

---

[28] 2 Cor. 12:9.
[29] *Homiliae*, 15, 4; *PL* 76, 1133.

"To bear all adversities and losses and to desire no prosperity in this world — all this is not according to man's natural inclination. If thou lookest unto thyself thou canst do nothing of this sort of thyself. But, if thou confidest in the Lord strength will be given thee from heaven and the world and the flesh will be made subject to you. Set thyself, therefore, to bear manfully the cross of thy Lord for the love of Him who was crucified for thee."[30]

Genuine patience in a man can come only from God. He acquires it because he draws near to God and God marks him with the sign of His own virtue. How incomprehensibly patient God is with the sins of men, with their frivolity and ingratitude! What an example of patience He gave us in His mortal life. Tertullian says: "I speak not of His crucifixion, for unto that end had He come. But was the endurance of outrage a necessary part of His dying? Yet out of love of patience He willed to die overwhelmed with suffering. He was spat upon, scourged, derided, clothed in ignoble garments, crowned with a yet more ignoble crown. What wonderful and faith-begetting tranquillity of soul! He, who had willed to conceal Himself under the aspect of man, imitated nothing of man's impatience. It was by this characteristic above all, O Pharisees, that you should have recognized the Lord: no mere man could have displayed such patience. All these striking traits, which in pagan eyes are so many objections to our faith but for us are the proof and vindication of that faith, show very clearly to those who have the faith, show — not by words and precepts, but by suffering endured by the Lord — that patience belongs to God's nature, and is the effect and manifestation of a quality which is proper to Him."[31]

The strength to be patient comes from contemplation of Him who came unto our miseries. But not only did He suffer; the third day He rose, His labors ended, death conquered, Himself in glory resplendent. From Him then we learn that man has two lives in the flesh: one before death with which we are all acquainted, another after the resurrection of which

[30] *Imitation*, Bk. 11, C. 12.
[31] *De Patientia*, C. III; *PL* 1, 1365.

we know nothing. He came in the flesh and assumed its burdens, in order to open our eyes to that other life which has no trials. By suffering and dying in this life, He shows us its true function; by rising, He teaches us that the life we lead before death is not to be loved for its own sake, but merely endured for the sake of unending life.

"The very Lord of prophets and apostles, forgetful as it were of His divine glory, how did He act?" asks Macarius. "Becoming an example for us He wore upon His head in great contumely a crown of thorns, He endured the spittle, the blows and the cross. If thus the Lord lived on earth, you too must imitate Him; and in this manner lived the prophets and apostles; we also, if we wish to be built upon the foundation of the Lord and the apostles, ought to imitate them. For the apostle says in the Holy Spirit: *Be ye imitators of me, as I am of Christ.* If you love the praises of men, and ambition the marks of honor, and seek an easy life, you have wandered from the way. You must be crucified with The Crucified, you must suffer with Him who has suffered, in order that you may likewise be glorified with Him in His glory. It is necessary that the bride suffer with the Spouse and thus become companion and fellow heir of Christ. Without suffering, adversity, and the straight and narrow way it is permitted no one to enter the city of the saints, to find rest, and reign with the King forever and ever."[32]

---

[32] Pseudo-Macarius, *Homiliae,* 12, 4–5; *PG* 34, 560.

7. Reparation

"Who his own self bore our sins in his body upon the tree: that we, being dead to sins, should live to justice" (1 Pet. 2:24).

WHAT Christ our Lord came on earth to do, each soul incorporated into Him by baptism is called to share and imitate, "according to the measure of the giving of Christ."[1] To appreciate the great dignity of a Christian let us first see the function of Christ on earth.

As the Head of man, Christ's first duty was to offer the Father fitting adoration in the name of mankind. Even though the liturgical law of Moses was to cease, He kept its requirements. He often spent the night in the prayer of God. His death on the cross was perfect worship. Before He died He took away the priesthood of Aaron and appointed a new and everlasting priesthood to care for and offer the perfect sacrifice He had ordained. With the assurance of a great duty accomplished He could say: "I have glorified thee on earth."[2]

As the second Adam, Christ offered fitting thanks for the good and perfect gifts which forever descend from above from the Father of lights.[3] He was ever mindful of gratitude to God. Before He multiplied the loaves and fishes He gave thanks. Before He raised Lazarus from the dead, lifting up His eyes to heaven, He said: "Father, I give thee thanks that thou hast heard me."[4] Before He broke the bread and constituted the undying memorial of His love, He gave thanks.

In a true sense His entire sojourn on earth was a plea to

[1] Eph. 4:7.
[2] Jn. 17:4.
[3] Cf. James 1:17.
[4] Jn. 11:41.

the Father of mercies on behalf of poor benighted men who had lost themselves in the snares of their passions and the darkness of their desires. How touchingly He illustrates His intercessory function when He prays: "Holy Father, keep them in thy name whom thou hast given me: that they may be one, as we also are one. . . . Father, I will that where I am, they also whom thou hast given me may be with me."[5]

In His earthly mission, however, adoration, thanksgiving, and petition were subordinate to the one great purpose of offering satisfaction for sins. Divine justice and wisdom had decreed that sin's infinite insult to the Creator be wiped out by an equally infinite act of reparation. Since mere man could never possibly have done this, Christ, the Head of man, had to come and, in the name of mankind, offer God a sacrifice of infinite worth which paid the forfeit of sin and blotted out the handwriting of the decree that was against us.[6] Like us in all things, sin alone excepted, He took upon Himself the burden of human sin. "He was wounded for our iniquities, He was bruised for our sins: the chastisement of our peace was upon Him, and by His bruises we are healed."[7] Thus does He purchase peace by His cross. The point of emphasis, however, is not so much that the God-Man made atonement, but that atonement was made by Him who had no need of forgiveness. The Lamb of God who taketh away the sins of the world is unspotted and unde-filed. For we have a high priest, holy, innocent, undefiled, and made higher than the heavens, who needs not daily to offer sacrifices first for his own sins, and then for the sins of the people.[8] Such was the supreme task of Christ, the offering of reparation for the sins of others. Everything in His mortal life centered around and took meaning from this prime function of vicarious satisfaction.

Since the Church is Christ living on through the ages, the chief activities of Christ will be carried on by the Church until the last man is saved and the number of the elect is filled up. The liturgy of the Church is the continuance of

[5] Jn. 17:11, 24.
[6] Cf. Col. 2:14.
[7] Isa. 53:5.
[8] Cf. Hebr. 7:26–27.

the adoration of Christ and the fulfillment of His statement: "The hour cometh, and now is, when the true adorers will adore the Father in spirit and in truth. For the Father also seeketh such to adore Him."[9] Not only does the Apostle command that thanksgivings be made for all men,[10] but the Church daily sings in the Mass: "It is truly meet and just, right and available to salvation that we should always and in all places give thanks to Thee, O holy Lord, Father Almighty, Eternal God." Surely Christ transmitted a duty of intercession and petition to His Church when He said: "Amen, amen I say to you: if you ask the Father anything in my name, he will give it to you. Hitherto you have not asked anything in my name. Ask, and you shall receive; that your joy may be full."[11] Although it is not certain that God invariably grants every petition of the Church, since Christ is the One Mediator whose petitions infallibly are "heard for his reverence,"[12] nevertheless can anyone doubt the intercessory power of the Beloved Spouse?

We are all convinced that the Church carries on, and that each Christian should engage in, Christ's work of adoration, thanksgiving, and petition. What may not be so clear is the necessity of continuing His labor of satisfaction to the end of time. For may it not be objected: Did not Christ offer Himself but once and dieth now no more?[13] Nevertheless, the messianic function of satisfaction is not to cease until all the elect are gathered into the Body of Christ. Since the Church is Christ continued, she is ever to do in a finite way that which He did in an infinite way. True, the sacrifice of redemption will never be renewed in the blood of Christ, yet the Church is ever to renew that sacrifice in an unbloody manner and the members of Christ are to continue the work of reparation. He performed the essential and irreplaceable part of reparation by His sacrificial death. They, members of a crucified Christ, contribute an accidental part: they are to fill up those things which are

---

[9] Jn. 4:23.
[10] Cf. 1 Tim. 2:1.
[11] Jn. 16:23–24.
[12] Hebr. 5:7.
[13] Cf. Rom. 6:9.

wanting to the sufferings of Christ.[14] Therefore, since sin abounds, the Spouse who is made one with Him labors at a labor of love to wipe out that sinning.

In every age preachers have bewailed the degeneracy of morals. Such a complaint today is strongly backed by the hard facts of contemporary life: in quantity and heinousness of sin this age has few, if any, equals in the history of Christendom. To accustom the imagination to the extent of present-day sinning let us reflect that a gram of radium emits 37 million alpha particles a second and 1332 billion in an hour.[15] It would be foolish to exaggerate; yet, how many sins must hourly assault the patience of God, rising from the 2265 million human beings who now inhabit the globe.[16] There are nearly that many tongues, wagging almost constantly, and how sinfully! "The tongue is a fire, a world of iniquity. The tongue is placed among our members, which defileth the whole body . . . being set on fire by hell."[17] And sins of thought. "But the things which proceed out of the mouth, come forth from the heart, and those things defile a man. For from the heart come forth evil thoughts, murders, adulteries, fornications, thefts, false testimonies, blasphemies."[18]

What unspeakable things man is doing! The Deism of the eighteenth century has run its natural course and spawned the atheism of today. "We see today, what was never before seen in history, the satanical banners of war against God and against religion brazenly unfurled to the winds in the midst of all peoples and in all parts of the earth."[19] Hitherto the impious atheist locked his foul secret in his heart because his Christian neighbors would not endure his blasphemies. "Today, on the contrary, atheism has already spread through large masses of the people. Well organized, it works its way even into the common schools; it appears in theaters, and in

---

[14] Cf. Col. 1:24.

[15] Cf. Lise Meitner, *Fortune,* March, 1946, p. 141.

[16] According to the *World Almanac,* 1950, p. 218, the population of the world is 2,264,563,771.

[17] James 3:6.

[18] Mt. 15:18–19.

[19] Pius XI, *Caritate Christi Compulsi.* Cf. *Social Wellsprings,* ed. Husslein (Milwaukee: Bruce, 1942), Vol. II, p. 264.

order to spread still more it makes use of its own cinema films, of the gramaphone and the radio. With its printing presses it prints booklets in every language; it promotes special exhibitions and public parades; it has its own political parties and its own economic and military systems. This organized and militant atheism works untiringly by means of its agitators, with conferences and projections, with every means of propaganda secret and open, among all classes, in every street, in every hall. It secures for this nefarious activity the moral support of its own universities, and holds fast the unwary with the mighty bonds of its organizing power."[20]

With the very basis of human order and decency so flagrantly attacked, is it any wonder that the seven deadly sins have swept over this age like the bursting of a dam? Divine and natural law is repudiated both by totalitarianism, which substitutes a rule of brute force trampling on every human right, and by the democracies, which rely on expediency and opportunism as the basis of rule. God is severely excluded from the councils of the nations. With diabolic pride new leaders erect their statues everywhere and fill every home with their pictures, offering themselves to their people in place of the God they endeavor to destroy. These men have not been heathens but baptized and apostate Christians.

Many nations, once strong and powerful, now tremble for their very existence upon the brink of the cataclysm because lust has eaten into their vitals and robbed them of virility. Fornication before marriage, contraception and adultery in marriage, followed by divorce and remarriage are wrecking their homes and withering their strength. Instruments of contraception are a seriously important item of manufacture: tremendous incomes flow from supplying the means of gratifying lust. How significant of the change of public morals is the attitude of the armed forces toward incontinency: in 1917 it was an evil to be tolerated; in 1941, a necessity to be pandered to. The crime records of our great cities, especially of crimes against the person, show an alarming upswing. Decent citizens clamor for personal protection. Women fear to attend evening services in their churches. At so tender an age boys and girls

---

[20] *Ibid.*, pp. 264–265.

learn to be drug addicts and criminals. What brazen, open, and cynical disregard of truth! The telling of falsehoods is adopted as a weapon of public policy upon the principle that, if one tells big enough lies often enough, some of them will be effective. Hate replaces Christian charity. Actions, which between individual persons are blameworthy by any rational standard, are praised if they are done on behalf of one's country. Not only Communism teaches class hatred as a fundamental doctrine: Christian sergeants tell their trainees they cannot be good soldiers unless they hate the enemy with a personal hatred.

In the name of Liberalism, the greed which Christian society once firmly bound by the bands of justice and charity, was let loose to reproduce the economic woes of the 1930's. This greed is still rampant and it begets mutual distrust, which blights all human dealings; as is envy, which makes a man consider the advantages of another as losses to himself; and narrow selfishness, which orders and subordinates all things to its own advantage without consideration of the rights and needs of others. No wonder Pius XI could say: "Old-time fidelity and honesty of conduct and mutual intercourse, extolled so much even by the orators and poets of paganism, now give place to speculations in one's own affairs, as in those of others, without reference to conscience. In fact, how can any contract be maintained and what value can any treaty have in which every guarantee of conscience is lacking? And how can there be talk of guarantees of conscience when all faith in God and all fear of God has vanished? Take away this basis, and with it all moral law falls, and there is no remedy left to stop the gradual but inevitable destruction of peoples, families, the state, civilization itself."[21]

Let no one say that all modern sinning takes place outside the fold of Christ. While some heroes, under stark oppression, manfully uphold their Christian faith, many, many others succumb to the threats of Caesar and apostatize. In our midst, the lure of riches, social prestige, and pagan pleasures annually take their toll. That some of the faithful are infected

---

[21] *Ibid.*, pp. 272–273.

by the pestilential air they breathe is clear from this: they resent and refuse to listen to a preacher who plainly tells them their faults or reminds them of the fire of hell — a thing unheard of in their fathers. A bountiful God gives every man 1440 minutes a day; 10,080 minutes a week; how many men cannot give God 60 minutes in a week! We must stand ashamed for abuses of Christ in the Blessed Sacrament; for sacrilegious Communions; for the sacred Host raised on high by offending hands; for pious exteriors hiding gross and hypo-critic hearts; for indulgences in sin until faith is lost; for vile surrenders of the clerical and religious state. May not our Lord say with the Psalmist: "Even my friend in whom I trusted, who ate my bread, hath lifted his heel against me."[22] "If my enemy had reviled me, I would verily have borne with it. And if he that hated me had spoken great things against me, I would perhaps have hidden myself from him. But thou a man of one mind, my guide and my familiar, who didst take sweetmeats together with me: in the house of God we walked with consent."[23] Of such persons, St. Gregory Nazianzen says: "I consider far worse those who in the more perfect way fall."[24]

"The men of Nineve shall rise in judgment with this gener-ation, and shall condemn it: because they did penance at the preaching of Jonas. And behold a greater than Jonas here."[25] None other than the Mother of God has warned this age.

No wonder, then, the Mother of God appeared on May 13, 1917, at Fatima and asked the three children: "Would you like to offer yourselves to God to make sacrifices, and to accept willingly all the sufferings it may please Him to send you, in order to make reparation for so many sins, which offend the Divine Majesty, to obtain the conversion of sinners, and to make amends for all the blasphemies and offences committed against the Immaculate Heart of Mary?"[26] On the

---

[22] Ps. 40:10. Cf. new Latin psalter.

[23] Ps. 54:13–15.

[24] *Carminum Liber* I, Sect. II, VV 222–223; *PG* 37, 663.

[25] Mt. 12:41.

[26] V. Montes de Oca, C.S.Sp., *More About Fatima* (Westminster, Md.: Newman, 1948), p. 11.

feast of St. Anthony, June 13, 1917, she appeared again and said to the children: "Sacrifice yourselves for sinners, and say often, especially when you make sacrifices: 'Oh Jesus, it is for love of You, for the conversion of sinners, and in reparation for the offences committed against the Immaculate Heart of Mary.'"[27] She granted the children a most horrendous vision of hell and said: "You have just seen hell where the souls of poor sinners go. . . . When you see the night illuminated by an unknown light, know that it is the great sign which God is giving you, indicating that the world, on account of its innumerable crimes, will soon be punished by war, famine, and persecutions against the Church and the Holy Father. In order to stop it, I shall ask for the consecration of the world to my Immaculate Heart, as well as Communion of reparation on the first Saturdays of the month. If my requests are granted Russia will be converted, and there will be peace. Otherwise, an impious propaganda will spread its errors through the world raising up wars and persecutions against the Church. Many will be martyred, the Holy Father will have much to suffer; several nations will be wiped out. . . . The outlook is, therefore, gloomy. But here is a ray of hope: My Immaculate Heart will triumph."[28]

How long will God withhold His avenging hand? It cannot be forever. St. Jerome reminds us: "The longer the space of time wherein we forget God, so much the greater the punishment of the sin."[29] God would not be God if He did not punish sin. He punishes sin for two main reasons: to lead the sinner back to the right way; to restore the order overturned by sin and secure the divinely chosen purposes which sin has temporarily thwarted. God rained down brimstone and fire upon the five cities of the plain "whose land for a testimony of their wickedness is desolate, and smoketh to this day."[30] Moses doubted the word of God and was denied entrance into the promised land. Oza touched the ark of the covenant and was struck dead upon the spot. David sinned, and his child by Bethsabee died. How often did Israel wor-

---

[27] *Ibid.*, p. 20.
[28] *Ibid.*, pp. 58–59.
[29] *Comment. in Jeremiam*, Lib. I, C. II; *PL* 24, 698.
[30] Wisd. 10:7.

ship Moloch and Astarte, and for its idolatry was delivered over to the rod of the stranger. Because the Pharisees would not believe Him, Christ said to them: "Therefore I say to you, that the kingdom of God shall be taken from you, and shall be given to a nation yielding the fruits thereof."[31] The Jews at the judgment seat of Pilate cried out against Him: "Away with him; away with him; crucify him,"[32] and they were cast adrift to wander through the world without king, high priest, temple, or sacrifice.

Will the Christian world afford another instance of action too little and too late? Good men soberly ponder what the future may have in store. Helplessness overwhelms them when imagination conjures up the possibilities of disaster and they say: "What can I do?" Instead of yielding to apathy they should feel an imperative call upon the most secret powers of their being. They are summoned to a high duty. Man has sinned: man must do penance. Let us reflect over and over again upon the unity of all men. We are one by nature: whereas each angel exhausts in himself the perfection of his form, the perfection of the human species is not exhausted by one or many men but only by all men. Although each angel constitutes a distinct species, all men constitute the single species, man.

Grace effects a unity yet more wondrous. All men belong to Christ because He purchased them by the blood of His cross. He invites all to come to Him and be born again, and those men who avail themselves of His saving blood and are baptized, He clasps to Himself so that they can live with His life. He and they form the Body of Christ: as the hands and feet of a man live by the life of the entire human body, so by grace the members of Christ live a divine life. When, then, one member of a body suffers, the other members suffer with it. When the hand is sick, the feet, head, and heart must help to heal it. Sinners are sick members of the Body of Christ. What sinners cannot or will not do for themselves, the healthy members must do for them. They who rejoice in the life of the Body must plead and do penance that the

---

[31] Mt. 21:43.
[32] Jn. 19:15.

sick members be not cut off forever. Every Christian has an obligation of vicarious satisfaction on behalf of Christians and non-Christians and, in order to meet the present crisis, two mighty weapons are put in his hands, prayer and penance. Pius XI says: "Prayer, then, and penance are the two potent inspirations sent us at this time by God that we may lead back to Him mankind that has gone astray and wanders without a guide."[33]

The doctrine and its practice is nothing new in the Church. St. Augustine says: "By divine judgment anyone may be punished, not for his own, but for the sins of others."[34] St. Bernard says: "It seems indeed that sometimes a kind of liberty exists in our tribulations, namely, when with voluntary and big-hearted charity we take upon ourselves the burden of penance for the sins of our neighbors, sighing for them, fasting for them, scourging ourselves for them, ourselves restoring what we have not stolen."[35]

Early in the thirteenth century the Cistercian mystic, St. Lutgarde, was favored with an apparition of our Lady which bears a startling resemblance to Fatima. So anguished did the Mother of God appear that the saint cried out: "What ails thee, O my dearest Lady, that thy face should be so haggard and so pale, thou, who art full of grace?" The Mother of God replied: "Behold, my Son is once again being crucified by heretics and bad Christians. Once again they are spitting in His face. Do thou, therefore, do penance, and fast seven years, and appease the anger of my Son which hangs heavy over the whole earth."[36] To save Christendom from the Albigensian heresy and to recall Christians from their sins, the saint thrice undertook a fast of seven years.

In the following century St. Catherine of Siena said: "As Thou Lord didst bear the pains that we had deserved, so I will bear the punishment for my spiritual children."[37] She wrote to a vacillating disciple: "Begin a new life, and I will

---

[33] *Social Wellsprings,* Vol. II, p. 274.

[34] *Contra Julianum,* Lib. III, c. 19; *PL* 44, 722.

[35] *Sermones de Diversis,* XXXIV, 3; *PL* 183, 631.

[36] Thomas Merton, *What Are These Wounds?* (Milwaukee: Bruce), pp. 39–40.

[37] Johannes Jörgensen, *Saint Catherine of Siena,* trans. Ingebord Lund (New York: Longmans, Green, 1938), p. 133.

take upon me all your guilt and melt it with tears and prayers in the fire of the love of God and do penance in your stead."[38] In 1377, the pressing need of Christendom was the return of the Pope, Gregory XI, from Avignon to Rome. At the entreaties of Catherine he started his journey to Rome but he stopped halfway. When he kept delaying for political reasons and was almost on the point of turning back, in a fiery outburst of the love of God the saint begged God to visit on her whatever fault the Pope was guilty of in delaying if only He would move him to go to Rome. For many years St. Teresa of Ávila made the grand motif of her life the acceptance of sufferings which rightly belong to others.

On December 27, 1673, our Lord appeared to St. Margaret Mary and said: "My divine Heart is so passionately in love with men that it can no longer contain within Itself the flames of Its ardent charity. It must pour them out by thy means, and manifest Itself to them to enrich them with Its precious treasures, which contain all the graces of which they have need to be saved from perdition." The following year He appeared again brilliant with glory. His five wounds shone like five suns. Flames darted from all parts of His humanity, and especially from His breast, which He opened, disclosing to the saint His Sacred Heart, the living source of these flames. Speaking of the ingratitude of man, He said: "This is more painful to Me than all I suffered in My passion. If men rendered me some return of love, I should little esteem all I have done for them, and should wish, if such could be, to suffer it over again; but they meet my eager love with coldness and rebuffs. So you at least console and rejoice Me, by supplying as much as you can for their ingratitude." During the octave of the feast of Corpus Christi, June 16, 1675, St. Margaret Mary was on her knees before the choir grate, her eyes fixed on the tabernacle. Suddenly our Lord appeared on the altar and laid bare His heart to her. "Behold," He said, "this Heart which has so loved men that it has spared nothing, even to exhausting and consuming Itself, in order to testify Its love. In return I receive from the greater part only ingratitude by their irreverence and sacrilege, and

---

[38] *Ibid.*

by the coldness and contempt they have for Me in this sacrament of love. And what is most painful to me is that they are
hearts consecrated to Me."

In our own time the Mother of God appeared to St.
Gemma Galgani and said to her: "Jesus my Son loves you
very much and wishes to confer a favor on you. Can you
render yourself worthy of it? I will be a Mother to you. Will
you show yourself a true daughter of mine?"[39] And she
covered her with her mantle. At the same instant Jesus
appeared with all His wounds open, whence issued not blood
but flames. The flames touched the hands, feet, and heart of
the girl and impressed the sacred stigmata upon them. Later
the wounds of the scourging were also reproduced in her body;
the marks of the thorns on her head; the wound Christ
received from carrying His cross on her shoulder. In her
ecstasies she would often plead for mercy for some poor soul
who was resisting grace. She would bargain with the Lord:
"Jesus, give me this soul. In exchange I will give you three
years of my life."[40] She protested she was willing to give the
last drop of her blood to prevent the offenses of sinners.

There is something quite understandable in the fact that
divine wisdom has often chosen a woman to be a victim of
reparation. The role fits a woman's great reserves of love, her
ability to make enormous sacrifices, to endure, and to do for
others. The part of women in the Passion of Christ was to
console and sympathize with Him. Hence it is that so many
congregations of religious women have been founded to
sustain the part of reparatrix, Good Samaritan to God and
man. Ruskin could never understand convents. He saw no
use in the sighs and prayers of cloistered women. Like millions of so-called practical people, Ruskin had small appreciation of the value of the prayers and expiations of women.
What women can effect before God, an incident of the battle
of New Orleans illustrates.

In January, 1815, while General Andrew Jackson went out
with a meager force to meet the British troops under Sir
Edward Packenham, seasoned veterans of the Napoleonic

---

[39] Herbert S. Kramer, S.M., *Crucified with Christ* (New York: Kenedy,
1949), p. 101.
[40] *Ibid.*, p. 106.

wars, the wives and mothers of New Orleans crowded the chapel of the Ursuline convent on Chartres Street. All through the night of January 7 they prayed, and they wept more than they prayed. For the chances of Jackson's little force seemed hopeless indeed. Many of the women hoped that when the British marched into the city they would see their men among the prisoners — alive. Inspired by the calmer Ursuline nuns, the women stormed heaven for the success of American arms and the safety of their city. The statue of our Lady was placed over the main altar. On the morning of January 8, the chaplain, Father Dubourg, offered Mass for the victory of Jackson in battle. Through their superior, the Ursuline nuns made a vow to have a Mass of thanksgiving sung each year, if their prayers were granted. At the Communion of the Mass, a messenger from the battle rushed in and shouted the news that the British had been completely crushed. The Mass, which had begun with the sadness of a requiem, ended as a triumphant thanksgiving. At its conclusion Father Dubourg intoned the *Te Deum* which the people joyfully sang. Jackson wrote personally to Father Dubourg stating his belief that the victory was "a signal intervention from Above." And he requested the administrator of the diocese "to order a solemn service of thanksgiving at the Cathedral, in thanks for the signal help that we have received from the Supreme Master of events." Jackson and his staff came to the convent to thank the nuns for their prayers. In our own New Orleans, the Mother of God now rejoices in a new title and shrine because of her prompt response to the prayers and tears of women.

The duty of reparation, however, is not reserved to women; it falls upon all. We read in the prophecy of Jonas: "The word of the Lord came to Jonas the second time, saying: Arise, and go to Ninive the great city . . . And Jonas arose, and went to Ninive . . . and he cried and said: Yet forty days and Ninive shall be destroyed. And the men of Ninive believed in God: and they proclaimed a fast, and put on sackcloth from the greatest to the least. And the word came to the king of Ninive; and he rose up out of his throne, and cast away his robe from him, and was clothed with sackcloth, and sat in ashes. And he caused it to be proclaimed and published in Ninive from the mouth of the king and his princes, saying:

Let neither men nor beasts, oxen nor sheep, taste anything: let them not feed, nor drink water. And let the men and beasts be covered with sackcloth, and cry to the Lord with all their strength, and let them turn every one from his evil way, and from the iniquity that is in their hands. Who can tell if God will turn, and forgive; and will turn away from his fierce anger, and we shall not perish? And God saw their works, that they were turned from their evil way: and God had mercy with regard to the evil which he had said he would do to them, and he did it not."[41]

The parallel between what is left of the Christian commonwealth and the incident related by the prophet is well nigh perfect. The fact of present sin is unchallengeable. The threat of punishment hangs over us as well. The unspeakable evils which have happened in the countries taken over by Communism will be repeated wherever Communism works its will. It is idle to ask: "Who is to blame for our plight?" Generations long dead, whose selfish deeds wrought the split of Christendom and hence its gradual decay, have their share of the blame for the evil situation of today. But dead men can offer no works of satisfaction. It is idle also for one to say: "This is no affair of mine. I lead an upright life. I am not contributing to this brazen upsurge of sin." It is human to try to avoid a common burden. But the need of averting the divine anger is a duty of all because danger threatens all. Nobody can shrug off the obligation with the comfortable thought that he need not bother since enough people will be found to take care of it. Each Christian should be deeply convinced that God wants him to take personal part in this work. The men of Ninive took no chances: they all had a share in appeasing God. It is evident that as long as the unbelievers in our midst are unconverted they will do nothing to alleviate the situation. The obligation, then, clearly falls upon Christian men and women; not upon some, but upon all.

As the king of Ninive himself gave so shining an example of the performance of penance enjoined upon all, does not also the office of the priest single him out to lead the way in this pressing business? It is impossible to accept the priest-

---

[41] Jonas 3.

hood and avoid a duty of atonement. "For every high priest taken from among men, is ordained for men in the things that appertain to God, that he may offer gifts and sacrifices for sin."[42] The saintly Pontiff Pius X reminds the priest: "Nor must our prayers be confined to our own needs, for in the fearful deluge of crime which overflows on all sides we must earnestly implore and beseech the Divine Mercy, praying with insistence to Christ, who is prodigal of grace in the adorable sacrament of the altar: 'Spare, O Lord, spare Thy People.' "[43] Pius XI says that, as Christ ever lives to make intercession for us, the priest, like Him, "is public and official intercessor of humanity before God . . . And never did humanity in its afflictions stand more in need of intercession and of the divine help which it brings. Who can tell how many chastisements priestly prayer wards off from mankind."[44]

To the whole Christian world is addressed the request of Our Lady of Fatima: "Pray, pray very much, make sacrifices for sinners. Remember that many souls are lost because there is nobody to pray and make sacrifices for them."[45] Every person in the state of grace is constantly performing acts such as obedience to law, fulfillment of duty, endurance of the crosses of life, all of which have reparatory value. By a morning offering and its constant renewal through the day all of one's good acts can be directed to the end of reparation, and thus, in a general way a person can participate all day long in the continuing atonement of the Church, the myrrh which the Beloved sends up to her Spouse.

Everybody has heartaches and bitter hours to endure. St. Elizabeth of Portugal had to put up with the numerous infidelities of a royal husband. A good man may be burdened with an alcoholic wife or a wayward son. Although the list of human woes is never fully told, one of the saddest mysteries is the waste of suffering. While everyone suffers, so few profit from suffering. Many fail to reap even the natural profit of becoming a more integrated person. Skid Row is peopled by

---

[42] Hebr. 5:1.

[43] *Exhortatio ad Clerum,* August 4, 1908, *Acta Sanctae Sedis,* v. 41, p. 565.

[44] Encyclical letter, *Ad Catholici Sacerdotii, A.A.S.,* v. 28, n. 1.

[45] *More About Fatima,* p. 29.

those whom difficulty has bewildered. But in last analysis all suffering is wasted which is not endured in union with the cross of Christ. Only thus is human pain capable of producing everlasting value. How do we bear our troubles, grudgingly or wholeheartedly with Christ? If we rebel at times and partially oppose them with earthy methods of escape, their supernatural value is negligible. If we take them submissively, thankful that we are asked to bear a part of Christ's burden, they instruct us, they mellow us, they form us in the image of Christ. United to the atonement of Christ, they too are acts of supernatural atonement. Here is the first practicable method of making reparation. It is open to all. Every Christian can adopt it. But although everyone suffers, unfortunately not everyone offers reparation.

In a more particular manner we can dedicate special prayers to the explicit purpose of expiation. For example, Our Lady of Fatima asks that all the faithful daily recite the rosary. The movement to revive the family rosary is worthy of all praise. During this salutary devotion, which makes so strongly for family solidarity, the older members can consciously and easily fulfill a duty of reparation which the younger members should come to know at an early age. A second means is self-denial and deliberate assumption of sufferings and humiliations. How many and of what kind these mortifications ought to be is for *prudence* to judge. Just as every good Christian asks himself at the beginning of Lent, "What mortifications will I practice?" so now even more seriously should he determine the reparatory mortifications which will become a more or less permanent part of his life.

A recent author has distinguished between necessary and voluntary mortifications. He calls a necessary mortification one which is inevitably bound up with some required act. By a required act he means one that is necessary not only in the strict sense of meeting a moral obligation or resisting temptation, but in the broad sense of being requisite for self-rectification. Voluntary mortifications are those which a person assumes completely of himself: they are commanded neither by law, by precept, nor by necessity. This author praises necessary mortifications; he frowns upon voluntary mortifications for the reason that they contain a danger of spiritual pride. His rejection, however, of voluntary mortifications seems contrary to the received tradition of Christian asceticism. Good Christians have often chosen corporal austerities in a measure far beyond the demand of any necessity and the Church has lauded their action. The argument against voluntary mortification, that it might lead to spiritual pride, could be applied to discourage the practice of many virtues — perpetual chastity, voluntary poverty, and the like. Who will say that the extraordinary penances of the great "victims of expiation" were not completely voluntary? The plea of Our Lady of Fatima seems to call precisely for voluntary mortifications.

The distinction between necessary and voluntary mortification, however, reminds us of a sensible precaution to be taken by one who is attracted to reparation. He asks himself, "What can I do?" Two courses are open. First, he can courageously, even joyously, accept the inevitable sufferings of his life, and to these add some *voluntary* acts of penance. A second course may appeal to enthusiastic souls, namely, to request of our Lord great sufferings like loss of peace, health, fortune, or even life. The first course is sane and reasonable and within the scope of any pious soul. It is dangerous, however, to enter upon the second course without having proved oneself in the first. One can be deluded that he wants great and vague sufferings in the distant future, when as yet he does not stand up manfully beneath the actual crosses God gives him. If God should grant such a rash request the soul is ill-prepared to bear the suffering. The person wilts under it, complains and wonders why the trial did not take some other form. Only after a person has given solid proof of generosity and fortitude in the first way, should he think of offering himself as a "permanent victim" of great sufferings.

Satisfying for the sins of others is not a frill of piety. It is an essential action of the Mystical Body of Christ. St. Paul was full of it. Did he not wish to be anathema, if only his brethren in the flesh would accept the true faith? St. John Vianney took upon himself the shortcomings of his parish. Reparation is the backbone of devotion to the Sacred Heart. There is a startling parallel between the utterances of our Lord to St. Margaret Mary and the messages of our Lady in our own time. There is the same appeal for reparation. How much greater is the need today? When was the Church of Christ more bitterly assailed and its faithful children more ferociously attacked? The mere recounting of the blasphemies of the last twenty-five years, the desecration of holy things, the torrential shedding of Christian blood makes the Christian wonder whether Satan has been unchained again among men.

Although the duty of reparation falls inexorably upon all, none of us should be saddened at the thought. Courageous acceptance of the duty brings at least two consolations. First, we learn by experience something of the mystery of suffering. As the cross of Christ is a mystery to all unbelievers, so also are all sufferings endured in union with the cross a mystery to all who do not believe enough. The mystery is this: nothing so effectively unites sin-laden man with God as pain endured in the company of Jesus. God comes to us in our pain. We hate the pain and squirm under it: we try to get out of it. If we merely fight it and cry out against it, we miss what God has for us. If we humbly take it and allow God to work His will with us by its instrumentality, He purifies and cleanses us and brings us that much closer to Himself. It is one thing to accept a statement of this kind as we read it in a book: it is quite another to have learned it by personal experience.

The second consolation is that our effort will not be in vain. What the Mother of God is asking Christians to do will evidently be done for she has promised that the cause of her Immaculate Heart will triumph. And triumph it will and in the way peculiar to God. From the most meager beginnings the cause of God grows slowly and slowly until it fills the heavens with a crescendo of success. The Fatima story begins with three children beholding our Lady standing on an evergreen oak and, despite the hindrances un-Christian men throw in the way, it culminates with seventy thousand people seeing the great miracle of the dancing sun. For a quarter of a century the facts are hidden. Almost suddenly they come to light and set reactions in train throughout the world. Even now we see only the beginning of good things: the ground swell of a mighty tide of prayer and reparation is setting in, which, God willing, will restore to the Christian world the faith and charity it has so sadly abjured. If anyone has doubted the genuineness of the Fatima story let him ponder the greatest news item of the twentieth century, more important than the German march into Poland: three times, in Rome, in 1950, the Holy Father saw the same miracle of the sun which the children saw in Portugal in 1917. This event may be the turning point of modern history: the unbelief of modern man is met by miracles and signs in the sky. Who can hope to stand against the living God? Or resist the allure of His Mother?

8. Friendship

"He that feareth God, shall likewise have good friendship: because according to him shall his friend be" (Ecclus. 6:17).

HUMAN things are copies of divine things. Man's being is a participation in Infinite Being. Man's life and action are little images of God's life and action. Man's most valuable powers — his ability to know and to love — are reflections of God knowing and loving.

Man's action is especially imitative of God, not only when he knows, but also when he loves and imitates the characteristics of divine love. Since God is not a lonely God dwelling in isolated splendor, there exists in Him the loftiest kind of love. This is the love of friendship, that mutual benevolence whereby one person seeks the good of another for the other's sake, and vice versa. It can exist only between equals. Its purpose is union as complete as possible. The means of achieving love's purpose is an interchange of life, the surrender of lover to beloved. Its end result is happiness in the union achieved.

Although God is one, unique, and simple, He enjoys the society, companionship, and affection of Divine Equals. For the Three Persons of the Most Blessed Trinity are incomprehensibly equal, each possessing the divine nature without limit. Father, Son, and Holy Ghost love one another, each for His own sake, wishing Infinite Good to one another and sharing it equally. As we cannot plumb the depth of the Divine Being nor comprehend the infinity of His intelligence, so we can only stand in awe of and adore the perfect love which God has for God. The love of the Three Persons is crowned not merely by a union but by a unity in one identical nature which has no parallel. In the unity, whereby the Three Persons share one divine life, consists their infinite happiness.

The relations of men with other men are to be modeled, in varying degrees of approximation, upon the personal relations in God. When they are so modeled, the great truth is apparent, that men were made not for competition, but for co-operation. As one divine nature is shared by Three Divine Persons among whom there cannot be the slightest friction, so human nature is shared by many individual persons who are intended to move and act together in utmost harmony.

What are man's great human relations? The first, because it most closely resembles the love of the Divine Persons, is charity. By charity the human soul, elevated by grace to share in God's life, loves his fellow man in Christ, desiring for him the divine good, supplying to him what he can in order to help him achieve the divine good. This most closely approximates divine love, not because by it a person seeks another with the greatest intensity of emotion, but because it is possible only by possession of divine life, and that which it communicates is not human but divine good.

Perhaps we should call this a divine-human relation, since it is possible only because God has invited man to be His friend. That man should be the friend of God is a true marvel of the universe: God endows man with divinity to make him capable of His friendship. A man's most sacred treasure is the friendship of God. Seeking perfection is the endeavor to convert that friendship into deepest intimacy.

The most important of purely human relations derives from human love of friendship. Even if God had not intended that men should be His friends and so be bound to one another by grace's bond of divine friendship, He would have, and He does, urge them to seek happiness in ties of mutual love for other men. The Author of nature has impressed upon the human heart a craving for this relationship whose loftiest human form is found in the bond of husband and wife. From this completest kind of friendship, wherein mutual giving is so comprehensive and inclusive, stems the blood tie of parent and child, brother and sister, a relationship that is meant to be, not a mere instinct of natural affection, but also a rational regard for one another's welfare. Relatives are to be friends.

It may seem strange to those who are not acquainted with the language of the Scholastics to list family affection as a species of love of friendship. The usage is real and justifiable. People, however, usually restrict the word "friendship" to the voluntary association of persons who, without the tie of blood or matrimony, develop mutual esteem and good will. It is founded upon a certain agreeableness of companionship and harmony of tastes; it is fostered by interchange of confidence and goods. In this sense we now use the word. The relation assumes its characteristic mark from the things which friend exchanges with friend. The nobler and more spiritual the things exchanged, the loftier the relation. Unless the enduring motive of the relation is the good of one's friend, the association scarcely deserves the name of friendship. As family affection is the first of purely human relationships, this is the second.

Now we cannot be friends to all men, since we cannot have in common with all the same opportunity of association, personal knowledge, and harmony of tastes which friendship demands. However, a fundamental tie of good will binds all men. Nature so demands. The outward expression of this good will calls for exercise of the natural virtue of friendliness. The equity of human intercourse obliges a person to act in a befitting and pleasant manner toward all with whom he deals. He is to speak to and act agreeably toward his fellow man, unless some good and sufficient reason obliges him at times to displease him.

From these three relationships we distinguish our obligation of friendliness to all men, of friendship toward our friends, of family affection toward our relatives, and we ask: "Are these human ties a help or a hindrance to our friendship with God?" How is the aspirant to perfection to use these relationships in order to draw closer to God?

We need delay little on the obligations of friendliness. As a moral virtue it stands in the golden mean between defect and excess. A person is deficient when his unreasonable action produces pain or unpleasantness in another. He offends by excess when he is too effusive and fulsome, or pours himself out upon undeserving persons, or at the wrong time, or in the wrong measure. This natural virtue is the foundation of international relations and demands recognition of the solidarity of the human race and good will toward all nations, even toward national enemies. Charity presupposes friendliness as basic to all human intercourse. Of charity there can be no excess. We cannot wish or give too much of God to our neighbor or be too closely united to him in Christ.

While obligations of supernatural charity like praying for all, doing good to the needy, forgiving enemies may absorb our attention, a danger can exist that in the quest of supernatural virtue we forget the demands of natural virtue. The aspirant to perfection must never fail to act as a lady or a gentleman. Whenever non-Catholics put Catholics to shame by the manifest superiority of their courtesy, something is wanting to the charity of those Catholics. As a means of practicing both friendliness and charity we should try to realize and revere the Most Blessed Trinity dwelling in everyone we meet.

Let us discuss at some length two things in relation to perfection: first, the family, and especially the conjugal tie; second, the bond of friendship.

FAMILY TIES AND PERFECTION

Does the family tie help or hinder us in becoming close friends of God? Is it true that, while the family tie helps to salvation, it hinders perfection? That hence, anyone desirous of perfection cannot be closely bound by family ties? That in practice the conjugal tie is incompatible with perfection? Does intense love for a human being prevent perfect love of God? These are questions of grave import, and confused and false answers have been given to them, with the result that a good deal of muddled thinking exists on the subject.

Christ our Lord says: "If any man come to me, and hate not his father, and mother, and wife and children, and brethren, and sisters, yea and his own life also, he cannot be my disciple."[1] The Albigensians appealed to this text to show that the married state is sinful in itself. Although the Church condemns this interpretation as blasphemous and heretical, do these words, nevertheless, prove that the quest

---

[1] Lk. 14:26.

of perfection means foregoing one's right to marry and surrendering family ties? Before answering we must ask, "What
is meant by being a disciple?" and, "Who are called to be
disciples?"

A disciple is any member of Christ, any branch of the Vine.
He has turned his back upon Satan and the world and he
has chosen Christ. He has been drawn to Christ by the
Father, he believes in Christ, he does His will, at least to
some extent. Without the previous action of grace, without
faith and baptism, discipleship is simply impossible.

We may, however, admit various levels of discipleship,
based upon a greater or less acceptance of His will. Leaving
sinners out of consideration, we may distinguish an ordinary
level of discipleship, consisting of those who habitually strive
to avoid mortal sin; a higher level of those who try to avoid
venial sin; and a highest level of those who try to avoid even
imperfections. These all are certainly disciples. For if they are
reckoned disciples of Christ who adhere to the faith despite
the sins they commit, all the more must we call disciples
those members of the Church who keep out of mortal sin.

Who are called to be disciples? Surely all men are called
to the faith, membership in the Church, and eternal salvation. Since all men are called to some manner of discipleship,
and since in the words quoted above Christ is speaking of
an essential condition of discipleship, the least which His
words can mean is this: no one may prefer father, mother,
wife, etc., to Christ. Rather than give up or forego membership in the Church one must actually sever the closest human
tie. For friendship with God is above all human relations.
That a person should actually give up his family in order to
keep the faith and cleave to Christ is an extraordinary demand
whose fulfillment calls for heroic virtue. Heroic virtue is not
ordinarily demanded and if the Gospel insisted that, as an
ordinary condition of discipleship, a man be without the
family tie, it would contradict the law of nature commanding
men to live a family life. What the Gospel requires is an
habitual frame of mind by which one is prepared to disregard
father, mother, wife, etc., whenever any one of them would
lead one into mortal sin.

The words of Christ have a second clear meaning: rather

than offend Christ even venially, one must choose to displease anyone no matter how dear. This represents a level of disciple-ship considerably above the first, for it requires no small control of self and exercise of virtue to avoid deliberate venial sin. It is a level, however, which all Christians should ambi-tion for the practical reason that, if a person aims only at avoiding mortal sin, he will not uniformly succeed. To save his soul a Christian must aim above the minimum requirement.

We may equate the first and second levels with the way of the commandments. Along these levels the ordinary Christian moves to salvation and maintains the ordinary family ties. These he need not habitually abjure. He must prefer Christ to them only upon the occasion when they present him with a proximate occasion of sin.

The third level of discipleship is that of persons who try to avoid all sin and follow the counsels of perfection. It is not true that these alone are disciples; but they are disciples in the fullest sense for they are closest to Christ. Concerning this class it has been said: first, that their number is very small; second, that the words of Christ given above refer to this class alone and mean: you must actually renounce father, mother, wife, etc., if you would aim at the perfection of a disciple of Christ.

As to the first assertion, it is true that the number of the faithful who ambition perfection is small. The reason, how-ever, is not the deliberate design of God but the weakness and pusillanimity of men. God wishes all men to be perfect but so many do not heed the invitation. St. Teresa says: "When I come to these wonders of God's greatness (graces of sublime holiness) . . . I cannot but feel keenly grieved at seeing what we lose by our own fault. It is true, His Majesty grants these favors to whom He chooses, yet if we were to seek Him as He seeks us, He would give them to all of us. He only longs for souls on whom He may bestow them, for His gifts diminish not His riches."[2] While Christ is desirous of offering perfection to all disciples, He can bestow it only as the disciple matures enough to be able to receive it. Disciples

---

[2] *Interior Castle*, Sixth Mans., Ch. iv, 16.

who co-operate with graces of the first level may expect graces
of a higher kind. Disciples who do not come to maturity in
Christ cannot expect the strong meat of the adult. If they
seldom co-operate with lesser graces, greater graces would be
useless to them. A father does not give his five-year-old son
the same kind of bicycle he gives his twelve-year-old son. It
would be useless, even dangerous, to the smaller boy. When
he grows bigger let him have it. So the souls which never
grow up in Christ, but remain stunted and immature, need
expect no great graces of holiness.

As to the second assertion, we doubt very much indeed that
the words of Christ are spoken to but a select few; from the
context it seems quite clear that they are addressed to all men.
They certainly, however, apply to persons aiming at perfection. These, like everyone else, are to "hate" father and mother
under penalty of not being a disciple. That some greater
degree of renunciation is required of them than of those who
walk the way of the commandments seems quite obvious.
What then does "hatred" of father, mother, etc., demand of
them?

The story of the rich young man in the Gospel gives a
most important clue. There we see, first, that Christ calls to
perfection those who have kept the commandments well.
Second, we learn the fundamental condition which a person
must fulfill, if he would draw very close to God. "If thou
wilt be perfect, go sell what thou hast, and give to the poor,
and thou shalt have treasure in heaven: and come follow me."[3]

The perfect disciple must give away his possessions and
come follow Christ. If these words are to be understood only
in a literal sense, then he who would be perfect must actually
strip himself of worldly goods. An inescapable corollary would
follow: he could not marry without worldly goods. Does then
the "hatred" demanded of him consist in renouncing matrimony and severing family ties in order to cling to God
alone? Is St. Paul suggesting the same thing when he says:
"He that is without a wife, is solicitous for the things that
belong to the Lord, how he may please God. But he that is
with a wife, is solicitous for the things of the world, how he

---

[3] Mt. 19:21.

may please his wife: and he is divided"?[4] Are we to conclude that such great abnegation of the heart is required of the perfect disciple that no married person nor anyone living intimately in the bosom of his family can aspire to perfection?

The history of the quest for Christian perfection may afford some enlightenment. The words of advice which St. Paul gave to the Corinthians regarding voluntary continence in marriage, virginity, and widowhood were considered by the first Christians as counsels to a higher life. He said: "The time is short: it remaineth that they also who have wives, be as if they had none. . . . Both he that giveth his virgin in marriage, doth well; and he that giveth her not, doth better . . . More blessed shall she [a widow] be, if she so remain, according to my counsel; and I think that I also have the spirit of God."[5] From the beginning Christians embraced the state of virginity which was in high honor in the Church. It is not surprising that the idea spread of calling to the priesthood by preference those Christians who were disposed to keep to this state and who were regarded as more perfect. The virgin and the widow remained in her own home. However, the great public movement toward the higher life began, when thousands of earnest souls interpreted literally the admonition of Christ, "Go sell what thou hast," and retired to the desert. These first efforts were highly individualistic and met with many trials and difficulties. The first thing which gave system and organization to these efforts was the establishment of a common or cenobitical life. The next great step, the thing which gave enduring substance to the movement, was the vow, the religious promise to obey a superior in one's quest for perfection. In the course of time other vows were added: chastity, military service, poverty, service of the sick, acceptance of slavery for the release of Christian captives or the like. So from centuries of experience there gradually evolved a "religious life" which has now maintained its substantial form for many hundred years. It is a canonically recognized "way of perfection" and at its core are the public vows of poverty, chastity, and obedience. In it the Church

---

[4] 1 Cor. 7:32–33.
[5] 1 Cor. 7:29, 38, 40.

offers the loving soul a sure, time-tried road to Christian perfection; we may call it an express highway to God. Of itself it is a higher and nobler state than the ordinary Christian life led without religious vows.

But the existence of this official "way of perfection" does not mean that perfection may be found in it alone. Religious life makes the acquisition of perfection easier. It affords the soul a peaceful shelter and gives facility in finding God. The vows make a direct and all-out attack upon the three great obstacles to perfection: pride, avarice, and carnal love. Nevertheless, any Christian in any honorable walk of life can become the intimate friend of God. Louis IX of France did not give away all his worldly possessions; he took no vow of religious chastity; he put himself under no superior; yet, he came very close to God. His is no isolated case: he is typical of the saint who lived in the world. Whoever keeps the commandments with all his heart, God will call to counsels of perfection. The counsels need not be of religious poverty, chastity, and obedience. There are other counsels, for in each virtue we may distinguish good which is commanded and good which is counseled. There are heroic counsels of patience, meekness, long-suffering, turning the other cheek, doing good to one's enemy.

Returning then to the fundamental law of perfection laid down by Christ, "Go sell what thou hast," we must say that it is not always to be interpreted in a literal sense. It is, however, always true in a spiritual sense; that is, he who would enter upon the way of perfection must free his heart of all inordinate affection for worldly goods. If literal surrender of worldly goods is not possible for an individual, this fact does not close the way of perfection to him; and if a person takes a vow of religious poverty and fails to cleanse his heart of such inordinate affection, he has not as yet truly entered the way of perfection. The essential prerequisite for attaining perfection, therefore, is not actual but spiritual poverty.

There are three great steps to perfection. The first is taken by resolutely preventing any material thing, any object less than man, from coming between one and God. The second, by allowing no man to hinder one from God. The third, by purifying from self every obstacle to God. Poverty of spirit

constitutes the first step. Concerning the second step, we
have already asked, "Are intimate family relations, especially
the conjugal tie, in themselves hindrances to perfection?"
They cannot be. If they were, then there would be an essential flaw in human nature and a direct opposition, an open
contradiction, between the law of nature and the counsels of
perfection. But there is no such flaw and such a contradiction
cannot be.

It is more difficult to attain perfection in the married state
than in the state of virginity. St. Paul gives the reason: "The
unmarried woman and the virgin thinketh on the things of
the Lord, that she may be holy both in body and in spirit.
But she that is married thinketh on the things of the world,
how she may please her husband."[6] True, this division of one's
heart between one's spouse and God is likely to happen, but
it need not. A man can love his wife in God and for God.
Their mutual love is intended by God to bring them closer
to Himself. There is something wondrously holy in the union
of Christian husband and wife. It is an imitation of the union
of Christ and His Church.

St. Paul says: "Wives [be subject] to your husbands as to
the Lord, because the husband is the head of the wife, as
Christ too is the head of the Church, himself being the saviour
of the body. Well, then, as the Church is subject to Christ,
so also should wives be to their husbands in everything.
Husbands, love your wives, as Christ also loved the Church
and delivered himself up for her, that he might sanctify her,
purifying her in the bath of water by means of the word, and
that he might present her to himself a glorious Church, not
having spot or wrinkle or any such thing, but holy and without blemish. Even thus ought husbands to love their wives
as their own bodies. He that loveth his own wife loveth himself. Surely no man ever hated his own flesh, nay, he doth
nourish and cherish it, even as Christ the Church; because we
are members of his body. 'For this shall man leave father and
mother, and shall cleave to his wife, and the two shall come
to be one flesh.' The mystery here is great — I mean in reference to Christ and the Church."[7]

---

[6] 1 Cor. 7:34.   [7] Eph. 5:22–32, Westminster version.

Jansenism had a low esteem of matrimony. In its eyes married people were only tolerated disciples who should be permitted to receive Holy Communion but rarely. It did not recognize the importance of matrimony, a sacramental charism intended to increase holiness and perfection in the Church. In this sacrament is the seed of perfection which awaits the warmth of divine grace and human co-operation to open into fragrant life. It is there as it is in the sacrament of Holy Orders.

Married people should constantly reflect upon the words of Pius XI: "For all men of every condition, in whatever honorable walk of life they may be, can and ought to imitate that most perfect example of holiness placed before man by God, namely Christ Our Lord, and by God's grace to arrive at the summit of perfection, as is proved by the example set us by many saints. This mutual inward moulding of husband and wife, this determined effort to perfect each other, can in a very real sense, as the Roman catechism teaches, be said to be the chief reason and purpose of matrimony, provided matrimony be looked at not in the restricted sense as instituted for the proper conception and education of children, but more widely as the blending of life as a whole and the mutual interchange and sharing thereof."[8] If then husband and wife set before themselves the lofty ideal proposed by the Roman Pontiff, they will help to purify and sanctify each other. They first co-operate with the lesser graces of matrimony given them to avoid mortal and venial sin. In this they exercise no small virtue, for dangers and temptations are grievous and multiple. Then God will give them graces of higher sanctity, so that the love which they bear each other, far from being an obstacle to intimacy with God, will become a sweet stimulus to draw nearer to God. Perfect love for a human being is a help to perfect love for God. The difficulty lies in their imperfect love for each other. Since they love their own selves too much and the other too little, they rise not to the pure love of God. Spouses do not love God perfectly because they first fail in mutual love.

---

[8] Encyclical letter, *Casti Connubii*, A.A.S., v. 22, n. 13, December 31, 1930, p. 548.

The conjugal love of Mary and Joseph was a mighty factor in their sanctification. The house of Nazareth shows how love of man and love of God blend perfectly together. Let no one, however, say that the wedded life of Mary and Joseph was so different from that of ordinary spouses that their example is of little use. God desired perfect chastity of them and for their compliance rewarded them with immense sanctity. God seldom desires the same thing of ordinary spouses but He will reward all proportionately with sanctity for giving Him what He desires of them. Sanctification comes of doing God's will. God does not will the same things of all His children but He makes holy all who do His will.

Anyone, therefore, old or young, married or single, lay or cleric, can become a disciple of the loftiest and most intimate kind. The invitation, "Go sell what thou hast," does not always involve voluntary choice of actual poverty; but in every instance it does demand purity of heart, the casting aside of disorderly desires for material things and selfish love of other people. The family tie is not of itself an obstacle to perfection. True, God pointedly asks some few to surrender it because it would hinder an apostolic or completely contemplative life. Speaking through the voice of nature, God signifies His desire that the vast majority of His children preserve the family tie intact: speaking through the Gospel, He signifies His desire that all be perfect. Hence He asks for the sanctification of the family tie and the achievement of perfection on the part of the vast majority within the family circle.

FRIENDSHIP AND PERFECTION

Let us now examine the relation between friendship and perfection. There are three kinds of friendship: the right kind which is based on charity; the wrong kind which is motivated by carnal love; and, as we should expect to find among men, an admixture of the good and the bad. Let us talk, first, about the wrong kind and, then, about the right kind.

We should not be frightened by the term "carnal love" and immediately give it an unsavory connotation. In a general sense, carnal love is the ministering to self of what the concupiscences crave. Applied to affection for other people it means loving or liking them according to the desires of nature wounded by sin and drawing therefrom satisfaction agreeable to unregenerate man. Its root is pride; it operates with no inconsiderable manifestation of the capital vices; and its ultimate object is the promotion of self.

There is a reprehensible simulation of friendship — an insufferable form of selfishness — wherein one offers another the tokens of friendship, not for the sake of the so-called friend, but merely for one's own pleasure or profit. The world is full of "business" friends and "social" friends, people who are simply used as steppingstones to another's utility. These friendships are unworthy of any man: no earnest soul would stoop to use another and abuse so precious a thing as friendship.

There is a genuine kind of friendship wherein a person really seeks the good of his friend and is willing to put himself out for his friend, but always at a price, and the price is some ministration to one's ego. The sop to self-love and the subordination of friend to self are often deftly concealed; nevertheless, these things underlie friendship founded on carnal love. The great object sought is pleasure in the friend's company, pleasure in doing for him, pleasure in giving him gifts. Take away the pleasure and nothing is left to sustain the friendship. When, then, deep conflict arises between one's own and the friend's interests and a definite choice must be made, the interests of self prevail. Merely carnal love cannot rise to the pure heights of total self-surrender. The charity which seeketh not her own is absent.

These friendships begin in the sense attraction of two mutually agreeable dispositions and are fostered and developed by imagination and sense appetite. We call them shallow or frivolous or sentimental as long as the manifestations of carnal love are merely on the surface. The first sign of carnal love is impetuosity. For sense rushes pell-mell to its object without waiting for the counsel of reason. The friendship is sudden in its origin and vehement in its first development. Second, it is all-absorbing while it lasts. The image of the friend is constantly in one's imagination. While the fever is on practically all other interests are subordinated to the friendship. One is always desirous of the friend's presence, either arranging new meetings and eagerly looking forward to them, or suffering desolation when his absence is prolonged. Third, it fluctuates as does all sense emotion, wavering between heights of desire and extremes of displeasure. While it hopes to be everlasting, it is often destroyed by separation and the formation of new attachments. So often it is put aside for a more recent attraction.

Perhaps all the attachments of youth are of this kind since youth is so much a creature of sense and imagination. For a while, these things do no great harm to a youth but as he comes to adult years he must learn to prune the dangerous excesses of carnal love and begin to elevate and transform his affections into charity. What is reprehensible is that people of mature years should continue to act in this respect like youths of sixteen.

Friendship, beginning in the senses, can quickly transcend sense and cast deep roots in the rational soul. Now it is the intention of nature that certain friendships be a natural preparation for matrimony. It is to be expected, therefore, that in their development elements of exclusive possessiveness and sexual attraction should manifest themselves. The sacrament of matrimony, which is to crown the relation, stands by to heal the attachment of the defects of disordered flesh. On the other hand, attachments which can never be blessed by matrimony may develop in similar fashion and, because they can never reach the healthful perfection of matrimony, manifest blemishes of frustration. The first of these is pride in which one desires to be loved totally for one's own sake, to have the friend wholly to oneself, or at least to hold first place in his affections. A natural consequence is a sensitive jealousy which shows ill will toward anyone who would appropriate any of the friend's affections. If the friend does not measure up to the demands of affection made upon him, anger — subtle revenge for real or fancied slights to one's ego — enters in to punish the friend for his deficiencies. Some ardent friendships are unsuspected substitutes for matrimony but it is absurd to say that all are such.

The error in these friendships lies in the predominance of carnal love, but this is not necessarily to be equated with sexual love. Freud was wrong when he reduced all the capital sins to one. Some unsentimental friendships are wrong because the common aim of the friends is unworthy, like the pursuit of worldly pleasure. We sometimes say that apart these two are fine persons but together they make a bad combination. Other friendships are wrong if the friends are unequal in virtue and the worse draws the other to his level. By their fruits you shall know them. A natural friendship is wrong if it fails to make the friends better men. Among adult Christians merely natural attachments ought not to exist. Friendship ought to be elevated to the supernatural and make the friends better sons of God.

Clearly, then, such friendships are dangerous for earnest souls. Tanquerey says: "They constitute one of the greatest obstacles to perfection."[9] They involve great loss of time. They make prayer difficult; sometimes, even impossible. What Father Gabriel says in this regard applies to all aspirants to perfection: ". . . who allows himself to be caught in the snare of a particular friendship puts a great obstacle in the way of his life of prayer . . . The more the heart is inclined to creatures the less free it is to occupy itself with the love for God. And as prayer consists chiefly in expressing our love for God, of necessity it will become less intense when there arise within us the evil tendencies aroused by our blame-worthy failures. In expressing its love, the soul will speak less energetically; God's company, once its sole desire, will be less relished, will even be found boring, whilst recollection will be rendered difficult thanks to the numerous distractions which will be born spontaneously from the new attraction for creatures."[10]

Very aptly and practically À Kempis sums up the situation: "If in all things thou seekest Jesus, truly thou shalt find Jesus; but if thou seek thyself, thou shalt find thyself, but to thy own ruin."[11]

Friendship based upon and motivated by charity is recog-

---

[9] Adolphe Tanquerey, SS., *The Spiritual Life*, 2 ed., (Westminster: Newman, 1948), p. 289.

[10] Father Gabriel of St. Mary Magdalen, *St. John of the Cross* (Cork: The Mercier Press, 1947), p. 135.

[11] *Imitation*, Bk. II, C. 7.

nizable by these qualities: (1) it is in God and for God;
(2) it is enduring; (3) it is a stimulus to virtue; (4) it
demands equality of virtue; (5) it knows no jealousy and
petty fears. These characteristics are worth examining in
detail.

1. St. Augustine has developed this first thought at length
in a letter written to his old friend Martianus who had just
become a catechumen. Taking as a text the definition of
Cicero: "Friendship is agreement about human and divine
things together with mutual esteem and good will,"[12] Augustine proceeds: "You were indeed, my dear friend, at one
time agreed with me as to human things . . . but as for
divine things of which I then possessed no gleam of truth,
our friendship was deficient as far as the important part of
this definition is concerned: for, although we had esteem
and good will, our agreement was about human and not
about divine things . . . But how shall I now express the
great joy I have on account of you, when I now have as
a true friend one whom for so long I have had as a kind
of friend? There is now agreement about divine things, because you who once shared with me so pleasing a temporal
existence, now begin to share with me the hope of eternal life.
. . . Thus it happens that when agreement in divine things
is wanting to friends, their agreement in human things cannot be full and true. For it must be that he who contemns
divine things has not a proper view of human things, nor
does anyone know how to love a man aright who loves not
Him who made man. And so I do not say that now you
are fully my friend having hitherto been partly my friend;
but it is reasonable to say that you were not even partly
my friend, when not even in human things were we bound
by true friendship. For in divine things, wherefrom all human
things take their right value, you were not my companion;
either when I myself rejected them, or after I began in a
fashion to relish that which you did still detest. I do not
wish to irritate you, and let it not seem absurd to you
that at the same time when I was eaten up with human
vanity, you were not as yet my friend, although you may

---

[12] *De Amicitia*, 20.

have seemed to love me very much; when indeed I was no friend to myself but rather an enemy; for I loved iniquity. True indeed is the divine sentence written in the holy books, *He that loveth inquity, hateth his own soul.* When, therefore, I hated my own soul, how could I have a true friend who desired for me the very things wherein I was acting as my own enemy? . . . Thanks be to God that at last He has deigned to make you my friend. For now along with esteem and affection we have perfect accord in human and divine things in Jesus Christ our Lord, our truest peace. All the divine commands He has included in two precepts: *Thou shalt love the Lord thy God with thy whole heart, and with thy whole soul, and with thy whole mind;* and, *Thou shalt love thy neighbor as thyself. On these two commandments dependeth the whole law and the prophets.* In the first is agreement about divine things, in the second is agreement about human things, together with mutual esteem and affection. If you firmly hold with me these two, our friendship is true and everlasting; and it will not only bind us together, but it will bind the two of us even to the Lord."[13]

2. It was laudable craving for the truly excellent which made Cicero long for immortality: for his actions, in the memory of grateful fellow citizens; for his writings, in the critical judgment of the scholars of all the race; for himself, in the bosom of God. Truly great things are lasting things; the things which run down and fall apart had in them from the beginning some essential defect. This criterion of being able to last in undiminished vigor is applicable to human relations. Real friendship endures. St. Jerome says: "Friendship which can cease, never was true friendship."[14] The Wise Man derides the notion of friendship which endures not. "There is a friend for his own occasion, and he will not abide in the day of thy trouble. And there is a friend that turneth to enmity; and there is a friend that will disclose hatred and strife and reproaches. And there is a friend, a companion at table, and he will not abide in the day of distress. A friend, if he continue steadfast, shall be to thee as thyself."[15]

---

[13] *Epistola ad Martianum,* 258; PL 33, 1071 ff.
[14] *Epistola ad Rufinum Monachum,* 6; PL 22, 335.
[15] Ecclus. 6:8–11.

Certain bonds of natural affection last a lifetime, because they are according to right reason; but, unless they are also according to supernatural faith and have something of supernatural charity, they will not survive into another life. Death will swallow them. For they who die in mortal sin become incapable of friendship or any noble emotion. Only the friendship of charity is everlasting. Even in this life it manifests its enduring robustness. St. Chrysostom says: "Whenever people are bound in friendship on account of merely temporal reasons, their union is neither ardent nor lasting; but pride, loss of money, jealousy, desire of vainglory or some such thing comes and breaks up the friendship. For it has found no root in the spirit. If it be of the spirit, nothing in this world would destroy what is spiritual. For the love which is through Christ is firm, unbroken, indestructible and nothing will be able to root it out — neither calumnies nor dangers nor death nor any such thing. For if he who loves in this manner were to suffer a thousand ills, he would keep before him the reason why he loves and he would never cease to love. He who loves that he may be loved in return, dissolves the friendship whenever something unpleasant happens. But he who loves for the former reason will never give it up. Wherefore Paul says: 'Charity never fails.' "[16]

Cassian is even more emphatic: "In all these [human relations] there is one kind of indissoluble charity, which is cemented neither by alluring charm, nor great offices and dignities, nor any kind of association whatever, not even by blood-relationship, but only by similarity of virtue. This it is, I say, which in no instance is ever broken up, which no separation of time or place is able to dissolve and destroy; not even death itself can tear it out. This is true and unbroken love which grows side by side with the perfection and virtue of the friends."[17]

3. The friendship must be a stimulus to virtue, since its unity consists in the friends willing and not willing the same thing, namely, never to displease God, always to do what pleases Him. No friends are so perfect as always to attain

---

[16] *In Matthaeum Homil.*, 61, 3; *PG* 58, 588.
[17] *Collatio* 16, 3; *PL* 49, 1014–1015.

this ideal, but the ambition to reach it is the bond between them. Such ambition is the natural outcome of charity whose ultimate purpose is union with God as He is. Hence the immediate purpose of this friendship is growth of the friends in intimacy with God.

4. The unity of every friendship demands a certain equality. St. Jerome says: "Friendship either finds or makes the friends equal. Where there is inequality, as lofty station on the one hand, and subjection on the other, there is not friendship but adulation. Hence we read in another place: *Let a friend be the same soul.* And the Lyric Poet, supplicating on behalf of his friend, says: *Preserve the other half of my soul.*"[18] The equality of this kind of friendship is similarity of virtue, as expressed in the words of the Psalmist: "God maketh men of one manner to dwell in a house."[19] St. Ambrose says: "You cannot be a friend to a man if you are unfaithful to God. Friendship is the guardian of good morals, the teacher of equality; so that a superior show himself equal to an inferior and an inferior to a superior. For between those whose virtue is unequal friendship cannot be; and, therefore grace must belong to each of them. Nor let authority be lacking to the inferior, if need should demand, nor humility to the superior. Let the latter hear him as an equal: let the former advise him as a friend and reprove him, not out of love of talking, but with charitable affection."[20]

5. Since the importunate demands of self would ruin such a friendship, it knows no jealousy. It is glad that the friend has other real friends, for it is not separated from the other branches of the Vine. It has a certain largeness of mind and peace, for it knows not the variations of passion. It goes its even way, in the manner of the magnanimous man of Aristotle, with measured gait, deep voice, and level utterance.[21] It gives its confidence, although it knows how to maintain a prudent reserve. It seeks no demonstrations of affection; it is sure of its friend, since it is founded on unwavering trust.

The priest in the ministry is strongly counseled to hold

---

[18] *Comment. in Michaeum,* II, 7; *PL* 25, 1219.
[19] Ps. 67:7.
[20] *De Officiis Ministrorum,* II, 22, 132; *PL* 16, 192.
[21] *Ethics,* IV, 3, 1125a.

fast to such a friend, especially among his clerical brethren. The advantages are obvious: comfort in trouble, reproof in delinquency, laughter in good season, constant stimulus to virtue. Scripture says: "The good counsels of a friend are sweet to the soul,"[22] and "Iron sharpeneth iron, so a man sharpeneth the countenance of his friend."[23] St. Ambrose says to his clergy: "Preserve then, my sons, the friendship you have begun with the brethren; there is nothing more beautiful in human intercourse. It is truly a solace of this life to have some one to whom you may open your soul, with whom you may share the deep hidden things, to whom you may entrust the secrets of your heart; to gather to yourself a faithful friend who rejoices with you in success, suffers with you in sorrow, advises you in difficulties."[24]

If we should now conclude that friendship, based on charity, is a help to perfection, perhaps someone may object and say that, while such friendship is good for the ordinary Christian, it is not for the aspirant to perfection. He may cite the words of Archbishop Martinez who says: "Some souls do not understand why or how affections can be an obstacle to perfection. They think that only those inclinations that tend to sin must be eradicated. This is how they reason: against which of God's commandments does this affection which I have in my heart fail? Against what precept does it fail? It is not against any. Therefore, there can be no evil in it. Let us grant that there is nothing present that can actually be called sin. Nevertheless, that affection is depriving our Lord of a portion of our heart; it is robbing Him of a share in our affections; and on this point God is most jealous."[25]

The good Archbishop writes with a sweetness and unction which clearly manifest the man of God. Obviously, he is speaking not of natural affection, which a child has for a parent or a brother for a sister, but of friendships and attachments which persons devoted to the interior life may form

---

[22] Prov. 27:9.

[23] Prov. 27:17.

[24] *Op. cit., PL* 16, 191.

[25] Most Rev. Luis M. Martinez, *The Secrets of the Interior Life,* trans. by H. J. Beutler (St. Louis: Herder, 1949), p. 30.

from time to time. Do his words mean this: you are incapable of loving such a person for God and in God; therefore, you are not to love him at all? We have already said that the words of Christ, "If any man come to me, and hate not his father, and mother, etc.," mean that any Christian must surrender affections which are proximate occasions of serious sin, that he is to allow no person to lead him into venial sin. But he who seeks perfection is to give up any attachment which is a cause of imperfection. No person is to come between him and intimacy with God. Is it true then that all affection for a human friend is necessarily disorderly? Is human nature so corrupt that all its love, except love of God, is necessarily intertwined with some shadow of evil?

There are those who sniff suspiciously at all forms of friendship and say that aspirants to perfection should have no friends; at least, not until they have attained a high degree of perfection. We have not seen the reasons for this attitude stated in this precise form, but we surmise they come to this: (*a*) the self-abnegation of which generous souls should give an outstanding example, the crucifixion of a life devoted to Christ, compels them to renounce friendship; or (*b*) the words of À Kempis may be adduced: "Jesus Christ alone is singly to be loved . . . Never desire to be singly praised or beloved; for this belongeth to God alone, who hath none like to himself."[26]

a) We must say again that the doctrine of self-abnegation can be misunderstood. It demands the removal of whatever is disorderly, the death of every impulse contrary to the will of God. Sometimes self-denial involves restraint of legitimate things but it cannot mean their utter destruction. It is not directly aimed against what is human and pleasant merely because it is human and pleasant, but only against what is superfluous and disorderly. To think of self-denial as the quest of unhappiness is to put sound doctrine into a bad light. This is the kind of doctrinal exaggeration that discredits true doctrine and leads to the abandonment of its practice.

Again, concerning the statement of St. Ignatius that a

---

[26] *Imitation*, Bk. II, C. 8.

man should be indifferent to all created things, two remarks
are in order. (1) He does not mean that a man should despoil
himself of feeling and affection — that is impossible — but
that he should cultivate an equilibrium of the will which
makes it ever alert to choose God's will. Indifference means
that no liking or disliking is to interfere with the accomplishment of God's will. (2) St. Ignatius adds an important
qualification to his words which is not always kept in mind.
He says that we are to be indifferent *insofar as it is permitted our free will and is not forbidden.* The one thing that
limits our free will, and hence the area of indifference, is
the will of God made manifest. Now must the will of God
impose only what is unpleasant and restrictive? May not
God's will sometimes indicate a pleasing course of action?
The underlying supposition of the opinion we are discussing
is that God's will does not so indicate. This is too extreme
a view. If friendship should lead the friends closer to God,
then God would bless that friendship. It would no longer
belong in the area of indifference.

The second argument that intimate friendship with God
renders intimate friendship with a human being impossible
deserves serious consideration. The problem is this: God's
love is so infinite that He can be the Bridegroom of every
soul, but the capacity of the human soul is so finite that
if it truly be the spouse of God it has nothing more to give
a friend.

Everyone will admit that God should come first, that no
human being should usurp the unique place which God
deserves in our hearts. Certainly sentimental and sensual
friendships that constantly lead one astray of God's will are
irreconcilable to close friendship with God. But may not
the charity which binds us to God also bind us to a fellow
creature in a close human way? They whose adverse opinion
we have been discussing would say that in theory such
charity is possible but it is unrealizable in practice.

The lives of the saints, however, show us that such charity
and friendship were realizable. St. Francis and St. Ignatius
gathered their first followers and held them by friendship.
St. Catherine of Siena lavished a wise affection upon her
followers. Surely hers was a spiritual affection but nonethe-

less human. Now the words and acts — especially the acts — of Christ our Lord are the model of the perfect life. Christ had several friends. There was Lazarus. When Jesus wept at his grave, the Jews said: "Behold how he loved him."[27] Christ was not shamming: He felt human grief for the death of a friend. Among the Apostles Christ showed special tokens of friendship for Peter, James, and John. And of these, Scripture says that John was the disciple whom Jesus loved.[28] Will Christ, who bids men follow Him closely, forbid them to do the human things He did Himself? Christ would not make so great a mistake of example as even to hint that there is in this respect one law for the perfect and another and a harder law for the imperfect. To say, then, that God is so jealous of human affections that He will not allow an earnest soul to bestow any part of them upon any-one but Himself is to make God over into the image of a man. When the soul loves God by ardent charity, its capacity to love is wondrously increased: something of the infinite love of God has been imparted to it, enabling it to love after the fashion of God, widely, broadly, unselfishly.

Our conclusion is, therefore: (1) Archbishop Martinez means by affections what we have described as sentimental or sensual friendships; (2) there is a blameworthy friend-ship which takes the aspiring soul away from God and there is a praiseworthy friendship which helps him to God. We accept the optimistic view of St. Aelred, the Cistercian abbot of Rievault in the territory of York, who began his little treatise *On Spiritual Friendship* with the significant words: "Here we are, you and I, and I trust there is a third in our midst, Christ."[29]

Perfection does not demand the destruction, but the ele-vation and supernaturalization of natural appetites. Man has an appetite for food and sleep but, because it sometimes runs to excess, it is not therefore to be uprooted. As a social being, man hungers in his soul to love men and to be loved by them. À Kempis says: "Without a friend thou canst not live happily."[30]

---

[27] Jn. 11:36. [28] Cf. Jn. 13:23.
[29] *PL* 195, 661. [30] *Imitation*, Bk. II, C. 8.

There are ascetics who, since food and sleep cannot be dispensed with, think that earnest souls should at least take no relish in these things. They think also that man's appetite to be loved should be satisfied only by the invisible God. This appears too dour and Jansenistic a view of life and seems to imply that man has a natural instinct which is bad, that God wants His children to be unhappy in this life. No; the unhappiness which He allows to befall them is merely what is necessary to cleanse them from defect, test their virtue, and build the Body of Christ.

Man's appetite for human love needs to be regulated by the will of God but it cannot be ripped out of a man nor denied a proper object to fasten upon. God desires that men should serve Him, not as angels nor unfeeling sticks and stones, but as men, as social beings with social needs and instincts. Many generous souls surrender the most intimate social relationships for the love of God but even they may not thwart all their social instincts without dehumanizing themselves. Quest of perfection ought to make one not less but more a man. There is a world of difference between being supernatural and being inhuman.

The Wise Man says: "A faithful friend is a strong defense: and he that hath found him, hath found a treasure. Nothing can be compared to a faithful friend, and no weight of gold or silver is able to countervail the goodness of his fidelity. A faithful friend is the medicine of life and immortality: and they that fear the Lord, shall find him."[31] Surely these words apply to all men. We note the sentence, "They that fear the Lord shall find [a faithful friend]." If the reward of fearing God is finding a faithful friend, why is he who both fears and loves God to be deprived of the reward?

Among aspirants to perfection, then, friendship is capable of promoting the glory of God in their own lives and in the lives of others. Friend helps friend to grow in virtue. Close association, which makes two given persons worse, can also make two different persons better. Since God deals with His creatures according to their natures, and since generous souls remain human in their quest for perfec-

---

[31] Ecclus. 6:14–16.

tion, God wills that they have human help and comfort.
Courage amid trials assuredly comes from speaking with
Jesus in the tabernacle; but poor man needs more — human
words and sympathy. Over and above the assistance of a
spiritual counselor, aspiring souls require an equal with
whom they can speak with the utmost freedom. For example,
religious vocations have been saved by the sane advice of
a sympathetic counselor of one's own age and standing. Persons have given up a religious vocation for lack of such a
friend. Friendship may be a means of advancing from the
lower to the higher stages of perfection. St. Teresa of Ávila
says: "It is a great evil for a soul to be alone in the midst
of such great dangers . . . I would advise those who are
giving themselves to prayer, particularly at first, to form
friendships . . . with those who are doing the same thing.
It is a matter of the last importance, even if it lead only
to helping one another by prayer . . . Now, if in their intercourse with one another, and in the indulgence of human
affection not even of the best kind, men seek friends with
whom they may refresh themselves . . . I know no reason
why it should not be lawful for him who is beginning
to love and serve God in earnest to confide his joys and
sorrows to another."[32]

Capacity for friendship can be a means of effecting great
supernatural good. Children and sinners are drawn to the
zealous soul in whom they detect a friendly heart. Con-
versions to the faith or from an evil life have been occasioned
by friendship. When one has a task of extraordinary difficulty, surely a friend who will share the burden does not
detract from the glory of God. When St. Ignatius was seeking for someone who would undertake the arduous mission
to the Indies, he chose his closest friend, Francis Xavier.
When he sent him, he knew that he would never look upon
his face again.

We distinguish between a defective friendship and a whole-
some friendship just as we resolve any other difficulty of
the ascetical life — by appeal to the will of God. À Kempis

---

[32] *Life of St. Teresa of Jesus,* trans. by David Lewis (Westminster:
Newman, 1943), Chap. 7, nn. 32–33, pp. 54–55.

says: "In me the love of thy friend ought to stand; and for me he is to be loved whoever he be, that appeareth to thee good and much to be loved in this life. Without me friendship can neither profit nor endure; nor is that love true and pure which I do not bind together."[33] The generous soul may recognize the will of God with regard to this or that friendship by honest consideration of his supernatural state and of the influence which the friendship exerts upon it. The will of God is neither whimsical nor arbitrary, nor is it always difficult to learn in detail. God wants the generous soul to become a better son. In conformity, then, with His plans for the good of all men, God desires his supernatural growth and the increase of his likeness to Christ. The friendship which makes him and his friend more Christlike He approves: that which makes him less Christlike He disapproves. In forming such a judgment one should be strict rather than lenient, remembering the caution of À Kempis: "That often seems to be charity which is carnal love."[34]

We have taken pains to develop this point at length for the reason that some teachers of asceticism tell their charges that all forms of friendship are forbidden them. In so acting they wish to prevent the formation of sentimental friendships, leaving to the experience of their charges or later instruction the discovery that the prohibition is not of universal validity. It is one thing to be silent upon points of instruction which may too easily be misunderstood: it is quite another thing to make universal prohibitions which do not square with the reality of things. This is one of the pitfalls to be avoided in moral instruction.

Let us conclude with a few remarks on the safeguarding of friendship. That we draw them from a teacher of ancient monks should cause no surprise. One cannot but admire the wholesomeness of these admirable men, especially the sound principles upon which they based human relations. At first reading their words sound at times too rugged or inapplicable to modern times, but closer scrutiny will reveal a timeless wisdom in them. For instance, the six points which we are

---

[33] *Imitation,* Bk. III, C. 42.
[34] *Ibid.,* Bk. I, C. 15.

about to quote from Cassian, on the means of maintaining friendship inviolate, could, with a few changes, be made into a practicable and cogent pamphlet for Christian spouses.

"The first foundation, therefore, of true friendship," he says, "consists in contempt of worldly goods and renunciation of all things we have. For it is most inequitable, even impious, if, after renouncing the world and all its vanity, one should prefer some worthless and superfluous possession to the precious treasure of a brother's love."[35]

He is saying what every newly married couple needs to hear — never let desire for money or any material thing become a source of discord. He is repeating the exhortation of Holy Writ: "Lose thy money for thy brother and thy friend: and hide it not under a stone to be lost."[36] "Say not to thy friend: Go, and come again: and tomorrow I will give to thee: when thou canst give at present."[37] Material things have each their price: a friend is beyond all price.

"The second is that each one should so deny his own will, lest considering himself to be wise and experienced, he should choose to follow his own rather than his brother's preferences." Since friendship is the unity of willing and not willing the same thing, it is maintained by a person preferring the friend's will to his own. How precious a principle and how practical! By neglect of it how many marriages have foundered! If the friends are ever animated by this principle, it will always be easy, in case of conflicting preferences, to see which of the two is objectively reasonable; for there will be no mist of bias and prejudice to hide the truth.

"The third is that one should realize that everything, even things he judges useful or necessary, must come second to the good of charity and peace." Since nothing which maintains charity can separate the friends from God, their immediate concern is the sustaining of their unity of minds and wills. The poison of unity is consideration of self. Only by surrender of selfish impulses is unity realizable.

"The fourth is that he believe that neither for good rea-

---

[35] *Collatio* 16, c. VI; *PL* 49, 1021.
[36] Ecclus. 29:13.
[37] Prov. 3:28.

son nor for bad reason may he ever be thoroughly angry."
Every moment that anger lasts it is killing love. A mother
gave her war-bride daughter, who was leaving for the United
States, this sole piece of parting advice. "Never, never go to
sleep angry with your husband." Anger and love are deadly
opposites. Whereas love moves to another for the joy of
union, anger looks on the object of wrath as evil, something
to be destroyed. "The anger of man worketh not the justice
of God."[38]

"The fifth is that, just as he tries to curb himself, so he
should, to the best of his ability, mollify even the unreasonable
anger of his brother for him, realizing that the bad mood
of the other hurts him just as much as if it were he who
was angry with the other." Since friend looks on friend as
his other self, that which perturbs one is equally the loss of
the other. Friendship cannot allow the dark divisive motion
of anger even to begin to part those who desire to be one.

"The last — which undoubtedly is the death of all vices —
is to think that one is going to leave the world this day.
This thought not only allows no passion to remain in the
heart, but it suppresses all motions of concupiscence and sin.
Whoever, therefore, fosters this thought can neither suffer nor
inflict the bitterness of anger and discord." Modern people
may smile at this advice as a piece of naïveté, or consider it
a pious but irritating prejudice. But far from being an *unreasonable* bias toward the next life, this is the only sensible
attitude. Is not the longest life in retrospect like a day at
the fair? Cannot any man die any day? Is not our little life
just a camping out, a getting ready for the real life? He who
daily thinks of death and orders his affairs by that sober
thought acts wisely indeed. He is foolish, and prejudiced by
present comfort, who adopts the opposite attitude.

In summary, the quest of perfection does not demand the
destruction of close personal relations but their sanctification.
Husband and wife, parent and child, brother and sister, friend
and friend, can remove all imperfection from their association: human association can help us to intimacy with God.
The problem is complex but soluble. Whoever builds his

---

[38] James 1:20.

friendship upon charity and maintains it by the methods suggested by Cassian, should be able to repeat with St. Aelred: "Here we are, you and I, and I trust there is a third in our midst, Christ."

As we advance in the love of God, the Holy Ghost pours more and more of the gifts of wisdom, understanding, and knowledge into our souls. God helps us to know more and more about Himself and our supernatural needs. At certain periods of our career we need the bolstering of good friends. As we pursue God wholeheartedly and co-operate with His graces, He will draw us closer to Himself. If we let Him, He will draw us so close that He finally asks us to let go of all else and to cling to Him alone. The time came when St. Teresa of Ávila gave up deep and affectionate attachments almost on the instant because God then desired that of her. This is the situation to which À Kempis refers: "Thou oughtest to be so dead toward persons beloved, as to wish as far as thou art concerned, to be altogether without human fellowship. So much the nearer doth man approach to God, as he withdraweth himself the farther from all earthly consolation."[39] God may snatch the soul for a time entirely to Himself that He may kiss it with the kiss of His mouth,[40] but He will return it to some manner of human fellowship: even in the beatific vision there is the secondary joy of the companionship of the blessed.

---

[39] *Imitation*, Bk. III, C. 42.
[40] Cf. Cant. 1:1.

9. Pleasure

"O how great is the multitude of thy sweetness, O Lord,
which thou hast hidden from them that fear thee! Which thou
hast wrought for them that hope in thee" (Ps. 30:20–21).

PLEASURE takes many forms. It shows itself in the absorbed
smile of a child patting his sand castle into shape; in the
ear-piercing screams of teen-age girls milling around the
current sensation; in the beaming countenances of parents
watching their son perform in the high school play. Its
grosser shapes hide in parked automobiles and tap rooms in
the dark of night. Although it is one of the elemental things,
unfortunately it is often misunderstood by those who claim
to know the basic facts of life.

We shall always have men and women who try to make
their lives an unending succession of pleasure. Since the
pleasant is their sole object of desire they laugh at duty
or obligation. So strenuously did ancient heathens pursue
pleasure that they made a god and a cult of it.[1] On the
other hand Puritan preachers have thundered against it as an
out-and-out evil. The Manichaeans identified pleasure with
sense activity and cursed it as the offspring of an infinite
evil principle. Manichaeanism never wholly dies out. The
dour and straight-laced will ever look on it with a sniff of
suspicion. How often they attribute the happiness of young
people to sin!

Pleasure, however, is neither the highest good nor a necessary evil, a kind of lovable scamp whom the heart favors
but the conscience frowns upon. As usual the truth stands
in the middle: pleasure has its good side and its bad side.

---

[1] St. Athanasius, *Oratio Contra Gentes,* 9; *PG* 25, 20.

The difference is very important. Salvation and perfection depend upon the practical attitude which one assumes toward pleasure. To solve the problem presented by pleasure we must first understand its nature.

Pleasure is not an evil. It is a good, an object of desire. Now a good is some reality pertaining to a being which enables it to be what it ought to be or which helps it to progress toward the fullness of its well-being. There are three kinds of good: primary, secondary, and tertiary. A primary good is called perfective good; secondary good, delectable good; tertiary good, useful good.

Perfective good includes the substance of the being, the powers or faculties it should have in order to measure up to what nature intends it to be, and all activity flowing from its powers which tend to improve it and enable it to fulfill its function and destiny. Perfective goods are always desirable for their own sakes. In a complicated being like man perfective good includes a huge collection of things — vegetative, sensitive, rational, and supernatural perfections. These constitute the Things of man. The Things of man are twofold: of nature and of grace. His natural goods include his rational nature and faculties, his acquired natural virtues, and every action he performs in accordance with right reason. These are sometimes called virtuous goods. His supernatural goods are his new nature of grace, the supernaturally infused virtues and gifts, and every supernaturally good act. These actions either directly help him to become an adopted son of God, or, if he is already one, they make him a better one. For they increase grace in him and enlarge his title to glory.

Tertiary goods are things outside the being which may help it acquire its due perfections. The same thing in one set of circumstances can be a help, and hence an object of desire, but in other circumstances its possession or use might be a hindrance. Then it is not good and ought not to be an object of desire. A lifesaving vest is very desirable in a disaster at sea but of no value at a formal dinner party. This kind of thing *becomes* good only by becoming useful, that is, as a means to the development and improvement of the being. Nasty medicine can help a sick person get well. Corrections and reproof can induce a man to get rid of defects. Money, position, reputation, and friends are good, and therefore, desirable to the extent that they help us become better men and better sons of God. There are clear circumstances when they become harmful either to our natural or supernatural well-being. Then they may not be objects of choice. For useful good may never be sought for its own sake. Of itself it cannot make us better. No one is a better man merely because he has an influential position, a well-known name, and powerful friends. Useful good is a means and nothing but a means to our proper development. Hence it is to be sought solely for the natural or supernatural well-being it can lead us to. The ghastly mistake of the world is to convert useful good into primary good, making money, position, influence, and the like the prime objects of desire. Deluded men imagine these things to be the Things of man whereas they are only tools of self-improvement, to be used when they help and put aside when they are no longer useful.

We all know secondary or delectable good from experience but most people have difficulty in analyzing and explaining it. The thing is also called delight, satisfaction, content. It is nobler than useful good because it exists in the agent and is desirable for its own sake. It is, however, less than perfective good. First, it is a dependent good which cannot exist by itself but depends on something else. Second, its presence in a man does not necessarily make him a better man. We may explain it in two ways.

First, it is something negative, the cessation of the want or dissatisfaction of appetite. Whenever we really want something and do not have it, appetite experiences an unrest which may range from slight frustration or unease to poignant pain. A little girl cries for her father gone to war. A young man craves to marry the girl he has quarreled with. A religious prays for relief from scruples. Now the satisfaction of appetite is in itself a good because appetite has been made by nature to seeks its satisfaction. But what will satisfy appetite? We could voluntarily surrender the quest for the desired object but that would not be the allaying but the suppression of appetite. We could be distracted by some new and greater pain or pleasure but that is not an allaying but a rechanneling of desire. As long as unsatisfied appetite keeps craving, only one thing will satisfy it. Appetite itself cannot do it; only the desired object. Only her father will dry the little girl's tears. Only marriage with his beloved will make the young man content. As long as his scruples continue, the religious will have no peace of mind. Grant the object of desire and the frustration of want is ended. The allaying of appetite in the possession of its desired object is delectable good.

We may look at the same thing in a positive way. A swallow rejoices in its flying, a swimmer in his swimming, a prima donna in her singing, but if there is no flying, no swimming, no singing, there can be no rejoicing. Pleasure is the joyous accompaniment of some fitting activity. Without the activity it could not exist. A girl receives her engagement ring and walks among the stars. After thirteen years of preparation a Jesuit scholastic reaches his ordination day and weeps for the joy of it. Lindbergh flew the Atlantic and Paris folded him in her arms. Pleasure is the natural accompaniment or sequel of having, doing, or being what the agent should have or do or be or, as in the case of a free agent, what the person thinks he should have or do or be. It exists by nature's explicit design. It is the lure which nature uses to draw sentient and intelligent beings to their proper good. Take away all relish from food and how many people would eat enough from a sense of duty? Children would not romp and play and so develop their bodies unless they found delight in play. If God were to abolish venereal pleasure in order to stop carnal sins the race would likely cease. Wondrous is the attractive force of pleasure. It is an elemental urge to action.

> What more felicity can fall to a creature
> Than to enjoy delight with liberty?[2]

There is a mistaken notion, however, that pleasure is the prerogative of sense alone, that only earthy and forbidden things are truly delightful. On the contrary, pleasure belongs to all conscious activity. Indeed, as there is a hierarchy of activity so there is a hierarchy of pleasure. Hence the nobler the activity the more pleasurable the delight which accom-

---

[2] Edmund Spenser, *Muiopotomos*, ll. 209–210.

panies it. The wordless content of a boy angling for catfish does not compare with the joy of Archimedes shouting in his bath because he has discovered the principle of the buoyancy of bodies. The radiance of a bride on her wedding day cannot hold a candle to the mystic raptures of St. Francis.

People should reflect more upon the higher delights of the spirit. They seldom savor the pleasure of thinking. Of course they do know that pleasure is basic to love. St. Augustine says "that is not loved which does not delight."[3] How could men and women marry if they found no delight in one another's company? The point is that God Himself uses delight to attract our love. "What is it to be drawn by pleasure?" asks St. Augustine. *Delight in the Lord and He will give you the requests of thy heart.* There is a certain pleasure of the heart whose sweet food is heavenly. For, if the poet could say, 'His personal pleasure attracts each man': not necessity but pleasure, not obligation but delight: how much more strongly ought we to say that to Christ a man is attracted who delights in truth, delights in happiness, delights in justice, delights in eternal life all of which is Christ? Have the senses of the body their pleasures and the soul none? If the soul has not its pleasures, whence is it said . . . *They shall be inebriated with the plenty of thy house: and thou shalt make them drink of the torrent of thy pleasure*? Show me a lover and he appreciates what I say. Show me one who yearns, hungers, and thirsts as a pilgrim in this solitude sighing for the fountain of the eternal fatherland: show me this man and he knows what I am talking about."[4]

Pleasure, then, is in itself a good. It is as natural a part of the universe as leaves in a forest, fledglings in a nest, hair and fingernails on a man. As a natural component of the universe, it is blessed by God. "And God saw all the things that he had made and they were very good."[5] It is not, however, an absolute but a dependent good whose worth is measured by the perfection which it accompanies. Therefore in the moral world pleasure resembles words, which are signs representing ideas. Strictly speaking no words are morally

---

[3] *Sermo* 159, 3; *PL* 38, 869.
[4] *In Joan. Evan. Tract.* 26, 4; *PL* 35, 1608.
[5] Gen. 1:31.

bad in themselves. They are morally indifferent. As words they are bad only if they fail in their function of representation. They become morally bad only when they are tainted by association with the evil of the action they represent or when a man makes them the instrument of an evil intention. The same is true of pleasure. For pleasure is not a primary but a secondary good.

People make two great mistakes about pleasure. The first is confusing pleasure with happiness. This is the mistake of youth which is so powerfully drawn by delight — a mistake, however, which often lingers long after youth's follies should be ended. Pleasure is only part of happiness: it is not its core but only its end product. The core is right action. A man is happy when he is and has and does what it becomes a man to be and have and do. He cannot be happy without pleasure but pleasure alone won't make him happy. Nor can he have lasting pleasure out of wrong things; only from right things. The happiness of heaven is not primarily delight but the vision of God as He is.

The second and more common mistake is to evaluate human goods and activities on the basis of the pleasure they afford and not on their capacity to make us better men. This is especially true of sense pleasure and the reason is that, since we are so close to the earth, the satisfactions of sense make too clamorous and insistent an appeal. People give their word they will attend a night meeting but sit home and watch television. Salary given is a form of evaluation, but how compare the salary of a Hollywood star and that of a first-rate physicist, or that of a professional ball player and a nun teaching in a parochial school? It is easy to choose a pleasant wrong and hard to face a disagreeable duty. Some unbelieving college professors say that that is good which feels good and that is bad which feels bad and that is the whole story of goodness and badness. Akin to these are our own pious hedonists who are drawn to God by delight. They seek Him with enthusiasm when they find sweetness in prayer and self-mastery but when the relish passes they give up prayer and self-conquest.

Pleasure presents an elemental problem which all men must solve in order to save their souls. Unless a man look

on pleasure as merely a secondary object of desire during
the time of his mortal pilgrimage, he stands to forfeit eternal
happiness and lose all pleasure. As befits a sinner on proba-
tion, he must be willing to embrace pain and forego pleasure
if, when, and for as long a time as it may be necessary to
gain sanctifying grace and persevere in it until death. Since
original sin has given him a bias toward delight and the
apparent goods of sense and a prejudice against pain and
discomfort, he must, through prudence, distinguish licit from
illicit pleasure and by temperance and self-control resist
the lure of the illicit and overcome his bias against unpleasant
duty.

The truly earnest soul solves this problem of pleasure and
salvation with one clear sure stroke. Since his interest is in
an enduring and imperishable happiness, he resolutely turns
his back upon all illicit pleasure. Fulfillment of duty, pleasant
or unpleasant, is his first objective. Pleasure is not the aim
but he hopes it will be the reward of his efforts. Since he
achieves this attitude only by the help of prayer, he learns
something of the sweetness of prayer and in an aura of spiritual joy and perhaps even of exultation he finds himself
strongly drawn to God. He enters the way of perfection and
soon learns about self-sacrifice and mortification. Initial enthusiasm carries him blithely over the first hurdles but once
this wanes he must face the problem of personal contentment. How will he stand prolonged periods of unhappiness,
how will he take surrender of old satisfactions, old ways of
thinking and doing? Much will depend on the instruction he
receives and his reaction to it.

Let us suppose he tries to be his own guide and to learn
from reading. He turns to St. John of the Cross and is
fascinated by his exposition of Christian perfection and the
uncompromising manner in which the saint solves the problem
of created pleasure. He sees that the saint's words are not
merely an explanation of doctrine but a baring of personal
experience. To John of the Cross the pursuit of perfection
means that the soul goes out in search of its true Lover, God.
It has no light to go by but the darkness of faith; it has
no comfort to sustain it until it will have found comfort unending. To the soul that loves, the darkness is light and

That light guided me
More surely than the noon day sun
To the place where He was waiting for me,
Whom I knew well,
And where none but He appeared.

O, guiding night;
O, night more lovely than the dawn;
O, night that has united
The Lover with His beloved,
And changed her into her Love.[6]

The end, union with the Beloved, is lyrically fair and enticing but the means are of grim and rugged iron. For the first practical step into the night of faith consists in this: "Strive always, not after that which is most easy, but that which is most difficult . . . and desire to be detached from all things, empty and poor for Christ's sake. This state is to be embraced with a perfect heart, and the will must conform thereto. Because if our heart be truly engaged herein, we shall in a short time attain to great joy and consolation . . . That thou mayest have pleasure in everything, seek pleasure in nothing."[7] Not for nothing have his fellow countrymen called the saint Doctor Nada, Doctor Nothing.

These and similar writings may produce in the beginner the impression that present delight is wrong and that henceforth he is to live devoid of satisfaction and delight. The doctrine of self-conquest with all its daily practical implications is not learned in a day and a year. One may misunderstand the paradox of St. Gregory Nazianzen: "My delight is to enjoy delights as little as possible."[8] Therefore while the beginner resolutely embraces a program of self-surrender, let him remember that he has not abjured his nature. Even here and now that nature ever tends toward happiness of which delight is a part. It is an imprudent asceticism which implies that a man should seek downright unhappiness in order to gain happiness hereafter. Since human nature craves happiness even now, there must be in the lives of those who seek perfection some sort of delectable good without which life

---

[6] *Complete Works of St. John of the Cross*, trans. by David Lewis (London: Longman, 1864), Vol. 1, p. 2.

[7] *Ibid.*, Chap. 13, pp. 49–50.

[8] *Carm. Lib.* I, sect. 2; *PG* 37, 655.

is totally inhuman and verges on the emptiness of the damned. Let us call it peace of mind, a least common denominator of satisfaction which keeps life from being pure misery.

Peace and satisfaction, however, cannot exist of themselves. They must come from things acquired, actions done, desires attained. You cannot be satisfied about nothing. So overwhelming is man's tendency toward happiness that, when he loses important objects of desire he will not long endure the misery of separation unless he find some compensating good and regain his equilibrium of content in the satisfaction of the substitute.

We have, therefore, a problem of substitution to be faced by everyone who makes a thoroughgoing change in his way of life. A sinner who has been indulging a guilty passion will bravely surrender the object of desire but the heart cries for something to take its place. If he finds no substitute he may easily return to his forbidden love. Catherine of Genoa made an instant resolve to give up the foolish and brittle pleasures of social life but her soul was in turmoil until she quieted it with prayer and her quest of God. Young people entering the novitiate surrender home and the ties of youth, a sacrifice which leaves the aching void of homesickness. But they cannot go on living in a vacuum which allows the tendrils of desire nothing to fasten on. Either they find a compensation for the home they gave up in the supernatural charity of a religious house and in the companionship of religious brethren or else they pack up and go home.

All along the line in real, personal, and intimate ways the following of Christ asks the surrender of natural goods. This, however, is no senseless deprivation inflicted merely for the sake of deprivation. It is the taking away of hay and stubble to offer gold and precious stones in their stead. True, the quest of perfection deprives us of some easy, pleasant things but, far from leaving us to shiver like shorn lambs in the winter of our discontent, it actually offers much more than it takes: perfect faith, hope, and charity, the moral virtues in their highest form, and Jesus Christ, the one Lover of the human soul. To the widows who had said farewell to worldly pleasure St. Augustine offered this consolation: "To carnal delights, therefore, there succeed spiritual delights in restored chastity: reading, prayer, psalmody, hope of the life to come, and a heart lifted on high."[9] Supernatural things have joys and satisfactions incomparably greater than any natural good. St. Gregory[10] aptly remarks that, before corporal delights are experienced they exercise an enticing fascination but once they are avidly enjoyed they beget satiety. Spiritual delights, on the contrary, have little attraction before they are experienced but once they are tasted they are eagerly sought for.

Furthermore, the means of attaining these supernatural goods amount to more than a mere denial of life and joy. Perfection indeed is the full flowering of the noblest activity of life. The effort for perfection is not the hamstringing of human efficiency but the release of our highest faculties from the obstacles which hinder their best functioning. Upon this process should attend a keen delight, not an empty, colorless discontent.

We may now state one of the chief difficulties which faces every beginner in the way of perfection. How is he to bridge the gap of unease and thwarted appetite caused by the abandonment of natural satisfactions, which must exist until he will have reached the firm enduring satisfactions of the supernatural life? He is like the homesteader of a hundred years ago who gave up his home in the settled east to find a new home in the west: how is he to manage in the meantime? In essence it is the age-old problem of adjustment to new environment, not of place and body, but of soul.

Some beginners, who have not much fortitude but a fair amount of shrewdness, will, for a time, make outward show of conforming to the exactions of the way of perfection, but, when opportunity presents, they lapse back into their natural satisfactions. They resign the quest for perfection. The reason may be that they misunderstood from the beginning. They subconsciously thought that the way would be a path of sunshine and roses. They did not seriously count on the endurance of pain.

---

[9] *De Bono Viduitatis Liber*, c. 21; *PL* 40, 447.
[10] Cf. *Homiliae*, 36, 1; *PL* 76, 1266.

Our attention and sympathy, however, are aimed at the ardent beginner who is eager to put on the Lord Jesus Christ but, overwhelmed with confusion and strangeness, imagines that he must resign himself to an unhappy life. With shining faith he embraces the totality of the cross and manfully strips himself of any created satisfaction which may draw him from the love of God which is in Christ Jesus.[11] He resolves ruggedly to endure the pain and loneliness even if the day will never dawn nor the morning star arise in his heart.[12] Cost what it may he will do the truth in charity, even if the peace of God which surpasses all understanding[13] is never in this life to be poured into his heart.

A soul so generous requires gentle instruction. Actually he is not going to live so bleak a life nor does God expect it of him. A very human and helpful lesson can be framed for him in the words of the poets. For poets are at times "hidden in the light of thought";[14] they have an insight into truth which rightly earns them the ancient name of Seer. As Christ in His agony sought the comfort of His friends, so the aspirant to perfection will not lack his times of consolation.

> Many a green isle needs must be
> In the deep wide sea of Misery,
> Or the mariner, worn and wan,
> Never thus could voyage on.[15]

It was originally intended that man be happy on this earth. For "the Lord God had planted a paradise of pleasures from the beginning: wherein he placed man whom he had formed."[16] Although sin drove him from paradise, it did not rob him of all delight and make the good life pure pain. Only he is bereft of all pleasure to whom God says irrevocably: "I know you not."[17] Despite the fall and the need of repairing its ravages in all of us,

> The world is so full of a number of things,
> I'm sure we should all be happy as kings.[18]

---

11 Cf. Rom. 8:39.
12 Cf. 2 Pet. 1:19.
13 Cf. Phil. 4:7.
14 P. B. Shelley, *The Skylark.*
15 P. B. Shelley, *Among The Euganean Hills.*
16 Gen. 2:8.
17 Lk. 13:27.
18 Robert Louis Stevenson, *Happy Thought.*

The beneficent God who rules all things by Divine Providence has a special providence for the just. He provides for their happiness both now and hereafter. We make a Calvinistic caricature of God if we imagine Him ever demanding present unhappiness of the just under penalty of His displeasure. God, who cannot be outdone in generosity, will not fail the soul who generously foregoes all illicit pleasure and mortifies his passions. Has He not promised the hundredfold in this life to them who sacrifice all for Him? Part of the hundredfold is delectable good in season. The earnest soul need never fear that if he faithfully pursue the will of God and follow divine guidance where it leads him he will fail of his share of pleasant days. He too will discover by sweet experience that the world is really full of a number of good things.

If he is given to studious pursuits he will make acquaintance with the giant minds who spoke the noblest thoughts of the human race and clothed them in language which never dies. If he is at least a reader, his soul will sometimes feel the divine touch as he reads Sacred Scripture or the lives of the saints. His heart too will be moved by instances of natural charm combined with supernatural virtue. He may, for instance, read of Thomas Kosaki, a Japanese boy of ten, who was taken prisoner with his father for confession of the Christian faith. He remained steadfast under torture, never wavering when the guards bound him, cut off one of his ears, and threw him bleeding into an icy cell. In the long cold night Thomas knelt in prayer and in the dawn he composed a letter of farewell to his mother which is now in the Vatican Museum. One of the most pathetic and heroic documents of childhood is this rice-paper scroll blurred by the tears of the boy — and of Pope Pius IX who, in 1862, when St. Thomas Kosaki was being canonized with twenty-five other martyrs of Japan, could not read this old letter without weeping:

To my honored and beloved mother:

It is with the greatest love and respect that I send this letter to you. By this time you will have heard that father and I are being crucified at Nagasaki. The edict of our execution has been published throughout the kingdom. There are 26 of us privileged to shed our blood for the holy faith. . . . Farewell, my dearest mother. I thank you for all the goodness you have shown me from the time that God gave me to you. Father and I are going to heaven, hand in hand, and there we shall wait for you.

Your loving son,
Thomas[19]

Cicero[20] reminds us how pleasing it is to read of the great deeds of others. There is surely this advantage to good reading: it keeps essential truths fresh in the mind. We may note that the Greek word for truth, ἀλήθεια, means literally a "not forgetting." Reading, however, should never be sought as an escape from unpleasant reality. For some unhappy people it is almost a narcotic.

The aspiring soul will never be denied the delights of nature: the eerie charm of dusk, the roaring splendor of autumnal woods, the odor of the earth in a spring rain, "the evening air clad in the beauty of a thousand stars."[21]

Certainly he will not be deprived of the pleasure peculiar to human association. He may possibly be blessed with a happy family life as were Mary and Joseph. Can anyone doubt the genuine happiness of Nazareth? Elizabeth Barrett Browning seems to doubt it when she writes of the "Child without the heart for play . . . who never sinned or smiled." But when Mary held her Baby up so that the passing children could call and wave to Him or when relatives tickled and fondled Him, are we to suppose the Baby Jesus gave them back just a stony stare? At the age of five did He avoid the village children and stay by Himself in the back of the shop to make little crosses with His little hammer?

Many saints found both sanctity and joy at home. That indeed is the place where the majority of Christians must find these precious things. Although the cross was deeply interwoven into the fabric of her domestic life, Elizabeth of Portugal drew immense satisfaction from her children and grandchildren. It will help perhaps to pause and savor the heroic details of what may well have been the most satisfactory hour of that gallant woman's life.

---

[19] *Catholic Digest,* December, 1939, p. 15.
[20] *Pro Archia.*
[21] Christopher Marlowe, *Doctor Faustus,* Sc. 18, 111–112.

Between her husband, the King of Portugal, and her son, the Infante, there had been bad blood for a long time. War broke out between them in 1323 and their forces met on the field of Alvalade. "The two armies were already engaged. Arrows and stones darkened the air. The dead and dying lay thickly on the field of battle. Soon father and son would have been in a deadly fight . . . 'All at once, a mule at the gallop tore a way through the combatants and opened a path in the horrible confusion amidst the glittering swords. The mule bore a woman. It was the Queen! Braving the missiles that were raining round her, she seemed a heavenly vision; alone, for no one dared to follow her; with no other weapon than her weakness; her hands joined in supplication. The effect produced was irresistible, everyone stood still and ceased to fight. Meanwhile the King and his son, touched to tears by so great heroism and love, made a reconciliation once more on the field of blood. Then, at the bidding of the Queen, the Infante kissed the hand of his father; and the King, in pardon, gave his son his blessing. And in this way was ended the patricidal struggle which had lasted five years.' "[22] It is difficult to imagine an earthly joy more deep and true than this.

Even if the generous soul gives up family life, he will yet meet resourceful, talented men and women and be in admiration of their humaneness, their sparkle, their *joie de vivre*. Perhaps youth will give him their confidences and he will be solaced by their guileless faces and winsome ways. To him, more than to other men, the variety and fascination of human characters in the flesh will be a book of life, easy to read and take delight in. For they who seek God unreservedly find an easy secret entrance to the human heart; saints are warmhearted.

Perhaps the aspiring soul may chance upon the pure pleasure of intellectual research as did St. Thomas and St. Albert the Great. What other thing can quite give the sense of worth-whileness which comes from concentration of one's powers upon the discovery of truth? Even if one seeks only a portion of the truth, say the solution of a problem in physics,

---

[22] *Saints Are Not Sad*, ed. by F. J. Sheed (New York: Sheed & Ward, 1949), p. 252.

politics, or history, he relishes life to the full; he would not exchange his situation with the bride of a month. What, then, if the truth one seeks is the One Immutable Truth! This is exactly the case of every aspiring soul. Be he learned or unlearned, he seeks, not perhaps as a scholar but certainly as one who prays, the inner secrets of God. He hungers after the reality of God, he wishes to discover the way of life in Him, and, although he must pass through the great darkness of faith before his mind is satisfied, satisfied it will be, if only he go on. While he awaits the ultimate satisfaction he will often be consoled and blessed.

Any gifted man can dedicate himself to the quest of beauty as did the young man at Harvard who wrote in his journal: "There is nothing in the world, for me at least, but art and beauty; if I cannot live for that, I had better die. I wish I could reveal the intense longing which I have to write something great: not for fame, nor that the world may praise; but to know — not to dream, or fancy, or hope — but to know that the Spirit of Beauty has laid her finger on me and consecrated me to her service."[23] What, then, if the beauty one seeks is the One Unchanging Beauty, the Source of all loveliness, the Immortal Fountain, whence must issue whatever word, or sound, or color, or line, or thought men call beautiful! Again this is the case of all aspiring souls. One needs no special talent — merely a generous response to grace! Fired by grace the heart pursues God with all its strength. It is impossible to do this for some length of time and not thrill to the divine touch. If faint little images of God set the heart pulsing with joy and even ravish a man out of himself, what must happen when God flashes upon him an authentic glimpse of His charm?

Truly, then, the saint is the real aesthete and the discerning critic of the beautiful. Love awakens and sharpens his instinct for genuine beauty. He alone experiences it in its highest manifestations. Oh the pity of it that so many souls with great natural capacity for the enjoyment of beauty waste it upon flawed and muddied copies of the real thing.

---

[23] *The Journal of Gamaliel Bradford*, ed. by V. W. Brooks (Boston: Houghton Mifflin, 1933), p. 5.

To them the Supreme Beauty means as much as the tragedies of Sophocles do to the ordinary race-track tout. What has happened to modern life that its centers of art produce such scoffers and so many moral derelicts? The great link by which faith bound society to God has been broken and since so many Western men "liked not to have God in their knowledge, God delivered them to a reprobate sense."[24]

It should be quite clear by now that God will not leave the generous soul to a dour and pleasureless life. He learns soon enough that a fair number of enjoined tasks and duties bring a surprising amount of pleasure and that he has, by and large, a greater chance of earthly happiness than has the ordinary Christian. Indeed he must be constantly on his guard lest the pleasure motive creep back into his life. That it may not do so, let him listen to the poet again:

> Ever let the Fancy roam;
> Pleasure never is at home.[25]

The first meaning of this line is that selfish pleasure is its own defeat. There is no master so exacting and delusive. For "pleasure is insatiable, and the more it is indulged, the greater the hunger it creates in its votaries."[26] It leads only to sad satiety and destruction. The cult of personal pleasure, pursued to monstrous extremes, ate away the traditional virtue of the Roman family and eventually brought low the Roman State. Through the exaggerations of the satirist we behold the grim facts: "Luxury, more cruel than the sword, has fallen on us and avenges a conquered world. Every crime and horror of debauchery has been in our midst since the day which saw the death of Roman poverty. . . . Venus in her cups no longer reveres anything."[27]

Solomon, who is represented as admitting, "I withheld not my heart from enjoying every pleasure,"[28] at the end had to confess, "therefore I was weary of my life, when I saw that all things under the sun . . . are vanity and vexation of

---

[24] Rom. 1:28.
[25] John Keats, *Fancy*.
[26] St. Jerome, *Comment. in Osee*, I, 4; *PL* 25, 850.
[27] Juvenal, *Satires*, VI, 292–300.
[28] Eccles. 2:10.

spirit."[29] Jeremias cried to Israel: "How long wilt thou be dissolute in deliciousness, O wandering daughter?"[30] No better word can describe the soul which is bent on its own pleasures. It flies out and spends itself upon a thousand fancies; therefore, it is dissolute, gone to pieces. Only the good will can be strong, for only the good will keeps the powers of the soul fixed upon their rightful objects. Only in this cohesion, arising from pursuit of truth and goodness, lies strength and integrity of soul. The bad will, intent on the wrong things, lets the powers break apart and scatter like the logs of a river raft when the binding chain breaks.

The end of the cult of pleasure is ever the same, says St. Jerome. "Will, therefore, hunger and gluttony, filth and cleanliness, sackcloth and silk have the same reward? Lazarus received evil in his life, and that purple-clad rich man, gleaming in his well fed body, enjoyed the goods of the flesh: but, after death, different places are their lot. Misery is exchanged for delight and delight is exchanged for misery."[31] The pleaser of self is always making a bad exchange. They say that in 1791 Benjamin Franklin was attempting to negotiate a loan for the victorious colonies and a certain Neufville made him an offer demanding as collateral all the thirteen colonies and all their revenues. An outrageous demand and an unequal bargain, one will say; yet, many Christians are willing to exchange their souls, not for the whole world, but for the pleasure of the moment, fatuously urged to destruction by what St. Basil calls "the demon of momentary pleasure."[32] God has declared his opinion of such a choice, "Thou fool."[33] Are there many who must regret for eternity just such a choice?

Terrible as it sounds, there is a ruthless logic in the matter: whoever follows through with the cult of self will find destruction no less than the ancient Romans. Many people fortunately stop short of the precipice: they draw the line at some pleasures; they do perform some unpleasant duties.

---

[29] Eccles. 2:17.
[30] Jer. 31:22.
[31] *Epistola* 48, 21; *PL* 22, 510–511.
[32] *Epistol. Classis I*, 42; *PG* 32, 356.
[33] Lk. 12:20.

But the principle remains unchallenged: to the degree that men seek pleasure in self, to that extent they frustrate their happiness.

If, then, one should not find his pleasure in self, where should he? Time and again men have admired the insight of the Greeks into fundamental realities. Our word for fullest happiness is *ecstasy* which derives from the Greek ἔκστασις, and means a "standing outside of self." We say truly that great joy makes a man beside himself. By commendable choice we have taken over the Greek ἔκστασις to express this thought of fullest joy, because a man finds unalloyed pleasure in going out of self and pleasing others.

The natural gentleman is convinced that this is true. A modern author[34] has called the cult of pleasing others an educated heart. That man has an educated heart who puts himself in the place of others, saves others embarrassment by forestalling their wants, gives them the exquisite pleasure that comes only from kindly deeds performed with style. The educated heart treasures up the likes and tastes of others and remembers them at the appropriate occasion. The educated heart spends time thinking out the exactly right gift, not for its intrinsic value but for its aptness and manifestation of forethought. The educated heart introduces people with such distinct articulation that both parties easily catch the names. It gives full and undivided attention to the person it converses with: it listens well and does not merely lie in wait to pounce on the other with its own narrative. It is said of a gentleman of the past generation that he understood the fourth dimension of kindness: whenever he put a friend of his wife aboard the streetcar, he always slipped the fare into her hand to save her from rummaging in her handbag.

The story is told of a Samoan girl, who naïvely attached herself to a visiting American family, simply because she liked them and wanted to do for them. After an acquaintanceship of only two weeks she made an overnight journey to be with them because she had heard that the children were endangered by a raging epidemic. So sweetly and completely

---

[34] Cf. *Reader's Digest*, October, 1941, pp. 81–83.

did she efface herself that she sought only their interests. Without her they could never have succeeded in the purpose that brought them to the islands — the making of a Polynesian cultural film. Her name meant, *She who wishes everyone well.* After they were parted because of immigration laws, a close friend of the family observed of her: "It was like having Christ in the house."[35]

Madame de Maintenon, who married Louis XIV to reform him, says of herself: "I had an excellent disposition, a kindly heart, in other words I was really what is called a good child . . . simply because I thought only of making myself agreeable. When I was older I lived in convents; you know how much I was beloved by my mistresses . . . because I did them services and thought of nothing but obliging them, and doing things for them from morning until night."[36] Looking back in old age she paints a similar picture: "I have never seen anyone who was like me in this respect. I was sensitive to the praises of the king and just as sensitive to those of a laborer. There is nothing I should not have been capable of to get well spoken of."[37] Although the good lady's motive was not the highest, yet her action was eminently wise: she sought her pleasure in pleasing others. Ampere, the friend of Ozanam, was so great of heart as to say: "I should possess everything in the world to make me happy did I possess nothing at all but the happiness of others."[38]

Mothers ought to be, and all good mothers are, the happiest people in the world because their natural office is securing the happiness of the family. If we have had the right kind of Christmas experiences we should know that we are never so happy as when we are making others happy.

The saints lived this altruistic principle. A secular friend of St. Lutgarde, the Cistercian mystic, had committed a sin and even after his confession had no peace of mind. He commended his cause to the holy nun who time and again

---

[35] Cf. *Reader's Digest*, March, 1942, pp. 41–44.

[36] Gamaliel Bradford, *Daughters of Eve* (Boston: Houghton Mifflin, 1930), p. 48.

[37] *Ibid.*, p. 37.

[38] Claude Williamson, ed., *Great Catholics* (New York: Macmillan, 1939), p. 332.

assailed heaven with her prayers on his behalf. Because her plea was unheeded she finally in desperation cried out to our Lord: "Well, then, either wipe my name from the book of life or forgive this man his sin."[39] Here was the same consuming interest in another which made St. Paul long so passionately for the conversion of the Jews: "For I wished myself to be anathema from Christ, for my brethren who are my kinsmen according to the flesh."[40] It is difficult to imagine greater selflessness.

The earnest soul may quiet any anxieties about the happiness or unhappiness of the way of perfection. If he does his duty and follows the inspirations of grace, he need never worry about himself. Let him abandon himself to Divine Providence, look to God for the supply of his happiness, and adopt the principle that his pleasure will be found in pleasing others. "Let every one of you," says St. Paul, "please his neighbor unto good."[41]

Of course among the others whom we strive to please God naturally comes first. For we are imitators of Christ who could say: "I always do the things that please him."[42] Obviously we err in pleasing others when by pleasing them we displease God. St. Thérèse of the Child Jesus was confidently sure that God would deny her nothing in heaven since she had denied Him nothing on earth. She was one of the rare souls who could say with absolute truth: "What have I in heaven? and besides thee what do I desire upon earth?"[43]

For the sake of the mature soul who has experienced trials and triumph, tears and consolation, progress and regression in the way of perfection, we return to the advice of St. John of the Cross: "Strive always, not after that which is most easy, but that which is most difficult . . . and desire to be detached from all things, empty and poor for Christ's sake. This state is to be embraced with a perfect heart, and the will must conform thereunto. Because if our heart is

[39] Thomas Merton, *What Are These Wounds?* (Milwaukee: Bruce, 1948), p. 168.
[40] Rom. 9:3.
[41] Rom. 15:2.
[42] Jn. 8:29.
[43] Ps. 72:25.

truly engaged herein, we shall in a short time attain to great
joy and consolation. . . . That thou mayest have pleasure in
everything, seek pleasure in nothing." Although these are the
words of a canonized Doctor of the Church, "all men take
not this word but they to whom it is given. . . . He that can
take it, let him take it."[44] This advice indicates a simple
rugged way: simple, in that only one purpose is sought;
rugged, in that not many have the uncompromising courage
to reduce it to practice. Teresa of Ávila endured twenty years
of desolation before she found the ease of perfect virtue:
indeed she was willing to live all her life without any
comfort. Perhaps in this uncompromising doctrine there is
that which fits the violence of the Spanish character and
the bleak, granitelike grandeur of the Spanish mountains. Be
that as it may, to him who can take and practice the doctrine
there must come the blessed consummation:

> He struck me on the neck
> With His gentle hand,
> And all sensation left me.
>
> I continued in oblivion lost,
> My head was resting on my Love;
> I fainted away, abandoned,
> And, amid the lilies forgotten,
> Threw all my cares away.[45]

Putting on Christ is no sentence of death. They who give
themselves to Christ without reserve truly taste and see that
the Lord is sweet. They do not seek Him for His sweetness;
yet only in Him will their craving for peace and delight be
satisfied. For "Thou hast made known to me the ways of
life, thou shalt fill me with joy of thy countenance: at thy
right hand are delights even to the end."[46]

---

[44] Mt. 19:11–12.

[45] *Complete Works of St. John of the Cross,* trans. by David Lewis,
Vol. 1, p. 2.

[46] Ps. 15:11.

10. Work

"Man shall go forth to his work and
his labor until evening" (Ps. 103:23).

A MAN was watching his small niece, on the floor at his
feet, move her paper dolls about in a rapture of energy,
and he said to her: "Margie, you are certainly working hard."
She flashed him a look of reproach for his ignorance: "I'm
not working. I'm playing!" He should have known that even
a child knows the difference between work and play. Play
is exercise of activity because it is pleasurable and heart-
easing. It regards only the present moment. Work looks to
a future end to be secured by effort and puts in train the
means necessary to accomplish a serious purpose. The fall
of man has robbed work of much of its delight.

The Church Militant works unceasingly, saying with her
Head: "My Father worketh until now and I work."[1] She
works to build herself, the Body of Christ, and to complete
the number of the elect. The Church Suffering labors at
purification and expiation. The Church Triumphant no longer
works but enjoys the unending now of eternity.

The activities of the Church Militant are serious. They
constitute work and fall into two categories: action and contemplation. According to St. Gregory Nazianzen,[2] Christianity
accepted this distinction from Greek philosophy which divided men into thinkers and doers and stressed the difference
between theory and practice. To the Greeks, the truly admirable man was the thinker who investigated truth for
the sake of truth and when he had found it spent his life

[1] Jn. 5:17.
[2] Cf. *Orationes*, 4, 113; *PG* 35, 649.

relishing it. He provided the right theories which ordinary men were to reduce to practice. Θεωρία, or contemplation, meant gazing upon the sources of truth. It was the loftiest exercise of the speculative intellect and the noblest activity of man. It was the prerogative of the best minds, an indispensable quality in the rulers of the State who should always be philosophers. Action was the workaday effort to fulfill the ends of life as proposed by the sages, the endeavor to realize their theories of conduct.

To the ancient Church, however, contemplation was more than philosophizing. It was the prayer of the speculative intellect, the highest energizing of the gifts of understanding and wisdom. It was imitation by the Church Militant of the restful activity of the Church Triumphant — loving gaze upon revealed truth. Action was its practical counterpart — the exertion, apart from prayer, which Christians put forth to make men friends of God and to advance them in that friendship. Upon the basis of this distinction the Fathers spoke of the active life, dominated by action, and the contemplative life, dominated by contemplation. St. Gregory says: "The active life consists in giving bread to the hungry, teaching the doctrine of wisdom to the ignorant, correcting the wayward . . . The contemplative life, however, consists in fostering the love of God and one's neighbor with all one's mind, but by abstaining from exterior action, clinging to the sole desire of the Maker, so that action is no longer pleasurable, but, laying aside every care, the soul yearns to see the face of its Creator . . . to rejoice in everlasting immortality in the sight of God."[3]

The Fathers compared the active life to Martha and the contemplative life to Mary. St. Augustine says: "You see . . . in these two women, who were both pleasing to the Lord . . . that two modes of life are illustrated, the present and the future . . . both innocent and praiseworthy: one full of labor, the other at rest, neither sinning, neither indolent . . . neither committing sins against which the laborious one must be careful, neither guilty of laziness of which the restful one must beware. There were, therefore, in that house

---

[3] *Homiliae in Ezechielem*, 2, 2, 8; *PL* 76, 953.

two ways of life and the Fount of Life. In Martha was the image of things present; in Mary, of things to come. What Martha was busied about, there we are; what Mary did, that we hope for."[4]

We recognize the same distinction today. For we speak of the contemplative life, which concentrates on prayer and whose ideal is Mary, and of the active life, which stresses good works and whose ideal is Martha. Although the division is not clear cut, since something of contemplation should accompany action and vice versa, nevertheless it is serviceable enough.

Naturally Christian asceticism has developed since the days of the Fathers. Its vitality is not satisfied with producing Marys who are exclusively contemplative or Marthas who are almost exclusively practical. Today it offers a more difficult ideal, a fusion of the more ancient concepts. It presents for imitation magnanimous souls like Philip Neri, Ignatius Loyola, Francesca Cabrini, who contemplate after the fashion of Mary and execute practical tasks with the skill of Martha. To appreciate the full nature of the work of the Church let us consider it as contemplation, as action, and in the combination called the mixed life.

CONTEMPLATION

We begin with contemplation because it is the more divine aspect of the Church's work. Not only does prayer involve direct dealing with God but we cannot pray at all unless God's grace solicits us to begin and accompanies us throughout. For "no man can say the Lord Jesus but by the Holy Ghost."[5] Just as liturgical prayers are Christ and His little ones praying in the Body of Christ, so the private prayer of the humblest member is the combined effort of Christ and this little one.

Progress in prayer is an incontestable sign of a healthy interior life. It is fair to evaluate one's interior by the level of prayer to which he has attained. Unless one says his vocal prayers well and earnestly speaks to God in his own words, he will not seriously think of striving for perfection.

---

[4] *Sermo* 104, 3, 4; *PL* 38, 617.
[5] 1 Cor. 12:3.

Once he has entered the way of perfection he will acquire some knowledge of, and skill in, mental prayer. Although agreement is lacking as to the logical method of dividing mental prayer, we offer this division of meditation, affective prayer, and contemplation, a classification which roughly corresponds to the generally accepted categories of earnest souls, namely, beginners, the proficient, and the perfect.

The beginner's stage is characterized by *meditation* in which discursive reasoning predominates. This is usually necessary for the beginner's spiritual formation. It is by learning to meditate that one is generally introduced to a life of mental prayer. Meditation may take the form of reasoning upon some truth of faith or incident in the life of our Lord or meditated reading or the slow reflective recitation of a vocal prayer.

The stage of the proficient is *affective prayer.* Here the role of the intellect is lessened; activity of the will is increased. The deduction of truths is partly replaced by intuition. The dominant note arises from the eliciting of sentiments of praise, reverence, gratitude, contrition, love, and the like. He who has attained this level of prayer begins to appreciate the statement of St. Teresa that mental prayer is an exchange of friendship with God, or the words of the other Teresa: "With me prayer is an uplifting of the heart; a glance toward heaven; a cry of gratitude and love, uttered equally in sorrow or in joy."[6]

Sometimes we meet in ancient writers what the author calls contemplation but is in reality affective prayer. Cassian says: "Contemplation is conceived in a variety of ways. For God is known not only through wonderment at His incomprehensible substance — a thing which is as yet hidden in the hope of His promises; but it is also perceived in the greatness of His creatures, or by consideration of His justice, or the help afforded by His daily providence; for instance, when with pure hearts we scrutinize His conduct toward the saints of every age; when with trembling heart we marvel at the power with which He governs, orders, and rules all

[6] *Soeur Thérèse of Lisieux,* ed. by T. N. Taylor (New York: Kenedy, 1912), p. 163.

things, at the immensity of His knowledge and insight which
no secret of the heart can elude; when fearfully we think of
the sands of the sea and the number of its waves, each measured and cognized by Him; when, lost in amazement, we
consider that the drops of rain, the days and hours of the
centuries, all the past or future stand revealed to His gaze;
when we think of the inexpressible mercy wherewith in
unwearied long-suffering He endures the numberless sins
which are committed every moment in His sight; when we
think of our calling whereby His gracious mercy joined us
to Him through no merit on our part; when, finally, in an
excess of wonderment we contemplate how many occasions
of salvation He has offered His adopted children. . . . There
are also innumerable other considerations of a similar nature
which arise in our minds according to the kind of life we
lead and the purity of our conscience, and by them God is
seen or held in a clean gaze."[7]

What Cassian refers to here is an habitual state of recollection and affectionate thought of God. When such thoughts
and affections accompany the soul all day long, at least upon
the fringes of consciousness, there is some justification for
calling that soul "contemplative." This contemplation, however, is not the mystic state. It results from the soul's own
activity and co-operation with grace. Whoever hopes for
perfection must earnestly seek this recollection. Its attainment is necessary, if one would advance beyond ordinary
mental prayer. To attain it requires humility and self-abnegation, purity of heart, and rectification of one's passions. To
maintain it one must cleanse from memory and imagination
images which distract from God. It is the normal background required if the soul is to receive the contemplation
which characterizes the mystic state and which we shall now
endeavor to describe.

The third great kind of prayer is that of the more or less
perfect. This is *contemplation* and it gives its name to the
contemplative life. It should not, however, be inferred that
very holy souls never meditate or that God never gives con-

---

[7] *Collatio* I, c. 15; *PL* 49, 505–506.

templation to beginners. Furthermore, it is well to note that
the term "contemplation" has been used in a broad sense
of genuine mental prayer without specifying whether it be
meditation, affective prayer, or mystic prayer: sometimes
the term refers only to mystic prayer. We shall use the
term in the broad sense and when we wish it to designate
a particular kind of mental prayer we shall add a properly
qualifying word.

We are familiar with natural contemplation. The eye rests
upon some attractive object — a mother looks upon her sleeping child or a traveler upon some gorgeous mountain scene.
The intellect fastens its attention as undividedly as possible
and the whole operation becomes involved in an aura of
emotion, such as love, wonderment, admiration. The emotion
need not be pleasant; it can be painful, as anyone can testify
who has sat a while beside the remains of a departed
loved one.

A similar process of the faculties is involved when the soul,
aided by divine grace, quietly, intently, simply, and lovingly
rests upon divine things. For surely if discursive study of
scientific truths or works of art can be followed by acts
of contemplation of the truth, the same may be asserted with
regard to the objects of faith. When this is done we have
contemplative prayer. Its essential element is intellectual. For
St. Thomas says that "contemplation is the simple act of
gazing upon the truth."[8] It is not a seeking after truth but
a survey of truth already possessed. Activity of the will precedes, accompanies, or follows it. For St. Augustine says
that the act of contemplating is a "pleasant wonderment at
a clearly perceived truth."[9] Contemplative prayer, therefore,
will arise when the will, aflame with divine love, directs the
intellect to fix its unwavering gaze upon divinity, and there
results a delight which renders love more intense. Hence
Richard of St. Victor defines contemplative prayer as the
"free penetrating gaze of the soul resting upon the objects
of wisdom."[10] If differs from meditation because it is not
reasoning but intuition, a leisurely look without the toil of

---

[8] *Sum. Theol.*, II–II, 180, 3, ad 1.

[9] *De Spiritu et Anima*, 32; PL 40, 802.

[10] *Benjamin Major de Contemp.*, I, 4; PL 196, 67.

discourse. It differs from affective prayer, which is characterized by a multiplicity of affections, because it tends to simplicity, a prolongation of one or other affection. Hence contemplative prayer is, in general, the elevation of the soul to God by simple and affectionate intuition.

Is there a contemplative prayer which the soul can achieve through its own initiative and with the aid of ordinary graces? Most writers say there is both acquired contemplation and infused contemplation. By the former they mean a non-discursive prayer in which the proficient can employ themselves *when they will.* It consists in thinking in a calm, simple manner of some divine mystery, especially of the Sacred Passion, and in making an act of love — all without any process of reasoning. By infused contemplation they mean a prayerful experience which *the soul is powerless* to initiate or even to revive once it has passed; its onset and duration depend solely on the Holy Ghost.

Some, however, deny there is such a thing as acquired contemplation. They say that contemplative prayer is always a mystical experience, that between the ordinary kinds of meditation and affective prayer on the one hand, and infused contemplation on the other, there is no intermediary. According to the more widely held opinion there is an intervening state of acquired contemplation, or the prayer of simplicity. Bossuet says: "The soul by her fidelity to mortification and recollection usually receives a purer and more interior prayer, which we call the prayer of simplicity, and which consists in a simple interior gaze, look or loving attention, directed toward some divine object, whether God in Himself or one of His perfections; it may be Our Lord Jesus Christ, or some one of His mysteries or some other Christian truth. The soul discarding all reasoning, then employs a gentle contemplation by which she is maintained in peace."[11] St. Alphonsus Liguori says: "At the end of a certain time ordinary meditation produces what is called acquired contemplation, which consists in seeing at a simple glance the truths which previously could be discovered only through prolonged dis-

---

[11] *Maniere Courte et Facile pour faire l'oraison en foi,* Oeuvres completes ed. by L'Abbe Guilaume (Lyon, 1879), Vol. 9, p. 581.

course."[12] This Teresa of Ávila calls the prayer of recollection and says that the proficient soul should employ itself therein when the waters of infused contemplation do not flow.[13]

Acquired contemplation has this in common with the ordinary forms of prayer that the faithful soul with the aid of grace can achieve facility in it. On account of its simplicity it resembles infused contemplation. They who hold that there are only ordinary mental prayer and infused contemplation are probably trying to say this: so different is infused contemplation from any other prayerful experience that it is in a class by itself. But precisely because it is so different, there ought to be some kind of prayer which is preparatory to it; and this is acquired contemplation.

Infused contemplation is the prayer proper to the mystic state. The soul that constantly receives this gift of prayer enters a new world. It is as if the soul in its journey to God has hitherto been able to guide itself by the human directives of the ascetical life and the ordinary inspirations of grace, but now God takes it into His own hands and bears it off into unknown regions to face ineffable experiences. The initiative of the soul falls from it and the Holy Ghost, operating through the *plenitude of His gifts,* takes over the guidance of the soul. But the soul does not become inert; it exercises a new and suprahuman kind of activity whose initiative, however, is in God.

They who have experienced infused contemplation are at a loss to relate it afterward. For the knowledge of God is difficult and mysterious, and their hearers or readers have no similar experiences with which to liken and compare such overwhelming contacts with God. The attempt to make this obscure matter plain is as if a man were born blind and, having received his sight, tried to describe the sensation of sight and objects of vision to another born blind. However, from the accounts of the mystics we may be able to piece together some reasonable description of it.

First, no virtue can merit it; no human endeavor can bring on the experience. St. Teresa says: "No matter how much we meditate and try our hardest . . . we cannot make this water

---

[12] *Homo Apostolicus*, Appen., I, n. II, 7.
[13] Cf. *Interior Castle*, VI, Ch. 7, n. 7 ff.

flow. God alone gives it to whom He chooses, and often when the soul is thinking of it least."[14] God has given it to boys and girls in their teens, even to children. It is God who begins and ends each particular instance of this prayer. God is the principal agent and the soul is the instrument; yet, an instrument intelligent and somewhat free.

Second, God produces indescribable effects of knowledge and love in the soul. In ordinary prayer the soul knows that it is communing with God but this knowledge is a *deduction* of faith and reason. In this prayer the soul experiences God present as a living reality. Here is the heart of the whole matter. What is the nature of this experience?

All agree that it is direct knowledge, an intuition, not a deduction. Some kind of experiential contact is made with God. Is the contact by means of some medium or is it immediate? Some say it is immediate. Of these some hold that it is like the beatific vision, but it differs in this, that it is vague and obscure, whereas the beatific vision is clear and distinct. Others liken it to sensation and call it a feeling of immersion in God, of seeing God, especially of tasting or touching God. According to Poulain it is a "spiritual sensation comparable to the sense of touch."[15] They say that the soul is as immediately aware of God as a sick person, awakening at night, knows the nurse is sitting nearby in the dark.

The better opinion is, however, that the contact with God is only mediate. Some say the medium is intellectual images infused by God into the soul. Others offer the following explanation. Through the ordinary graces of prayer the soul is only mediately aware that it is united to God and has supernatural gifts. By the light of infused contemplation it is immediately aware of its union with God and of the gifts. Now just as the soul by the light of glory becomes capable of seeing God immediately, who hitherto was present to the soul by His immensity and by grace but could not be seen on account of the lack of the light of glory, so by the light of infused contemplation the soul has an immediate consciousness of its union and gifts, which hitherto were

---

[14] *Interior Castle*, IV, 2.
[15] A. Poulain, *The Graces of Interior Prayer*, trans. from the sixth edition by L. L. Yorke Smith (St. Louis: Herder), Ch. IX, 1, p. 122.

present to it, and in the gifts as in a mirror the soul beholds God present and working in it. Thus upon the just soul, which possesses in germ the power of seeing God, two special lights can be shed. One is the light of glory, given in heaven, enabling it to see God as He is. The other is the light of infused contemplation, given in this life, affording the soul immediate awareness, not of God as He is, but of its union and the gifts: in the medium of these it is aware of God.

Whatever be the nature of this knowledge, the mystics describe it as a condition of "being plunged into the darkness of God." Compared to the noonday splendor of the beatific vision, infused contemplation is darkness. For its perception of God is but general and confused. It is darkness also in comparison with man's ordinary knowledge. For the mystic calls his contemplations a blind journey through darkness. He means that he goes out into the night of faith; that is, he leaves the mode of knowledge with which he has been familiar, and in this new prayer he has his first taste of the incomprehensibility of God. The new light of God thus given him is too much for his weak intellect, as sunlight is too strong for the eyes of an owl. He advances toward God by not understanding; for the process entails abstraction from sense and ordinary human knowledge. Can we wonder that the movement of ignorant men toward the transcendence of God is through a "cloud of unknowing"? Although infused contemplation of itself is accompanied by no new ideas and teaches nothing new, nevertheless it makes upon the intellect deep enriching impressions which cannot be forgotten and affords an insight into divine things which no study or reasoning could ever produce. For it is indeed a deeper penetration into, an unspeakable experience of, God.

As a consequence of this knowledge, the soul, snatched up by God, feels an increase of love which it has done nothing of itself to bring about. According to the degree of mystic union granted by God, this love may be quite calm, or it may be so intense that the will is ravished to God as to imperishable beauty, violently, yet freely. This union of intense love is the truly indescribable part of the experience. St. Bernard describes it as "a canticle of love . . . It is not a cry from the mouth, but the gladness of the heart; not a sound of the lips but the emotion of joy within; not a concert of words but of wills moving in harmony."[16] But sometimes in infused contemplation the soul sees both its union with God and its own deformity. Acutely conscious of its shabbiness in the presence of the divine riches, it experiences a sense of its own emptiness, even a horror of itself. That the soul should simultaneously experience great joy and intense sorrow is not to be wondered at.

If one human being can inflame another with deepest affection, what deeps of love cannot the omnipotent God stir up? This beloved was not necessarily made for this sole lover but every soul was made to rest in God alone. What then will happen to the fortunate soul which God touches, revealing to it some small facet of His lovableness, alluring it with some of the divine attraction? Truly is such a soul wounded by a dart of divine love!

The third characteristic is that the soul's action is of the utmost simplicity. The intellect cannot discourse. It simply looks at God or touches Him or just experiences Him. The will can only love Him and relish Him. This is to be expected in the prayer of the perfect. For the perfection of mental prayer is from multiplicity to simplicity in both its intellectual and volitional operations.

Finally, infused contemplation should be carefully distinguished from visions, ecstasies, locutions, revelations, raptures, and similar extraordinary things which may accompany it. For, strictly speaking, infused contemplation consists solely in the act by which the soul experiences God to be present and by which it clings to Him in love.

Three things, then, characterize this prayer: more or less passivity, experiential contact with God, simplicity. Moreover, the divine visitation may be brief or more or less permanent. It may be unspeakably sweet or full of distress. Sometimes the affection of love surpasses the illumination of the intellect, and vice versa: whence arises the distinction between cherubic and seraphic contemplation. It admits

---

[16] *Sermones in Cantica,* I, 11; *PL* 183, 789.

of varying degrees of intensity, rising from the prayer of quiet, which is the first mystic state, to the mystic marriage, which is the earthly culmination of the mystic state.

Undoubtedly, infused contemplation is a surpassing blessing which the earnest Christian may petition to receive; for it is a powerful help to holiness and generally produces great fruits of sanctity. It begets an insatiable hunger for God which only the beatific vision will satisfy. It is the most exquisite flower which blossoms in this life on the stem of Christian living whose seed is faith, a breath-taking preparation of the perfected soul for heaven, the climax of the interior life. Generally speaking, it is had only by those who have left the flesh far behind.

Let us not delude ourselves — here is no casual experience to be lightly treated of, but a high and mysterious matter for which space allows but a brief summary. We touch upon it, however, in order to stimulate further study. Most good souls will find profit in reading what the masters of mystical theology have said about it. Although some undisciplined or uninstructed souls, or flighty people who are prone to imitate the last thing they have read, may take harm from such reading, yet accurate knowledge of this matter is generally useful and consoling. Apart from direction to be given to others, it is consoling to learn about God's special rewards to His faithful ones and to admire the work of God in His children. Moreover, one can see that proper counsel is necessary not only for beginners: they who suspect they are entering upon this highway generally require skilled advice.

Does God intend that all generous souls attain to infused contemplation? The answer depends on the call of God. Let us distinguish between a proximate call to individuals and a remote and general call to all the just. Evidently many individuals have not a proximate call because they have failed to prepare themselves. They who have adequate preparation are called to the mystic state. Preparation in general consists in great purity of mind and heart, assiduous practice of virtue, great diligence in mental prayer, especially in affective prayer. St. John of the Cross adds three more particular signs: (1) "When one finds he cannot meditate nor exert his imagination, nor derive any satisfaction from it, as he was wont to do."

(2) "When he sees that he has no inclination to fix the imagination or the other senses on particular objects, exterior or interior." (3) "The third sign is the most certain of the three, namely, when the soul delights to be alone, waiting lovingly on God without any particular considerations, in interior peace, quiet, and repose, when the acts and exercises of the understanding, memory, and will have ceased, at least discursively, that is going from one subject to another, nothing remains except that knowledge and attention, general and loving, of which I have spoken, without the particular perception of anything else."[17] No one should lightly conclude that he is adequately prepared and therefore called to the mystic state. Although some prudent or learned priest might safely make such a conclusion about his own case, nevertheless the overwhelming majority of good souls would run a risk of great delusion if they did not seek the opinion of a spiritual director.

As for a general and remote call of all the just to infused contemplation authors are not in agreement. Some vigorously defend the universality of the call and say that as all men are called to salvation, so all the just are called to infused contemplation. God wills, they say, that every justified soul should attain such perfection of charity by the time he dies that he have no need of passing through purgatory in order to receive the beatific vision. To reach perfection one must endure the passive trials of the mystic state and attain some degree of infused contemplation. Their conclusion is that infused contemplation is the *sole* road to high sanctity, that the vocation to infused contemplation is contained in the vocation to the faith, that in itself it is not extraordinary but normal, that it is unusual only in that few attain it. The majority of Christians fail of it because they lack preparation. Some prayerful generous souls do not reach it on account of natural temperament, unfavorable circumstances, too many active occupations.

Others, with greater probability, deny the universality of the call. They say that the only sense in which a universal call is admissible is that no one is beforehand excluded by

---

[17] *Ascent of Mount Carmel*, Bk. II, C. 13.

God. Although many of these authors admit that souls who actually reach high sanctity have at least transitory touches of mystic prayer, yet they all contend that the mystic state is *only one of the ways* of reaching high sanctity, that for infused contemplation God chooses whom He will, that canonized saints had the perfection of sanctity who could not be reckoned contemplative. The passive trials of the mystic state are not required for one to pass from life immediately to the beatific vision: to say otherwise is to deny the efficacy of the sacrament of Extreme Unction received with fitting dispositions. Hence one may liken the mystic state to the religious life, which, while making perfection easier, is not the only way thereto.

Whatever be the solution of this controversy, the earnest soul ought not to worry about his attainment of infused contemplation as a permanent state. That is a consummation which he must leave in the hands of God. What is important, however, is his practical attitude toward this highest form of prayer. For the fostering of a profitable attitude three suggestions are offered.

For the first suggestion we turn to St. Gregory of Nyssa. Taking the words, *Blessed are the pure of heart for they shall see God,* he says: "It does not seem to me that God here proposes some face-to-face vision of divinity to the person who will have purified the eye of his soul, but more probably these sublime words suggest to us what The Word more plainly expressed to others, saying, *The kingdom of God is within you.* By this we are taught that whoever purges his heart of every creature and of all disordered affections will behold the image of the divine nature in the beauty of his soul. It further appears to me that through the few to whom He spoke, The Word offered one and the same counsel, namely, you men who yearn to contemplate the true good, whenever you hear that the divine greatness is exalted above the heavens . . . do not despair of being able to look upon that which you ambition. For your ability to contain God is the measure of your power to contemplate Him, since, in making you as He did, He incorporated that same power into your nature. For God wove into your being imitations of the perfections of His own nature. . . . But copious flaws have

overlaid the divine image and rendered useless to you a
power now concealed beneath deforming obstacles. If, therefore, by a diligent life you clean away the defilement that
has become emplastered upon your heart, the divine beauty
will again be resplendent in you. As happens with iron,
whenever it is stripped of its rust by the whetstone, that which
before was dark now gleams in the sun and gives forth
sheen and sparkle from itself, so whenever the interior man
. . . will have scoured away the rustlike defilement which
has flourished in the decay of his nature, he will again recover his likeness to his Archetype and be good. For that
which has likeness to The Good is thoroughly good. Gazing,
therefore, upon himself he sees in himself the object of his
aspirations. And thus will he be blessed who is pure of
heart, because, contemplating his own purity, he will see
the Archetype of purity in a pure image. For purity of heart,
mastery of passion, and absence of evil — that is being Godlike.
If therefore this is in you, God is totally in you."[18]

He who would "see" God must cleanse his heart. Since no
amount of desire or reading or instruction can bring us to
infused contemplation, we fix our effort on removing the
obstacles which impede it. These are selfishness, lack of
generosity, immersion in wordly concerns. They are overcome by cultivating great purity of heart, mind, and intention, by lively faith and religious recollection, by ardent love
and generosity.

The second suggestion is that each one perfect himself
in the kind of prayer which responds to his current needs
and capacity. Since the beginner needs a firm intellectual
foundation for his whole interior life, he devotes himself to
meditation and learns methods of prayer. He should realize
at the start that methods are means. Their function is to
lead the soul to God; once the soul makes contact with God,
He becomes the real teacher. If the beginner is diligent, he
usually becomes proficient in meditation. After one has
mastered meditation he may lose facility in it and find it
boring. He should then emphasize affective prayer.

The stimulant to affective prayer is the inspiration which

---

[18] *De Beatitudinibus,* 6; *PG* 44, 1269.

quietly seeps into the heart. Innumerable are the ways by which God enters deep within us. One is by years of faithful effort to pray. One is by endurance of trial in His company. One is by contact with souls who love Him very much. We may be denied personal contact with saints but we can find immense profit from their writings. The diaries, letters, and notes on experiences in prayer, left by the saints, are precious documents. It is difficult to read the *Memoriale* of Blessed Peter Faber and not be charmed and lifted to God. Out of these oddly written pages a delicate soul comes to meet you and the flavor of his simplicity and the warmth of his affection for God and His Church must penetrate even the casual reader. When he records little practices which helped him pray more profitably, we feel that we are looking at the careful minutiae of true love. How ingenuously he says: "On the feast of St. Elizabeth, Queen of Hungary, I had great devotion because there came to mind seven persons, together with the desire to remember them and pray for them without any consideration of their failings. They were: the Supreme Pontiff, the Emperor, the King of England, Luther, the Grand Turk, Bucer, Philip Melanchthon. The occasion of this resolve was that I had felt in my soul that the aforenamed were being judged by many; wherefore there arose in me a kind of holy compassion, coming from the good spirit."[19] The inspiration he affords consists not so much in our resolve to imitate each pious practice; but rather, from contact with so simple and loving a heart we cannot but love God a little more and aspire to pray as he did.

The third suggestion is that, whatever be our mode of prayer, we be thoroughly convinced that by mental prayer we do the work of the Church. For the Church works an unseen work not only through the efficacy of the sacraments but also through the prayerful lives of earnest souls.

As right action in the State depends on right theory and without right thinking the State perishes, so also, if we remove prayerful souls and contemplation from the Church, its public action is most seriously affected. Can anyone really explain Christian doctrine who has not at some time or other prayer-

---

[19] *Memoriale Beati Petri Fabri* (Paris: Gauthier-Villars, 1873), p. 22.

fully pondered it? Could the Pope effectively teach from the Chair of Peter unless long and deep contemplations preceded his utterances? Does not the urgency of the preacher's exhortation arise from the fervor of his interior prayer? Devotion to interior practices is the dynamo of the apostle, giving supernatural force and vigor to his exterior activities.

St. James says that "the continual prayer of a just man availeth much."[20] This means not only that fervent petitions bring down blessings on the Church, as the poet says, "More things are wrought by prayer than this world dreams of";[21] but also that the mere existence of prayerful activity even in one soul is of benefit to the whole Body of Christ. We are all bound by the tie of grace and live by one divine life. Hence the activity of the Holy Ghost in one soul is a communication of goodness to all who share the same supernatural life.

If anyone should ask, "What good do cloistered religious do for others?" we should explain how immensely the whole body of the Church is benefited by the Holy Ghost producing choice fruits of contemplation in one mystic soul. In our extrovert age we must keep emphasizing a truth which other times took for granted, namely, that whoever is withdrawn from active pursuits, whether in the cloister or in a third-floor back apartment, and finds God in uninterrupted prayer, is building Christ in the souls of other Christians. A contemplative religious house set up in a non-Catholic district is a mighty seed of faith. The old man or the old woman, who spends so much time in the rear of the parish church and seems to be of no use but to take the dog for a walk, may, by reason of contemplative prayer, be a most fruitful worker of the Church. Who could evaluate the contribution to the work of the Church made by the two mystics, the great Teresas?

ACTION

Since too many people erroneously identify work with external activity, we have been at pains to explain that contemplation is part of the work of the Church. It is genuine work although it is interior, supernatural, and so hidden that worldly men are scarcely aware of its existence. Now since

[20] James 5:16.
[21] Alfred Lord Tennyson, *Morte d'Arthur*, 247.

the Church is a visible society, it has also an external activity which complements its contemplation. We call it action and confess that it is so simple a notion that it defies definition. To get a clear grasp of military action or legal action we turn to soldiers or lawyers. So, to understand the action peculiar to the Church we turn to her spiritual writers where we find two traditional meanings.

First, the Fathers speak of action as the labor of self-conquest which a man must undergo before he arrives at contemplation. St. Augustine says: "Two virtues are proposed to the human mind, one active, the other contemplative. By the first, we move to the end; by the second, we arrive thereat. By the first, one labors at the cleansing of his heart in order to see God; by the second, one is at ease and God is seen. The first consists in keeping the precepts of mortal life; the second, in the knowledge of that eternal life. And for this reason the first labors and the second rests, namely, the first is busied with the purgation of sins; the second basks in the light of sins forgiven."[22]

Origen understands action in the same sense. Taking the sentence of Proverbs, *The beginning of the good way is to do justice*, he says: "Since the good way happens to be very long, the first thing you have to know about it are principles of action which may be expressed in the phrase, *To do justice*; as for what comes next, you have to know principles of contemplation wherein, I think, the good way terminates."[23]

This kind of action is proposed to souls who undertake to lead a spiritual life. The purpose of the spiritual life is that we become children of God who fully correspond to God's loving designs for us. God desires high sanctity for us and offers it, at least remotely. And at the end of the spiritual journey is contemplation of heavenly things. But the way is long and if we hope to arrive at contemplation, we must first vigorously practice action, that is, make ourselves just by purging injustices and by exercising solid virtue.

No one becomes a great surgeon or a finished concert artist overnight. He must go through an apprenticeship to get rid of defects and acquire necessary techniques. So also, no one

---

[22] *De Consensu Evangelistarum*, I, 5, 8; *PL* 34, 145.
[23] *Comment. in Joannem*, 1, 16; *PG* 14, 49.

can attain the higher reaches of the road to God unless he pass through the lower stages. Now the principles which guide the soul in the lower stages are rightly called active, because at that stage the soul must discipline itself. It exercises itself strenuously and exerts its own initiative. If, however, the soul progresses to the contemplative stage, training exercises disappear. The soul, schooled in humility and responsive to the infused gifts, hands over the initiative to the Holy Ghost. The relation, then, between the action we have been describing and contemplation becomes like that of training to perfected skill. We do not infer that the contemplative soul is inert and bereft of activity. But in comparison with its former state, the contemplative soul is quiet and rests in the hands of God: it has surrendered self-guidance in order to be directed by the illuminations of the Holy Ghost. Origen and Augustine, therefore, say that one must master the active or ascetical part of the way of perfection before one can arrive at its passive or contemplative consummation. The toil of the first stages of the journey they call action. We may call it private action, or living an ascetical life.

A second and more common usage employs action to designate any activity, apart from mental prayer, which the Church makes use of to induce men to co-operate with grace. This activity includes preaching the word of God, administering the sacraments, directing souls, regulating the various units of the Church, practicing the corporal and spiritual works of mercy. To distinguish it from the private action of which we have just spoken let us call this public action — all the *external* activity of the Church designed to reconcile men to God and make them holy and pleasing in His sight. The purpose of private and public action is the same: to make men just. Private action is mainly interior; public action is exterior. The former is directed at self; the latter, at the neighbor.

Between the public action of the Church, generally known as the active life today, and the private action of the individual, or the ascetical life, there is a very exact parallel. For the Church is to labor at the purification of men, the administration of the sacraments, the preaching of the Gospel, until the whole Church is ready for contemplation. This purification will be completed only in the next life when Christ presents His unspotted Bride to the Father. The individual also labors at self-purification until he obtains contemplation, if not in this life, at least in the next life.

Action, therefore, understood as the apostolate of the Church, stands in the following relation to contemplation taken in the broad sense. Contemplation is interior: action is exterior. Contemplation is completed within one's own soul: action goes out to another. Contemplation is turning from men to God: action is seeking out men. Contemplation requires quiet and repose: action flourishes amid the busyness of men. Contemplation is of itself supernatural: some of the phases of action are not supernatural. Who would say that taking a parish census and keeping Sunday school records were of themselves supernatural acts? Contemplation is interested in the end: action, in the means to the end. Contemplation is directed immediately at God: action, mainly at men. Contemplation emphasizes expenditure of spiritual energies: action, expenditure of physical energies.

Now action is more necessary than contemplation. For if the Gospel were not preached and the works of mercy practiced, how could men properly lead a spiritual life? Since action is more requisite to the essential purpose of the Church, it is the concern of more Christians. "It is commanded," says St. Gregory, "that there be offered for sin a lamb from the flocks or a wild goat. What is meant by a lamb but the innocence of the active life? And what is signified by a wild goat which clings to the heights and grazes on the remotest cliffs but the contemplative life? . . . It is well said that a lamb from the flocks be offered and not a wild goat from the flocks because the active life concerns many, the contemplative but a few."[24]

Contemplation as such, however, is nobler than action as such. Practical-minded Americans need to ponder well these remarks of St. Thomas: "The contemplative life is simply more excellent than the active. . . . The contemplative life becomes man according to that which is best in him, the intellect, and according to its proper objects, namely, things intelligible, but the active life deals with externals. . . . The

---

[24] *Moralium Lib.* 32, 3, 4; *PL* 76, 636.

contemplative life can be more continuous . . . and is more delightful than the active. . . . In the contemplative life man is more self-sufficient because he requires fewer things for that purpose. . . . The contemplative life is loved for its own sake but the active life is directed to something else. . . . The contemplative life consists in rest and leisure . . . and is according to divine things but the active life is according to human things. The contemplative life is according to that which is more proper to man, his intellect; whereas in the works of the active life the lower powers also, which are common to us and brutes, have their part. . . . Our Lord adds [another] reason when He says: 'Mary hath chosen the best part which shall not be taken from her.' "[25]

Contemplation is also more meritorious, as St. Thomas proves: "The root of merit is charity; and, while charity consists in the love of God and the love of our neighbor, the love of God is of itself more meritorious than the love of neighbor. Hence, that which pertains directly and immediately to the love of God is generically more meritorious than that which pertains directly and immediately to the love of our neighbor for God's sake. Now the contemplative life pertains directly and immediately to the love of God . . . whereas the active life is more directly concerned with love of our neighbor. Hence the contemplative life is generically more meritorious than the active life."[26]

For private action, or self-conquest, we should overcome ourselves to the extent of avoiding all deliberate sin. And whoever ambitions the fullest interior life and hopes that God may call him to true contemplation must purify himself to the utmost extent. But who is to undertake public action or the apostolate? Does it fall to all, or many, or only a few?

Some chosen souls are clearly not called to it. Cast in the role of Mary they work for the Church by seeking the perfection of the purely contemplative life. At the turn of the century the opinion was quite prevalent that the apostolate was the exclusive concern of bishops, priests, and religious. The last two sovereign pontiffs, however, have summoned all the faithful to engage in Catholic Action, the layman's partici-

[25] *Sum. Theol.*, II–II, 182, 1.
[26] *Ibid.*, 182, 2.

pation in the apostolic ministry of the Church. In his radio address, Christmas Eve, 1943, Pius XII said: "The progress of mankind in the present confusion of ideas has been a progress without and often against God; without Christ and even against Christ . . . Have not many Christians made concessions to those false ideas and ways of life which have been so many times disapproved by the teaching authority of the Church? . . . Is there anyone who has the right to say that he is blameless? Reflection on yourselves and your deeds, and the humble recognition of this moral responsibility will make you realize . . . how necessary and holy a thing it is to pray and labor in order to placate God and invoke His mercy and to *participate in the salvation of your brethren* . . . securing and acquiring for your fellowmen that interior peace which cannot be found except by coming close to the spiritual life of Bethlehem's cave. To Action, then, beloved children! . . . Let not your courage fail!"[27]

This appeal to the apostolic spirit of the layman has been necessary and consoling. For he has contacts with people outside the true fold and an entree into their lives which is denied the priest. The first steps in convertmaking often belong to the layman who can discreetly interest a non-Catholic friend in the Church and, when the opportune moment arises, invite him to accompany him to Mass.

While Catholic Action, in its name and practice, may be new to the twentieth century, its reality is only a return to the earliest ages of the Church. Therefore, whether one be lay or cleric, old or young, married or single, each should contribute to the work of the Church by some kind of external activity. We should often ask: "What shall we do that we may work the works of God?"[28] The first answer is — only that which authority approves of.

The reason is that since the Church is a great society, its work must be co-operative and co-ordinated. This is accomplished only by submission to proper authority. While priests and religious see that the blessing of authority is as necessary to apostolic work as breathing is to our natural life, a layman

---

[27] A.A.S., Vol. 36, n. 1, pp. 19–20.
[28] Jn. 6:28.

may not always appreciate this truth. When war was declared in 1917 ex-President Theodore Roosevelt proposed to raise a body of volunteers which would go to France as an independent command. The proposal was rejected because such a body could not be fitted into the hierarchic army under one supreme commander which the government was planning. So also, our work must fit into the general plan of the Church and it is so fitted by submission to authority. For the obedience of the individual to his proper authority links him with the Holy See, and where Peter is, there is Christ.

To accomplish this work three things are necessary: (a) a right attitude of mind, (b) a right intention of the will, and (c) a right principle of procedure. The right attitude of mind arises from "faith that worketh by charity."[29] Without vivid faith nothing is undertaken. Our faith, however, ought not to be partial but all-embracing. We should see not only the general problems of human existence in the light of faith but the lesser problems of daily life. St. Aloysius was very right when he applied to the minutiae of every day this unvarying norm: What has this to do with eternity?

The right attitude of will is a pure intention. Our intention is pure when it is directed solely to God's purposes and is free of the alloy of self-love. We must fulfill the exhortation of St. Paul: "All things whatsoever you do in word or in work, do all in the name of the Lord Jesus Christ."[30] Therefore one must triumph over the temptation of making apostolic work a means of satisfying self-love. Whether one is a religious holding an important post of administration, or a young lady helping her pastor by teaching catechism, the work should not become a means for getting pleasant things one likes or avoiding unpleasant things one dislikes. Both must be taken in stride: neither should cause one to deviate from the singleness of his original resolve.

We undertake some work out of love of God and in the course of it find many agreeable things — praise, affection, popularity. If we do not keep scrutinizing our motives, we may begin to seek these advantages for their own sake. To

---

[29] Gal. 5:6.
[30] Col. 3:17.

the extent that we do so, we are distracted from our main purpose and fail to keep before us the ideal of St. Paul: "I seek not the things that are yours, but you."[31]

On the other hand, it is not always easy to abound in the work of the Lord.[32] A person must overcome laziness, boredom, disillusionment. The pious will goes seeking the purposes of God and finds its enthusiastic expectations blocked by ignorance. It tries to help the weak-willed and they refuse to help themselves. It speaks courteously only to be rebuffed by bad manners. It gives magnanimously only to find ingratitude. Deep faith and deeper humility are required by the earnest soul in order to look upon the objects of its ministrations and say: "Are not you my work in the Lord?"[33] The pure and simple will, intent solely on God, moves steadily ahead through the obstacles which tend to impede its quest for the purposes of God. In proportion as our quest of these purposes grows slack, to that extent has the purity of our motives been vitiated.

As a right principle of procedure we offer two propositions: (1) as a mere man, the aspirant to perfection must look on his apostolic work as greater than himself and subordinate to it all that is human in him; (2) as a new Christ, called to perfect union with God, he must consider apostolic work of less importance than his own sanctification.

The first way in which we submit ourselves to the task in hand is by devotion — the giving of oneself to the good of others. What an example of devotion mothers give who, from dawn to night, busy themselves with home and family without a thought of self. So the earnest soul becomes devoted by subordinating his ego to the work, by viewing the work as more important than his convenience, by giving time, heart, and sweat that the project succeed.

Devoted work calls for a peculiar kind of humility. In every job there are a number of unattractive details which one cannot delegate to some lesser agent. No glory attaches to them. They call for no ingenious thinking or exercise of special charm. However, no necessary detail is unworthy of

---

[31] 2 Cor. 12:14.
[32] 1 Cor. 15:58.
[33] 1 Cor. 9:1.

the work of God. It is careful attention to these details which makes the difference between work well done and a mediocre performance.

The second way in which we submit ourselves is by giving our very best to the task. Everyone loathes a sloppy piece of work. We attain the efficiency of our best by an intelligent appraisal of what the work requires, the part we are to play in it, the things we are to do to fulfill that part, and the faithful execution of these requirements. For intelligent estimation of the work nothing can be substituted. For the fulfillment of the necessary means two suggestions are made: cultivate quiet of mind and be patient with difficulties.

We read in the Book of Kings: "And [God] said to [Elias]: Go forth, and stand upon the mount before the Lord: and behold the Lord passeth, and a great and strong wind before the Lord overthrowing the mountains, and breaking the rocks in pieces: the Lord is not in the wind, and after the wind an earthquake: the Lord is not in the earthquake. And after the earthquake a fire: the Lord is not in the fire, and after the fire a whistling of a gentle air."[34] In work we seek God, not by agitation but activity, not by anxiety but repose of mind. God is not in the strong wind nor the earthquake nor the fire but in the whistling of the gentle air. He who is intent upon the will of God does not unduly exaggerate the importance of his work nor speak of what he does as if no one else did anything. Good work is done without fuss. It is planned beforehand and it is done systematically. It proceeds without worry about the result. The result is in the hands of God.

In his work one may face three human difficulties. The first is lack of appreciation. No one is so foolish as to work *for* the commendation of a superior or the gratitude of beneficiaries; yet, when the occasion calls for either of these and it is withheld, one feels cheated. Suppose the ladies of the Parent-Teacher Association raise funds to equip the cafeteria of the parish school and never get a real word of thanks from the pastor! Suppose a priest defrays the expenses of the education of a promising boy and after the boy has become a great success hears nothing from him! Our Lord has

---

[34] 3 Kings 19:11–12.

forewarned us: "When you shall have done all things that are commanded you, say: We are unprofitable servants; we have done that which we ought to do."[35]

A second difficulty is paying too much attention to fellow workers. It is only human to compare one's efforts and rewards with the efforts and rewards of others; human indeed, but unprofitable. For who can rightly evaluate a worker's merits but He who reads the human heart? In the scene upon the lake shore after the Resurrection, "Peter, turning about, seeth the disciple whom Jesus loved following. . . . Him therefore Peter saw, and saith to Jesus, 'Lord, and what of him?' Jesus saith to him, 'If I wish him to remain until I come, what is it to thee? Do thou follow me.' "[36] Peter is not to worry about what may happen to John; his duty is to follow Christ. If we simply follow Christ, we have neither the time nor the inclination to busy ourselves with the fortunes of others. Paul said to Timothy: "Look well to thyself and thy teaching"[37] —paternal advice to mind his own affairs!

The third difficulty is disappointment. As nothing is more stimulating than success, so nothing is more likely to paralyze effort than failure. He who works for Christ must endure disappointment, for Christ endured it first. He was so discouraged over Jerusalem that He wept. How must He regard the failure of Israel to assume its messianic function of bringing the whole world into the kingdom of God? What does He think of the millions of souls for whom He shed His blood in vain? These are mysteries of God.

Our disappointment may be ill-founded. We may feel sure that our efficiency is achieving results; but we may not realize what are proper results in the work of God. Our yardstick for evaluating results may differ from God's. We look for the execution of a project in a way that meets with man's approval. God looks for something else — how closely does the worker come to doing the divine will? In this sort of work a man is only an instrument: God is the principal Agent. He has selected the good which He wants done in the

---

[35] Lk. 17:10.
[36] Jn. 21:20–21, Westminster version.
[37] 1 Tim. 4:16, Westminster version.

world. It is His ends, His aims, His designs, which are to be fulfilled, and often these are well hidden from us. A worker's efficiency, therefore, cannot be reckoned according to the praise or blame accorded for achieving or failing to achieve visible results. The one thing which matters is whether he honestly tried to learn the will of God and gave his best effort for the love of God. As for the actual results, God will take care of His projects. He sees to it that they get done. When a man sets out to do his own will in these things, he is a failure in the work. When he tries to do the will of God, he is a success in the work.

Besides, God sends us disappointments to cure us of arrogant self-reliance. When we imagine we are all-sufficient, it is "as if the clay should think against the potter, and the work should say to the maker thereof: Thou madest me not: or the thing framed should say to him that fashioned it: Thou understandest not."[38] Disappointments, accepted in the spirit of faith, are steppingstones to sanctity; they are the discipline which teaches humility. What we shudder to look back upon as a bitter blow to pride may be very pleasing to God, for it was the occasion of drawing us out of self and teaching us to rely on God. Once our failures have taught us humility, we may have some value as an instrument of God. For "the foolish things of the world hath God chosen, that he may confound the wise . . . And the base things of the world, and the things that are contemptible, hath God chosen, and things that are not, that he might bring to nought things that are: that no flesh should glory in his sight."[39]

What, now, about the earnest soul, the new creature called to perfection, who considers his external work to be of less importance than his own sanctification? We admit that he is right, that the principle is true, but do we cherish it as a practical principle which daily influences our lives? People penetrate to a real knowledge of practical truths in proportion as they put them into practice. In moral matters knowledge flows from practice. Thus, St. Thomas repeats over and over again that we acquire prudence, or knowledge of the right

---

[38] Isa. 29:16.
[39] 1 Cor. 1:27–29.

thing to do, in proportion as we order our appetites and exercise the moral virtues.[40]

How then can we prevent work from interfering with our personal sanctification? The answer is — by wisely combining action with contemplation.

ACTION AND CONTEMPLATION COMBINED

It is helpful to keep in mind the succinct phrase of St. Gregory Nazianzen: "Contemplation is a beautiful thing, action is a beautiful thing."[41] The reason is clear: both lead to God and both were so admirably united in the life of our Lord. In the daylight He worked miracles in Capharnaum: He often spent the night in the prayer of God. At suppertime He instituted two sacraments: in the dark He went to the garden to pray "according to his custom."[42]

The Church, therefore, does not intend that a hard and fast line always be drawn so that this one gives himself only to action, and that one only to contemplation. Although God calls some few to an exclusively contemplative life, it is His design for the vast majority of His children that they unite both elements in their lives. In saints like the Curé d'Ars we are edified by a wondrous fusing of a high degree of contemplation with most vigorous action. This is the most excellent manner of life, as St. Thomas says. This is his argument: "As it is better to enlighten than merely to shine, so it is better to give to others the fruits of one's contemplation than merely to contemplate."[43]

Between action and contemplation there is a mutual exchange of efficacy. St. Gregory says: "As the reasonable order of life is that we move to the contemplative life from the active life, so usually the soul turns again with profit from the contemplative life to action, so that the soul inflamed by contemplation may more perfectly pursue the active life. Action, therefore, ought to carry us to contemplation: however, what we have pondered in our meditations should from time to time, recall us more vigorously to action."[44]

---

[40] Cf. *Sum. Theol.*, I–II, 65, 1.
[41] *Orationes*, 14, 4; *PG* 35, 864.
[42] Lk. 22:39.
[43] *Sum. Theol.*, II–II, 188, 6.
[44] *Homiliae in Ezechielem*, 2, 2, 11; *PL* 76, 954–955.

From this we gather, first, that the climax of an active life should be contemplation. Action, zealously pursued with a mind intent on God, is not a hindrance but a help to acquiring skill in contemplation. Worth-while experiences in Catholic Action or well-motivated exercise of the apostolate should make communion with God easier. Greater intimacy with Christ is a reward for zeal. Did not our Lord promise through St. Margaret Mary: "They who shall promote this devotion [to My Sacred Heart] shall have their names written in My Heart never to be effaced"?

Second, for action to be effective, it needs the preparation of contemplation. The soul with great ambitions in the field of action should first be thoroughly steeped in contemplation, which supplies action with the necessary interior force. The labors of St. Francis Xavier are explained by the depths of his devotion to prayer. Immediately after Paul was converted he did not begin his apostolate but retired for three years into the deserts of Arabia.

Third, action must be refreshed by periods of contemplation. To devote an hour of a busy day to mental prayer is to join action and contemplation. Setting aside a fixed period for weekly or monthly recollection, devoting a number of consecutive days each year exclusively to spiritual concerns are common means of vitalizing action with contemplation.

Finally, contemplation needs a realistic outlet in action. St. Gregory shrewdly notes how action serves as a test of the virtue acquired during a period of contemplation. "It often happens," he says, "in the case of holy persons that, when they see themselves brought to compunction by great graces from heaven, they imagine themselves to be perfect. They think themselves obedient but the reason is that no one has put any hard commands on them. They believe themselves patient but no one afflicts them with injury and hardship. And it often happens that these people take up a spiritual ministry against their will and are brought to rule the faithful. And when they have been tossed to and fro by great trials and thoroughly disturbed in soul, they find themselves quite imperfect, they who, free of trial, deemed themselves quite perfect."[45]

---

[45] *Homiliae in Ezechielem,* 2, 7, 12; *PL* 76, 1020.

This happy combination of action and contemplation certainly existed in the early Church. St. Augustine is speaking from his own experience when he says: "As to these three modes of life, the contemplative, the active, and the combination of both, although, so long as a man's faith is preserved, he may choose any of them without detriment to his eternal interests, yet he must never overlook the demands of truth and duty. No man has a right to lead such a life of contemplation that he forgets in his own ease the service due to his neighbor; nor has any man a right to be so immersed in the active life that he neglects the contemplation of God. The charm of leisure must not be indolent vacancy of mind but the investigation or discovery of truth . . . And in the active life, it is not the honors or powers of this life that we should ambition, but we should aim at using our position and influence, if these have been honorably attained, for the welfare of those who are under us . . . And therefore holy leisure is longed for through love of truth; but it is the demand of charity to undertake requisite business. If no one imposes this burden upon us, we are free to inquire into and contemplate truth; but if it be laid upon us, we are compelled for charity's sake to undertake it. And yet not even in this case are we wholly obliged to surrender the sweets of contemplation; for if these were to be withdrawn, the burden might prove to be intolerable."[46]

In the life of the earnest soul, then, a place should be found for both contemplation and action. As our action should measure up to lofty standards of excellence, so also should our contemplation. While we pray, there should be a genuine turning away from creatures to cling to the Creator alone; while we are not engaged in formal prayer, there should be an unswerving effort to walk in the presence of God; at all times, indeed, there should be the loving endeavor to advance our friendship with God. But how much action, how much contemplation should be put into our lives? It requires no small prudence to discover the proper balance, no small fidelity to maintain it. God indicates the proportions of this balance in a general way through the duties of our state in life; more particularly, by the voice of grace, speaking in the

[46] *City of God,* B. 19, c. 19; *PL* 41, 647.

heart of each one, sweetly summoning him to the perfection which God intends for him.

Our natural temperament inclines us to excess; in the case of a few, in favor of contemplation; in the case of the majority, in favor of action. Whoever is inclined to prefer the delights of contemplation should remember that even the monks of the desert were warned: "Neglect not the active life; otherwise contemplation will fall off."[47] The lesson is imparted naïvely, yet forcefully and with matchless humor, in this tale of the desert. "A certain brother came to the Abbot Silvanus on Mount Sina; and seeing the brethren at manual labor, he said to the old man: 'Labor not for food which perishes. For Mary has chosen the best part.' The old man said to one of his disciples: 'Zachary, give the brother a book and take him to an empty cell.' When three o'clock came, the monk looked out the door to see if they were sending some one to call him to eat. When no one called him, he came out to the old man and said to him: 'Father, have the brethren eaten today?' The old man replied: 'Yes, they have eaten.' 'And why,' said he, 'have you not called me?' The old man said: 'Because you are a spiritual man and have no desire for material food; we, being of the flesh, wish to eat and by this means we are able to work. You, on the other hand, have chosen the best part who wish to spend the whole day in meditation and have no desire for material food.' When the monk heard this, he bowed penitently, saying: 'Father, forgive me.' The old man said: 'Assuredly Martha is necessary to Mary, for through Martha Mary also is praised.' "[48]

Overemphasis upon action is by far the greater danger. It is easy to become so engrossed in activities that one neglects the legitimate needs of his own soul. Those who are vigorous in action may profit from two suggestions for maintaining a proportioned balance of action and contemplation.

The first object of anyone's apostolic zeal ought to be himself. Well-ordered charity demands that he first secure his own salvation, that he never endanger it for the sake of helping others. Our Lord has warned us that the gaining of the

---

[47] Thalassius, *Centuriae*, 2, 32; *PG* 91, 1440.
[48] *Apothegmata Patrum, De Abbate Silvano*, 5; *PG* 65, 409.

whole world, which conceivably could include the saving of many souls, would avail us nothing if we lost our own soul.[49] St. Paul tells us of the precautions he took, lest while preaching to others, he become a castaway.[50] The need of self-sanctification before one takes up the active life is thoroughly inculcated in the great appeals to the apostolic life. The first fruit of St. Ignatius' meditations, on the Kingdom of Christ which so clearly contains the apostolic vocation, and on the Two Standards where the exercitant beholds Christ sending His disciples to scatter His sacred doctrine throughout the world, is some high point of personal sanctification. In the first, he who would be distinguished in the service of Christ must first act contrary to his own sensuality and carnal love. He is not set aflame with the thought of the soul's value, but in his mouth are put the words of this high prayer: "It is my deliberate determination, provided it be to Thy greater service and praise, to imitate Thee in bearing all injury and insult and all poverty both actual and spiritual." In the second meditation, the exercitant concludes with the very earnest prayer that he be received by Christ in the highest spiritual poverty and, if God so wills, in actual poverty, that he be allowed to bear injuries and opprobrium in imitation of Christ.

The second thought is that the greatest good we can do for others is our own sanctification. Neglect of our own perfection makes us that much less an apostle. It is more in accord with the divine plan and more effective of good in the universe that earnest souls attain the perfection which God expects of them than that they be expert workers for the Church. If they become in their interior lives all that God desires them to be, one need never fear that the external works of the Church will be neglected.

There is no point in underlining the defects of those who yield to the pressure of the active life and neglect contemplation. They are not always stimulated to compunction by the high-lighting of their failings. To strengthen their resolve to pray they need to see the brighter side of the picture. If we take that practical norm, "By their fruits you shall know

---

[49] Cf. Mt. 16:26.
[50] Cf. 1 Cor. 9:27.

them," then the American aspirant to perfection has done a giant's work. Since the foundation of the hierarchy in 1790 he has changed the American Church from a mission of London to one of the brighter jewels in the crown of the Church Universal. The American Church is equipped with sees, parishes, parochial schools, convents, abbeys, universities, colleges, high schools, hospitals, orphanages, pious societies, confraternities, sodalities, associations for the promotion of Catholic Action, and the like. And what is the human explanation of this wondrous growth? Hours, days, and years of unremitting toil — and humble prayer. How much of these fruits are due to action? How much to prayer? God alone knows. Would the results have been even more fruitful had the contemplation been more and the action less? God alone knows. But perhaps we do know that the time has come for an increase of contemplation without a decrease of action.

11. Acedia

"By slothfulness a building shall be brought down, and through the weakness of hands the house shall fall through" (Eccles. 10:18).

ALL the things that God created, He made to engage in action of some sort. God wills that the atom of gold, the molecule of salt, the rose, the cat, the man, and the angel should not merely exist inertly, but should· act according to their proper natures. They do not begin in possession of the fullness of their well-being; they must move toward that, as toward their proper destiny. The motion to their destiny is the expansion and flowering of their nature. It is simply themselves acting as God intends they should act. All things less than man, unless prevented by some external mischance over which they have no control, function easily and without strain. It is no trouble for a bird to act as a bird or a cat to act as a cat — unless, of course, malice or accident robs them of the satisfaction of their natural instincts. Whoever heard of a squirrel unhappy in its native habitat or of a cow with a nervous breakdown? The natures of these beings have not been hurt.

Yet man, the lord of visible creation, finds it hard to act as a man. It takes noticeable effort to be prudent, just, temperate, and brave at all times. The reason for the difficulty is intrinsic to man: his nature has been wounded by sin. Like an automobile which has lost its wheel and body alignment in an accident, human nature often functions poorly. Indeed, some people are so badly disturbed by life's vicissitudes that they become dispirited by the pain of living and sigh inordinately for eternal rest. They imagine that the blessed end of life is a blissful minimum of activity. Since they feel that their lives are only painful scramblings, they imagine heaven to be the chance to crawl into a quiet room and hang out a huge sign: Do Not Disturb! Waking in heaven, they will sit in the spring sunshine and doze and nod and once in a while take a sleepy look at God.

Let us not misinterpret the *At Rest* cut upon Christian tombstones or the *Eternal rest grant unto them, O Lord* of the Mass for the dead. Eternal rest is rest from the anxiety, toil, and fretting for an end not yet achieved. It is cessation from strife and worry, but it is by no means cessation from activity. On the contrary, heaven involves the most intense and pleasurable activity conceivable. Here on earth, the spirit acts fitfully, groaningly, laboriously. In heaven, as truly befits an immortal thing, it will function easily, perfectly, ceaselessly. In the final possession of God, human activity will be endless, for the intellect will always discover new facets of reality in the infinite being of God, and with newer and ever refreshed surges of love the will will ever revel in love's union with divinity.

Unfortunately, as free beings, we are capable of both wrong and right action. Nature employs two means of inducing us to embrace right action and avoid wrong action. The first is appeal to reason. She shows us the inherent rectitude or reasonableness of right action; the unreasonableness, the nothingness, of wrong action. The second means is a system of pleasures annexing to right action and a system of pains attaching to wrong action. Since man loves pleasure, and since pleasure is the reward of right action, man is drawn to right action — vegetative, sensitive, intellectual, and even moral action — by the secondary motive of its pleasurableness. Since man hates pain, and since pain is the penalty of wrong action, man has a secondary motive for avoiding wrong action.

The system operates ineffectually now, not because it is in itself poorly designed, but again because man has thrown his nature out of joint. Original sin seems to have switched pleasure to vice and pain to virtue. By failure to act aright a man becomes insensitive to the pleasure of right action: by constant wrong action a man is perversely captivated by the pleasure of wrong action. The consequence in his intellect is confusion concerning the relative values of sense action, intellectual action, and volitional action. He may be entirely ignorant of supernatural action. He may think the pleasure to be more important than the action from which it springs. The consequence in his will may be contentment with sense action and sense pleasure and the rudest kind of intellectual activity: he may never experience the highest and most pleasurable activity.

Nevertheless, God's system of pleasures and pains is fundamentally sound: it will work its purposes. Our present concern is not to explain why it sometimes seems to misfire but to point out that absence of a certain type of pleasure is indication of the lack of activity to which the pleasure belongs. If a man's body is quite inactive, he will feel heavy and sluggish. A person without intellectual interests has no concept of intellectual delight. Stimulate the activity and its connatural pleasure is aroused. During the war, men in their thirties, forced from comparative bodily inactivity into strenuous physical exertion in the armed forces, recaptured an *élan* and a physical exuberance of living to which they had long before said good-by. Sometimes a college boy, who has been an indifferent student, chances upon an attractive field of study and discovers problems which arouse his curiosity. For the first time in his life he becomes intellectually awake and he experiences the keen pleasure of mental pursuit. He may be so smitten with relish of intellectual conquest that he chooses a life of scientific research. The same may be said of volitional activity. A man can give in to his passions and for months be swept into a bad life. His will follows in the wake of animal appetite like a puppy after its young master. He deplores his weakness. He promises he shall check himself, but he does nothing until some calamity brings him to his senses. He then puts the brake on passion. His will assumes its rightful dominance. He now experiences the peace of a good conscience. He is happy in doing the right thing.

So also a person who has never acted supernaturally has as much idea of supernatural joy as a Senegalese has of the delights of skiing. There is supernatural joy and it signifies supernatural activity. It results from charity's presence and operation in the soul. There is no substitute, for example, for the peace of a long-needed and really good confession. A very genuine satisfaction accompanies the realization that one has mastered some obnoxious fault. Devoted persons who see

Christ in His afflicted poor and offer them the charity of Christ are often rewarded with a peculiar serenity and cheerfulness. Sometimes an almost ecstatic thrill accompanies the dedication of one's self to God by religious vows or the sacrament of Holy Orders. A very deep content which no adversity can shake may accompany the daily effort to do God's will in all things.

Everyone who has dedicated himself to the pursuit of perfection, or whose state of life is tantamount to such dedication, should ask himself this practical question, "How often and how intensely do I experience supernatural joy?" The question must be rightly understood. The reference is not to sensible consolation, the occasional ice-cream cone which God gives to His children of the supernatural life: persons of a sentimental turn prize it very highly. We refer to the joy which lifts up *the soul*, when the intellect is vividly touched by the light of faith and the will responds to the inspiration of charity; it is the sweetness which the soul experiences upon the ingress of the good spirit; it is the relish of exercising divine activity; its fruit is increase of faith, hope, charity, or the exercise of solid moral virtue.

Of many possible answers to our question, let us indicate four which are typical of recognizable groups of people. A first type includes persons who experience frequent changes of consolation and desolation. This variety of spiritual emotion betokens intense volitional activity. The person is making and trying to keep good solid resolutions. These ups and downs of the spirit often accompany great changes in one's manner of life. Beginners often experience them. So do persons who are passing into the unitive or mystic way.

A second type includes a few who endure long and deep desolation. This condition in earnest souls is often a severe test, preparatory to the reception of great graces.

A third type includes some happy souls who, having survived the ordinary trials of the spirit and having attained solid virtue, now run joyously but evenly along the way of God. Saints, like Robert Bellarmine, who have been blessed with a naturally optimistic temperament, prove that sanctity is not unhappiness.

Finally, there are persons who have difficulty remembering

when they last experienced spiritual joy. They are strangers to the joys and sorrows of the interior life.

There are three general causes of the lack of supernatural joy: the evil one tempting us, God teaching us and testing us, and our own neglect. For the fourth class, just mentioned, the cause of their lack of joy and sorrow is very probably personal neglect. Although the soul is adorned with grace, it feels dull and apathetic. The reason is that its supernatural activity is very limited. As the body reacts to lack of exercise with dullness and torpidity, so does the soul. If a person, who once vigorously pursued the interior life, now seldom resorts to mental prayer and self-examination, need he wonder if his interior life has become drab and lusterless? He is cheating himself of a keen satisfaction which the desire of perfection entitles him to. We do not say that joy of the spirit is an end in itself. It is only a help to perfection. It is a meaningful, though not infallible, sign of the presence or absence of true well-being of the spirit. It is like noise and the normal small boy. If we notice he is very quiet, we presume there is something wrong with him. The fact that now a person knows so little joy of spirit can be a just indication that he does little supernaturally.

Lack of spiritual activity and its accompanying relish causes a vacuum in a person's life and a corresponding boredom. The vacuum must be filled. Active persons cannot be satisfied with inactivity. A zestful woman, whose energies have gone into the raising of her children, once the children are raised, must turn to parish activities or civic affairs to find a proper outlet. The man, who retires from the active direction of some large corporation, if he is wise, takes up fishing or gun collecting or some other hobby. So the person, who once had high spiritual ambitions and allowed them to decay, gives his will other objects of desire. If he is a layman, he lapses back into semiworldly pursuits. He remains interested in the Church's activities, but mediocrity repossesses him. If he is a priest or religious, he substitutes for God the work of God, and pretends there is no difference. He quiets the hunger of his soul by multiplying external ministries. Or he devotes himself to research and the solution of intellectual problems. He may go on for quite a while without realizing what he is missing. But not forever. Sooner or later the problem of the wreck of his interior life must catch up with him.

We squirm beneath the realization that we are failing, especially in a lofty enterprise to which we promised the utmost devotion. How we hate to be confronted with evidence of our remissness. When a husband's devotedness falls off, he dreads his wife's reproaches. If a man has pledged a group of friends his out-and-out co-operation in some worth-while undertaking and fails to keep his word, he is uneasy in their company. So anyone who is letting his ambition for perfection drift away dreads to be all alone with God, or even with himself, for he must apply to himself the words of the Wise Man: "I passed by the field of the slothful man, and by the vineyard of the foolish man: and behold it was all filled with nettles, and thorns had covered the face thereof, and the stone wall was broken down."[1] If he avoids the uncomfortable scrutiny of his soul one time, the problem which he is running from will assail him some other time. It may lay hold of him when he is well along in years and no longer has the physical ability to distract himself from himself. Some day he must squarely face the question, "What have I been doing with my interior life?" No one can forever avoid answering this question who once seriously pledged himself to the pursuit of perfection and has slackened in that pursuit.

Startling as it may seem, it is of more concern to the Church of God that they who have gone along the way of perfection should persevere therein, than that newcomers be persuaded to enter upon it. The former are the older children of the Church; they are closer to her, and have, as it were, prescriptive rights in her. Furthermore, it is as profitable to the Church to bring back persons who have relaxed their efforts to the pursuit of perfection as it is to stir up new enthusiasm for it.

This statement will doubtless be challenged, perhaps upon the principle that it is too late to teach old dogs new tricks; that the attempt would be like throwing good money after a bad investment. We cannot agree. Time, care, energy, and much of God's grace have gone into the formation of these relaxed persons. Although their spiritual efficiency has unfor-

---

[1] Prov. 24:30–31.

tunately been impaired, it can be restored by the correct approach and the grace of God. The problem is like that of converting an old farmhouse into a modern dwelling. A good deal of money may be required to scrape off the hideous stucco, to replace broken sashes, to throw down useless partitions, but the edifice has inherent possibilities. Its walls and floors are firm and solid; it was originally built with beautiful lines. Could not a competent architect restore its former beauties? So also it is our firm conviction that men and women, who are no longer active in the pursuit of perfection, could be reactivated, and with great profit to the Church of God.

The connection between action and pleasure has been emphasized so that active souls may be encouraged to persevere and inactive souls to become reactivated. It is important also to note the relation between lack of activity — sloth — and sadness.

We all know from personal experience that many times we see the better thing to do and fail to do it. The reason for failure to act is inordinate love of self. Doing the right thing involves surrender of something which pride or envy or avarice is loath to part with. So also the self-surrender may impinge upon sloth.

Sloth is as much a source of moral weakness as is lust or anger. A man may be subject to sloth of the body. His natural temperament inclines him to avoid unpleasant exertion and to seek ease and comfort. If he habitually yields to this inclination, he becomes a lazy man who fails by omission. Persons who are inclined to be lazy seldom begin the quest of perfection. Aspirants to perfection are usually active and vigorous persons. It is not sloth of the body they need to fear so much as sloth of the spirit.

Aspiring souls do not first become slack in performing exterior duties. The first attack of sloth is upon the interior life. Spiritual sloth tries to make spiritual activity unattractive. It inclines one to excuse himself from part of his daily program of prayer. It makes the execution of resolutions distasteful. By making self-mastery appear too arduous, it slows down one's all-out effort for perfection. By yielding to the obstacles to interior activity which the three concupiscences keep throwing in his way, a man can surrender his exercises of piety one by one. If he comes to this pass, neglect of external duties can follow easily. He cuts himself off from the abundant flow of supernatural energy. Whenever he is habitually neglectful of external duties, the reason is that the inner pendulum of the spiritual life has ceased to swing. Spiritual laziness has bred bodily laziness.

Notice of sloth, or acedia, appears in the first accounts of the fathers of the desert. The word "acedia" is a transliteration of the Greek ἀκηδία, which in classic Greek meant "indifference," a "state of not caring," the "result of grief or exhaustion." It bears much the same meaning in early ascetical writing. The first reality which the word designated for the Greek-speaking anchorite of the East was the languor of the body, brought on by the heat of the noonday sun and the wait until three o'clock to break one's fast. In their minds, acedia was the noonday devil, spoken of by Holy Writ.[2] It came to mean also torpor of the will in the exercise of good works, induced by lack of divine love and joy therein. Cassian said that it was the sixth great problem[3] of the monk and he described its symptoms in minute detail:[4] loathing of the place where the hermit dwelt; boredom with his cell; contempt of the brethren; laziness and tardiness at manual work; wandering outside the enclosure; neglect of spiritual reading; sighing that nothing in the place helps him; imagining that elsewhere he would be better off; desiring to be put over others; disregard of monastic discipline; dislike of fasting, solitude, prayer, and mortification; drowsiness and frequent sleeping; idle visits and conversations; long and unprofitable pilgrimages; dangerous friendships; desire and solicitude for his relatives; urging others to join him in giving up the monastic life. These are particular illustrations of the general theme: "My soul hath slumbered through heaviness."[5]

In a sermon to his monks on the feast of the Ascension of our Lord St. Bernard contrasts two types of monks: "You can certainly notice in almost every religious congregation men

---

[2] Cf. Ps. 90:6.
[3] Cf. *De Coenobiorum Instit.* X, I; *PL* 49, 359.
[4] Cf. *ibid.*, C. 2; *PL* 49, 365 ff.
[5] Ps. 118:28.

filled with consolation, abounding with joy, always pleasant and cheerful, fervent in spirit, day and night meditating the law of God, frequently looking up to heaven and lifting pure hands in prayer, solicitous to follow conscience, devoted to good works; to whom discipline is lovable, fasting sweet, watching short, manual labor pleasing, the whole tenor of whose austere life seems refreshment. On the other hand, you find men fainthearted and relaxed; who wilt beneath the yoke and need the rod and spur; whose joy is slight, whose sadness fainthearted; brief and rare their compunction, animal-like their thinking, tepid their life; their obedience lacks devotion, their speech prudence, their prayer true heart, their reading personal profit: whom, in a word, as we see, the fear of hell scarcely checks, or shame holds back, or reason bridles, or discipline compels. Does it not seem to you that the lives of these men are like a hell, because, with their intellect opposed to their desires and their desires to their intellect, they must put their hands to the work of the strong, they who are not sustained by the food of the strong, they who are certainly partners in the tribulation but not in the consolation."[6]

It remained, however, for St. Thomas properly to analyze and describe this capital vice, which is a problem by no means peculiar to hermits and monks: it is a universal obstacle which every pious soul must encounter and overcome. First, he speaks of a general kind of sloth, "an oppressive sorrow which so burdens a man's mind that he wishes to do nothing."[7] In this wide meaning, sloth is not a special but a general vice. For example, the reluctance of the body which a person must overcome to obey the laws of fasting belongs to this general kind of sloth. So also does the difficulty inherent in practicing any particular virtue, like humility or almsgiving. To understand sloth as a special vice let us recall that a certain order ought to exist among spiritual goods; that is, the act of each virtue ought to be directed to a supreme spiritual good which is the divine good. A special virtue produces this order — charity. As it is fitting for each virtue to find pleasure in its own good, which is its proper act, so it especially belongs to charity to possess that joy by which a person rejoices in the

---

[6] *In Ascensione Domini Sermo* V, 7; *PL* 183, 318.

[7] *Sum. Theol.*, II–II, 35, 1.

divine good. Similarly, then, the difficulty or sorrow which a person encounters in performing any act of virtue belongs, not to any special vice, but to every vice; sorrow, however, in attaining the divine good about which charity rejoices, belongs to a special vice. And this is sloth properly so called.[8]

As charity has a special fruit — joy — which makes its practice interesting and attractive, so also it has a special hindrance — sorrow relative to the attainment of the divine good. By charity a person tends to order all his actions unto God. He fails in charity insofar as he neglects to order this, that, or the other action so. A great cause of the failure is the unpleasantness which he finds in the attempt. Unpleasantness in doing a certain thing leads one not to do it.

Aristotle puts his finger upon a central motive of human conduct when he says: "No one can spend his days with one whose company is painful, or not pleasant, since nature seems above all to avoid the painful and aim at the pleasant."[9] In the presence of the unpleasant a person naturally tends first to shun that which causes the unpleasantness, and then to seek that which will afford him pleasure. St. Thomas states this principle in his explanation of the consequences of acedia. He accepts the opinion of St. Gregory who cites six pernicious effects which may follow from acedia, namely: malice, spite, faintheartedness, despair, sluggishness in regard to the commandments, and wandering after unlawful things.[10] He vindicates St. Gregory as follows: "In the avoidance of sorrow the order followed is first that a man fly from unpleasant things, and second that he even struggle against such things as cause sorrow. Spiritual goods, which are the object of the sorrow of acedia, are both end and means. Avoidance of the end happens through *despair*. Avoidance of the goods which are means to the end, in matters of difficulty which come under the counsels, happens through *faintheartedness*, and in matters of common righteousness, happens through *sluggishness about the commandments*. The struggle against spiritual goods which cause sorrow is sometimes with men who lead others to spiritual goods themselves, and this is *spite*; and sometimes

---

[8] Cf. *ibid.*, a. 2.

[9] *Ethics*, VIII, 5, 1157b.

[10] *Moralium Lib.* 31, 45, 88; *PL* 76, 621.

it extends to spiritual goods themselves, when a man goes so far as to detest them, and this is properly called *malice*. In so far as a man has recourse to external objects of pleasure, the daughter of acedia is called *wandering after unlawful things*."[11]

How clearly is this doctrine borne out in everyday life. What an obstacle to salvation is acedia! The sinner finds sorrow in the injunction: "If you love me, keep my commandments."[12] So he is careless in observing the divine law and his appetite wanders after unlawful things. The procurement of sinful pleasures is so thoroughly organized because many men desire them and will pay handsomely for them. If the sinner finds absolutely no pleasure in divine things and logically pursues the worship of material things, he will come to a dislike, horror, and detestation of divine things, such as we find among Communists. The final consequence of seeking happiness outside of God can only be despair. The despair of ancient pagan civilization, which was its outstanding characteristic, was born of its abandonment of God. The emptiness and pessimism of modern existentialism is another cult of despair. Lack of charity is symptomatic of all heresy, and it is characteristic of heretics to manifest spite against Catholic teachers and maliciously to distort Catholic doctrine.

What a hindrance to perfection acedia can be. How realistic is St. Thomas when he says that in matters of counsel a person yields to sloth through faintheartedness. When adherence to the resolution to order all one's actions unto God no longer produces consolation, how is one to face the boredom, apathy, or even disgust which sets in? Faintheartedness in the presence of the unpleasant or painful is the first serious test which the resolution of the earnest soul must encounter. He too has a natural bias toward the pleasant and for him also the practical dictates of charity can involve unpleasantness. He can give in to sloth and fail to keep his resolution. He can be lured by the idea that "the faraway hills are green" and can experience a tendency to wander after unlawful things, that is, for persons, places, and actions which his resolution has declared out of bounds for him.

[11] *Sum. Theol.*, II–II, 35, 4, ad 2.
[12] Jn. 14:15.

Silently, insidiously, without much heed paid to it, a condition of relaxation can develop in a person. Of course he is always aware of the beginnings of the defection, since the first yielding to sloth is deliberate and overt. Some unusual occurrence — some new temptation, recreation, change of residence, death of a loved one — causes him to make a notable surrender of his resolution. After he has recovered from the chagrin of his first defection, the second defection comes more easily and with less surprise at his weakness. Smaller defections may grow into larger defections, until he is no longer conscience-stricken by his failures. He loses his sense of guilt for the failure of his resolution; in fact he finds his new way of acting quite pleasant and agreeable.

The downward course is never that of a stone falling from the roof, quickly and precipitately. Moral decline follows a zigzag course. The person has periods of remorse, amendment, and renewed activity. He has intervals of consolation and renewed hope. The first remedies may be effective. He may even advance for a time. But if he has not solved the central problem of how to continue active in the face of desolation, of how to seek God even when God seems grim and distant, he lapses again. Then he comes to fall into the second class of men, mentioned by St. Ignatius in his meditation on "The Three Classes of Men." He is not of the first class, those who know what ails them but who make no effort at curing themselves. He is willing to do something, but his measures are only partial and ineffective; they do not strike at the root of things. When his halfway measures fail to produce the desired result, he is content to drift along, deluding himself that he is doing much, whereas he is doing next to nothing. Conscience may then give its last effective protest and self-dissatisfaction sets in. But self-accusation produces no result, for he has slipped down to the first class of men who do nothing. His dissatisfaction has begotten only irresolution. As Scripture says: "The sluggard wills and wills not."[13]

Then the whole cast of his thinking may undergo a change. He wants peace of soul, to be at ease with himself. Since he must chide himself constantly for not living up to lofty

---

[13] Prov. 13:4.

ideals, why not trim down the ideals so that conscience will be easier to live with? From their high staff he hauls down the ideals of a happier day and for them substitutes meager ideas of his own devising. Of this Cassian remarks: "It must be ascribed to negligence, when, thanks to some previous lukewarmness wherein we have acted carelessly and remissly and in cowardly idleness have fed upon noxious thoughts, we make the soil of our hearts bring forth thorns and thistles, so that upon their emergence we are, as a consequence, made sterile and devoid of all spiritual fruit and contemplation."[14]

After he has rationalized away the need of ascetical practices, he looks back upon his former fervor with a kind of pitying contempt. "Was I not foolish then," he says to himself; "now that I have gotten that foolishness out of my system, I can begin to live and be of some use." Certain resentments, which resemble the spite and malice which St. Thomas speaks of, take hold of him. He feels a kind of ill will toward fervent persons. He looks down upon another's ascetical practices. He dislikes words like "mortification," "abnegation," "self-denial." So he justifies the remark of Thalassius: "Acedia is a belittling on the part of the soul: the soul becomes a belittler which is too fond of pleasure."[15]

Since the joy of spiritual accomplishment no longer spurs him to action, dissatisfaction, bred of inaction, tends to produce more inaction. As a frog is captivated by a light held before it in the dark, or as a bird is fascinated by the eyes of a watching snake, so he can become immobilized in the toils of his own inactivity. Each slackening of effort produces further and further inaction. As in the economic depression of the thirties each failure led to the collapse of more and yet more businesses until there was a real stoppage of the wheels of industry, so the number of his spiritual failures can increase until he acquires the habit of spiritual inaction. He passes from the state of willing and not willing to a state of simply not willing.

Then things are really bad. A person who brightly and earnestly entered upon the way of perfection may so surrender to spiritual sloth that he becomes completely indiffer-

---

[14] *Collationes*, IV, 3; *PL* 49, 586.
[15] *Centuriae*, 3, 51; *PG* 91, 1453.

ent and apathetic. When he no longer cares, he is seriously
sick. The joy of supernatural action has faded out entirely,
so that he can now take a perverted acquiescence or even
comfort in his own misery. His condition is a true and
dangerous illness of the soul. It is the real acedia, the state
of being without care. His soul is like the physical state of
a person recovering from a bad case of grippe or virus
pneumonia — he feels so poorly that he cares about nothing.
When he comes to this, he gives up all hope of and struggle
for perfection. It is the despair of the aspirant to perfection.
He stops caring for and doing anything to maintain an interior life. He loses interest in prayer, in the acqusition of
virtue, in doing good to the neighbor — even in the good
opinion of others. Climacus calls the condition "the paresis
of the soul, the enervation of the mind."[16] The soul, in the
midst of supernatural plenty, is wasting with pellagra; the
will is paralyzed. From this apathy and cessation of volitional
activity results a pitiable melancholy. Just as intense joy
flows from intense activity of the will, so a corresponding
depression follows from complete will-inertia.

The most extreme manifestation of the ill is fearful terror
of God's judgment. The victim may be haunted by the conviction that he is already condemned to hell. He is on the
verge of final despair. He then requires the attention of a
skillful physician of souls no less than a psychopath needs
a good psychiatrist. Although the disease will seldom go to
this extremity, it will leave the sufferer open to serious
temptation, as St. Thomas has explained. The outer wall of
precaution has disappeared, the ordinary safeguards have
been spurned; nothing prevents temptation from swarming
in. With his courage very low, the victim may quickly tire
of the effort of resistance and say: "There is no point in
resisting. I may as well give in." Like an overwearied and
demoralized soldier, who has thrown away his pieces of
equipment in the course of his army's rout, he is tempted
to sit down where he is and let the enemy take him.

Someone may object to the length of this description,
contending that the portrayal of human weaknesses is no
inspiration to exalted living. We assert, on the contrary, that

---

[16] St. John Climacus, *Scala Paradisi*, XIII; *PG* 88, 860.

these matters serve very useful purposes. First, we need the reminder that we live in a real world; that it is only in this real world, where faults and weaknesses abound, that we work out salvation and perfection. It is not good that one should read only what soothes his likes. Instead of helping, it hurts an adult to close his eyes to the actual realities of human existence and, by a process of eliminating the nasty and unpleasant, to construct in his mind a rose-colored world. Second, ascetical writings need not always be inspirational. As Holy Writ[17] reminds us, there is a time for all things; there is a time for inspiration, and a time for common-sense admonition and practical advice. Besides, the inspiration which ignores the pointed facts of life cannot be substantial and enduring. Third, the dangers of acedia are actual, potent, and menacing. They threaten every earnest soul. A person who thinks that these dangers are nonexistent for him should remember that one of the Apostles surrendered completely to a capital vice, that one of the first deacons fell away. If a man knows the illness which is likely to strike him down and takes no precaution, he is being foolish. Hence the serious reminder that we are prone to spiritual sloth should serve as a useful prophylaxis.

The ancient fathers offered some strong and simple remedies. We read in *The Spiritual Meadow:* "Another brother went to the monastery of the Abbot Gerasimus, of which the Abbot Alexander was the head, and said to him: 'Father, I wish to leave the place where I dwell because I am overwhelmed with sloth.' The Abbot Alexander answered him: 'This is a natural sign, my son, that you bear in mind neither the eternal punishment nor the kingdom of heaven, for [if you did] you could suffer no sloth.'"[18] There is something naïve and robust in the advice: think seriously of heaven and hell, and sloth will not overcome you.

The anchorites thought that acedia was their special plague which they would be rid of, if they assumed the cenobitical life. Men took up the cenobitical life and, although monastic life took away many opportunities of indulging the vice, it did not make over human nature. For

---

[17] Cf. Eccles. 3:2 ff.
[18] John Moschus, *The Spiritual Meadow,* 142; *PG* 87, 3, 3004.

we hear St. John Damascene offering this advice to eighth-century monks: "If you wish to overcome acedia, work hard meanwhile at some small handicraft, and take up spiritual reading, and pray assiduously with strong hope of obtaining blessings; keep in mind the souls in their last agony, the violence and suffocation of sins, how unmercifully they are punished and tormented, and thus you will find relief from your ill."[19]

Cassian suggests other remedies. He says that the monk who is thus afflicted should be dealt with kindly and humanely. The severity of authority should be tempered with paternal solicitude.[20] Invoking the example of St. Paul, he offers his monks manual labor as the great cure. He cites the example of the Abbot Paul who, although he lived too far away from the cities to sell his woven palm-leaf work, nevertheless exacted of himself a daily stint of work, as if he had to live therefrom. At the end of each year when his cave was full of finished pieces of work, he set it all on fire.

Cassian concludes his remarks upon acedia by telling this story of himself. When he was a young monk, he said to the Abbot Moses that yesterday he had been so beset by the onslaught of acedia that he could shake it off only by the determination to betake himself to the Abbot Paul. Whereupon the Abbot Moses said to Cassian: "You have not freed yourself from it; but you have delivered yourself over to it. For all the more severely will it henceforth afflict you, a deserter and a fugitive, whom it has seen flying in defeat from the battle: unless for the future, whenever the attack arises, by not deserting your cell or yielding to sleep, you will have chosen to overcome its afflicting heat at its customary time, but, by endurance and conflict you will have learned to triumph."[21]

Cassian stoutly sums it all up: "Experience shows that the onslaught of acedia is not avoided by flight but overcome by resistance."[22] Commenting on these words St. Thomas

---

[19] *De octo spiritibus nequitiae,* 8; *PG* 95, 82.
[20] Cf. *De Coenob. Instit.* X, C. 15 ff.; *PL* 49, 381 ff.
[21] *Ibid.,* 397.
[22] *Ibid.,* col. 398.

says: "The assaults of sin should be overcome, sometimes by flight, sometimes by resistance: by flight when a continued thought increases the incentive to sin, as in lust . . . By resistance, when perseverance in the thought diminishes the incentive to sin, which incentive rises from some trivial consideration. This is the case with sloth, because the more we think about spiritual goods, the more pleasing they become to us, and forthwith sloth dies away."[23]

From the traditional teaching of Christian asceticism we gather the not very startling conclusion that sloth is overcome by counteractivity. This general answer, however, requires a discriminating application to particular cases, for not every kind of activity will answer. The fathers of the desert, for example, fought noonday sluggishness with manual labor, but we need not infer therefrom that relaxed persons today will necessarily regain lost fervor by imitating the amiable boondoggling of the Abbot Paul.

In any case, however, the first counteractivity is action of the intellect. For continued torpor of spirit comes from diminution of practical faith, that is, from failure to keep the truths of faith and the counsels of the Gospel before one's mind and operative upon one's conduct. The first antidote to spiritual laziness is vigorous thought. One must keep exercising the mind upon the deposit of faith, and try to find new insights and application in the principles of asceticism. Well-known truths are liable to grow stale and unprofitable. They need not; for no man can exhaust the breadth and depths of revealed truth. But unless we keep freshening them for ourselves, they will exert no new influence on us.

Here is a grave difficulty of the ascetical life: as a person gets older he gets bored reading and hearing the same stock explanations of the same truths. How is a man to avoid the staleness and overcome the tedium? The saints succeeded. They kept discovering more reality and fresh wonders in God's revealed word. Why? First, because they kept doing the truth in charity. Then they made themselves progressively more docile to the inspirations of the Holy Ghost, whose gifts opened to them more and more of the

---

[23] *Sum. Theol.*, II–II, 35, 1, ad 4.

hidden things of God. They learned more about God because they hungered after Him.

The second remedy is that a person have the fortitude to continue active, despite a natural inclination to become inactive. It is easy to be alert and vigorous when one feels bright and joyous, but we all tend to become inactive when action loses its relish. It requires no special virtue to row along with a fast current, but a man must strain and sweat to make headway when the tide sets full against him. Joy in supernatural action carries one along swiftly: lack of joy is a mean tide to pull against. Yet faith and reason keep demanding action of him even when his feelings incline him to inaction. God is still to be sought, even when He seems remote and dour. Resolutions are to be kept, even when one is downcast and desolate. When boredom, apathy, and dis-inclination descend upon a person, he must apply the soldierly remedy of St. Ignatius, *agere contra,* doing the exact opposite of what slothful nature inclines him to.

It is a mistake, however, to think that the principle of *agere contra* must be applied to every situation and every choice in life. Sometimes what God wills for us is very pleasant. It can be virtuous to follow the joyous impulses of nature and grace, for God can sweetly draw us by the cords of Adam. An ailing man may think that he should fight his indisposition and stay on his feet, when reason is crying out that he should go to bed and give himself a chance to recover. The inability to distinguish the wrong time from the right time to apply this principle often leads inexperienced people to abandon it. It is not an all-out attack upon human happiness; it is the goad to use when nature lags unreasonably. When aridity urges a person to shorten prayer, he wins by praying on a little longer. When waywardness tells him to omit thanksgiving after Holy Communion, he kneels down and tries to find God even in an imagination full of dis-tractions.

Since sloth is the aversion of the soul, not from every spiritual good but from the divine good, its function is to slow down, even to put a stop to the operation of charity. Hence the third and greatest remedy for sloth is vigorous and intrepid charity: vigorous, in that it struggles against inaction; intrepid, in that it refuses to yield to the deadening effects of sadness.

There is charity which is obligatory — the keeping of the commandments as a divine good — and it leads to salvation. A person commits a *sin* of sloth, not when he is disinclined to perform an act of virtue to which he is not obliged, but when he is sorry he has to do something for God's sake and fails to do it. He conquers sinful sloth whenever he overcomes his repugnance and disinclination, and seeks the divine good as God commands him.

There is a charity which is counseled — and it leads to perfection. A person exercises such charity not only when he keeps the law of God for God's sake, but especially when he tries to order all his actions unto the love of God. This simple and earnest quest of the soul for God in all things is our movement toward perfection. Sloth slows us down when we should run to God; it makes us stand still when we should ever move to Him. The reason is that we are saddened by the vigilance, effort, and self-surrender which such motion entails. Our comfort, or the attractiveness of creatures for their own sakes, draws us aside from the single-minded quest of God. These things set up a counterattraction, so that moving straight to God at all times appears irksome and a burden. The soul which is now relaxed was once enamored of the idea of doing all for God, urged on by the wondrous attraction of God. But on account of the soul's neglect to work the superabundant works of charity, God has lost for it His old attractiveness. The clouds have hidden the Sun of Justice. So the soul fails to move toward God as once it did. How now will it overcome its inertia for loving God superabundantly? How is the inertia of any nonmovement overcome? Simply by movement. In our case by the movement of charity, and by perseverance in the movement of charity. The person simply goes ahead with blind faith and, despite the retarding force of old habits of apathy, begins again to render God a superabundant love. He returns to doing what he formerly did, to loving God as best he can in all things, and by the goodness of God, the attractiveness of God once again casts its spell upon him.

Three things, then, kill sloth: vigor of faith, fortitude in the face of sadness and unpleasantness, the activity of charity. By faith we look up and are encouraged, beholding from afar the mansions of bliss prepared for us. By fortitude in the face of sadness we ride over our fear of embracing God's will and make ourselves constant in keeping resolutions. By charity's activity we put our volitional life on a par with our life of faith, and so assure ourselves a complete and satisfactory life. For as boredom is born of a lethargic will, so joy will follow from a resurgent and resolute will. "Therefore," as St. Paul says, "brace up the hands that have grown helpless, and the knees that totter, and make straight paths for your feet, so that that which is lame may not be put out of joint, but rather be cured."[24]

But no man can do any of these things by himself. He will never rise from his listlessness, unless God grants His supporting grace. He must ask God to breathe a new heart into him. Left to himself he is buried in his apathy; but let God touch him anew and he rises out of his old dead self. St. Bernard says: "There are persons who have wearied of spiritual pursuits . . . and walk the ways of the Lord in sadness . . . if the merciful Lord draw near us in the way we walk and He who is from heaven begin to speak of heaven, and sing to us some pleasing portion of the canticle of Sion, and tell of the city of God, of the peace of its city, of the eternity of its peace, of the state of eternity — I say to you that the joyous tale will be as a vehicle to carry the sleeping and torpid soul, so that from him who hearkens it will drive boredom from the soul and weariness from the body."[25] The oil of the Spirit alone can soothe the troubled heart and restore forgotten vigor. This is any man's for the asking. "Cast away from you," says the prophet, "all your transgressions, by which you have transgressed, and make to yourselves a new heart, and a new spirit . . . For I desire not the death of him that dieth, saith the Lord God, return ye and live."[26]

Pursuit of perfection is not renunciation of happiness. Everybody is entitled to a modicum of happiness even now,

---

[24] Hebr. 12:12–13, Westminster version.
[25] *Sermones in Cantica*, XXXIII, 4; *PL* 183, 947.
[26] Ezech. 18:31–32.

and it seems fitting that a man should find it in his chosen work. If he has wisely chosen his career, an engineer should find his satisfaction in his professional work; a singer, in his singing; a housewife, in the conduct of her house. Should not the aspirant to perfection find happiness in efficient effort for perfection? A good stonecutter likes to cut stone. A good violinist likes to play the violin. A saint should be happy making himself like to the Son of God. As the old Irish lady said: "If we do what we are supposed to be doing we'll be happy in the doing of it." By the same token, if we do not do what we are supposed to be doing, let us not be surprised if we are unhappy.

Spiritual sloth is the redoubtable enemy of every high-minded person. The effort to give God our all is like making a clearing in the tropical jungle. We work hard, under the impulse of His love, to clear out a small cultivated space, but, as soon as we stop working, the jungle moves in on us again. How shall we maintain a constant level of effort? How shall we keep the love of God operative in our hearts? We need, at least from time to time, the joy which is the precious gift of the Holy Ghost. But we must not expect the gift unearned. Joy is born of action. It is the fruit of vigorous faith, manful fortitude, and charity operating under the inspirations of divine grace.

12. Fishers of Men

"And Jesus said to them: Come after me, and I will
make you to become fishers of men" (Mk. 1:17).

AN AIR of awe and paradoxical dignity surrounds the phrases,
the "Seal of the Fisherman," the "Throne of the Fisherman."
To some Evangelicals the Throne of the Fisherman is set up
in Babylon, the land of antichrist; on it sits the great harlot.
The words evoke for them the mystery of dark powers and
the efficiency of malevolent forces. To us they represent the
summit of human dignity, the primacy of the Vicar of Christ,
the headship of him who is first among the fishers of men.
He is so great because it is so great a thing to be a fisher of
men. By the power of God, the occupation of ignorant,
horny-handed men becomes the symbol of God's own work.

Through the mouth of the prophet God had promised:
"Behold I will send many fishers . . . and they shall fish
them,"[1] First among these fishers is the Peerless Fisher who
sits in Peter's boat and from it teaches the multitudes. The
Second Person of the Most Blessed Trinity, who proceeds
from the Father by an eternal procession, proceeds also in
time to fish for the souls of men. He compares His mission
to a net cast into the sea gathering together all kinds of
fishes.[2] He angles for souls, enticing them to Himself that
He may heal them of the wounds of sin and restore to them
their divine adoption. He makes provision that, after His
personal mission is completed by His sacrificial death, the
work of fishing for souls will go on until the end of time.
His Galilean companions will leave their nets and boats
by the shore of the lake for the sake of a world-wide enter-

---

[1] Jer. 16:16.
[2] Cf. Mt. 13:47.

prise; they will go and teach all nations and baptize them in the name of the Father and of the Son and of the Holy Ghost.

In the two miraculous drafts of fish recorded in the Gospels, one before and the other after the resurrection of our Lord, the seerlike mind of Augustine[3] rightly sees a sublime mystery. The first incident represents the Church laboring in this time: the net takes in all manner of fish, good and bad; the bark of Peter is almost submerged; the net is broken by schism. The second incident represents the Church after the resurrection of the dead. The Sea of Galilee is time and the world of men; the shore is the end of time and life eternal. The net is let down on the right side at the command of Christ and is filled, but never broken, with the souls of the just. It is Peter, the Roman bishop, who hauls the net ashore. The one hundred and fifty-three great fishes are the full number of the elect.

In order that the souls of men may be safely landed on the shore of eternity at the feet of Christ, they must enter the net of the Church. Men, laboring under Peter's immediate direction and ultimately under Christ's command, manipulate the net. For this task Christ calls all apostolic men. As he invited James and John to leave the boat of Zebedee to become fishers of men, so through the ages He will touch young men and women and draw them apart to share in a sublime work. Apostolic men consist of the Apostles, their successors in the hierarchy, and all men and women who have been dedicated by the Church to the saving of souls. These all are the full-time fishers of men. All the members of the laity who, under the direction of the hierarchy, engage in Catholic action are part-time fishers of men.

To appreciate the sublimity of the vocation of the full-time fisher of souls, let us compare it to other occupations. Like the Holy Trinity, depicted by St. Ignatius in the meditation on the Incarnation, let us look over the race of men and behold what men are doing and evaluate their activity. Some are mouthing silly sounds into microphones in hope of rousing sillier laughter. By road and rail and airways many are racing from place to place. For what? Most of

---

[3] Cf. *In Joan. Evan. Tract.* 122, c. 21, nn. 6–9; *PL* 35, 1961 ff.

them, for money; some, for lust; some, for power; some, for they know not what. Some are telling lies in courtrooms. Some are aiming, or learning to aim, lethal weapons at their fellow man. Some are standing guard over slaves. Some are tilling the fields. Some are tending the machines which produce the bright objects of human desire. Some are mending broken bodies. Some are laying brick or making butter or selling haberdashery. Many are doing useless things. Some are doing harmful, even execrable things. Some are doing what is necessary to maintain the life which lives by bread. A few are adding to the intellectual possessions of the race.

Are any doing irreplaceable work? In the sphere of nature — the life of birth and death and taxes, of work and play, of eating and drinking — multitudes of decent people are so engaged. But the activities of mere nature, necessary as so many of them are in their own way, avail not unto life everlasting. In the sphere of faith, thanks be to God, many of the faithful are building the kingdom of God for the saving of their own and others' souls. But of these, how many are *professedly* dedicated to the kingdom of God? So many are doctors, mothers, stenographers, and mechanics first. Yet, the one profession which is irreplaceable in the realm of faith is fishing for souls. He or she who fishes for souls is rendering a service to men, akin to that which the God-Man has rendered. For the fisher for souls is the human instrument of men's salvation, the ordinary external assistance given by Divine Providence to men to prepare and dispose them to co-operate with the inspirations of the Holy Ghost, so that, if they lack sanctifying grace, they may be led to it; if they have sanctifying grace, it may be increased in their souls. Co-operation with actual grace is the proximate goal, possession and increase of sanctifying grace is the ultimate goal of the labor of fishing for souls. Here then is the activity which matters. For upon the possession of sanctifying grace and nothing else does eternity depend. Unless men with the use of reason die in the state of sanctifying grace, it were better for them if they had not been born. Fishers of men exist in order that as many men as possible may die in the state of grace.

The fishers of men are divine instruments. They are vessels

of election who bring the name of God and the chance of
eternal life to men. They are human channels conveying
the clear waters of truth and salvation to the race. Hence
they deal with men in the most intimate relationship. The
necessity of their calling gives them the right to enter into
and walk on very sacred ground, the privacy of the souls of
men, the ground common to each soul and its Maker, the
hidden trysting place where the loving Creator whispers
to His creature. Therefore they treat with their fellow men
concerning the most vital of all human activity — the judgments of the intellect and the volitions of the will elicited
for the gain or loss of salvation.

They fish for souls by conveying knowledge of God's
revealed word to men and persuading them to submit to it;
by freeing them from scruples and solving doubts of conscience; by advising them with counsels of supererogation.
They fish for souls by quieting the turmoil of the will disturbed by sorrow; by rousing the will to shake off the chains
of sin; by spurring the will with hope of eternal bliss; by
proposing to the will the One Essential Good whose loss
or possession spells disaster or triumph. They fish for souls
by administering to them the sacraments which produce
the living God within them.

They also fish for souls who offer reparation to the divine
justice, thereby averting God's anger from men. They also
fish for souls who implore mercy for sinners, who, by the
unflagging petition of their prayers bring down the abundance
of divine grace. How fruitful of apostolic achievement is
a life of unremitting prayer. Is not St. Thérèse of the Child
Jesus, who never preached a sermon or administered a sacrament, copatron with Francis Xavier of all foreign missionaries?

In importance and sublimity no human occupation can vie
with this. The fishers of men pursue men, not that they may
get some mutable good from them, but that they may impart the Immutable Good. Here is a thought of utmost importance to be expressed in terms of "value." Since some
modern philosophers have only a sketchy knowledge of ancient Greek philosophy and are quite ignorant of Scholasti-
cism, they think that they have solved the problem of
good and evil with their doctrine of "value." Adopting their

word "value," let us inquire what is truly valuable in human experience. The question, however, is so vast that we can merely high-light its most significant phases. Let us consider the valuable effects which a man can produce, first in himself, and then in others.

Evidently those effects are more valuable personally which respond to a deeper human need and which last longer. Of all human needs none is comparable with salvation. Salvation is the ultimate need which swallows up all other needs. Whatever a man does which *directly* promotes his union with God in the beatific vision stands outside of comparison with any merely natural activity, excitement, thrill, or satisfaction. Acts of supernatural faith, hope, and penitence which lead a man to sanctifying grace are incomparably more valuable and choice-worthy than delivering the world's best political speech, than the lawful satisfaction of romantic love, or the creation of artistic wonders. A person can spend much time and effort upon self-improvement, for example, the enhancement of bodily charm, cultivation of personality or a talent for oratory, knowledge, conversation, influence, and a thousand other things. If the improvement is merely natural, it is short-lived: it certainly will not survive the agent's death. Only one kind of self-improvement is enduring, that which is effected by supernatural acts. The man who acts in the state of grace in a manner which accords with God's will, and from a motive of faith, wins an increase of grace and glory. The achievement is his forever — provided, of course, he saves his soul. Being in the state of grace and increasing in grace are a man's everlasting values. By natural power no man can produce such a value: to do so he must be endowed by God with power from on high.

What of the effects men produce for and in others? The Romans thought that they had founded an everlasting State, but Rome did not long survive the decay of Roman virtue. Horace was confident his songs were eternal; Cicero, polishing his *Pro Milone,* deemed his masterpiece deathless. But none of the treasures of art, no merely human works — States, United Nations, Red Cross societies, humanitarian endeavors — none will survive the Day of Judgment. The only human institution which will survive is the Church, and that is divine. But one man can do something of everlasting value for another. A nurse can baptize a dying baby and that soul will be the son of God forever. A priest can crawl through a sewer to put the holy oil on an unconscious sinner and that sinner dies in the state of grace. By the exchange of marriage vows a Christian man and woman can produce sacramental effects in the soul of each other which will be a source of lifelong grace and eternal merit. A friend can speak the seasonable reasonable words which enable the unbelieving mind to co-operate with divine illumination and make its first act of faith. A mother can pray unceasingly for her son, as Monica did for Augustine, and win for him the grace of conversion.

In the Mass of the dead the Church tersely reminds us: *their works shall follow them.* The naked soul brings into eternity only its works: its evil works for punishment, its supernaturally good works for reward and adornment. All natural values cease at the threshhold of eternity. No merely natural good avails anything unto life eternal. In this life the only value worth a second thought is supernatural good. It alone has a chance of surviving and it will survive only in the souls of the just. They, then, who are wholly concerned to make men just and to persuade the just to grow in the likeness of the Son of God, they are the true salt of the earth. They are the purveyors of the one enduring reality of existence. In comparison with a share in the nature of God, anything else which a man may have or desire is completely irrelevant to the one great business of life. In comparison with this divinely appointed commission of leading men to share in God, the opinions of the President of the United States, the speeches of the Prime Minister of England, the decisions of the Politburo are as valuable as copies of Emily Post in the landing barges of D Day.

Bishop D'Herbigny, who carefully weighed every utterance, once related that a Hungarian priest, a former classmate and confidant of Lenin, had this statement from Lenin in his last illness: "I have been mistaken. It was, I suppose, necessary to liberate a multitude of oppressed people. But our methods have provoked other oppressions and frightful massacres. You know, my most awful nightmare is to feel myself drowning in an ocean of blood of countless victims. To save our Russia, what we needed was ten Francises of Assisi. Ten Francises of Assisi and we would have saved Russia."[4]

Every earnest soul may view himself as standing in a double relationship to the sublime activity of fishing for souls. Either he is the recipient of apostolic ministration — the passive relationship, or in some measure, large or small, he shares in the apostolate — the active relationship. He is both fisher and fished for.

As an example of the passive relationship, let him see himself as a penitent in the sacred tribunal of Penance. It is a universal role: the Holy Father himself, cardinals, archbishops, bishops, priests, religious, as well as the humblest laymen, kneel before a man and make the sign of the cross and say, "Bless me, Father, for I have sinned." The gesture is significant of universal frailty and human insufficiency.

One's attitude toward this powerful instrument of perfection is of great importance. Some few look on the sacrament of Penance with dread. Some of the most painful experiences of their lives have been linked with sacramental confession. They who have had such experiences should do everything possible to erase impressions of anxiety and fear. They ought to see God in these afflictions, testing their faith and stimulating their hope. Thereafter, their faith should ever see in confession, not an instrument of torture, but of mercy and leniency. Their hope should behold God in it, giving them the medicine of the soul and the promise of intimate union.

For many good souls confession is routine. They confess every week or two weeks. They repeat the same formula, recite practically the same litany of little faults, and seldom experience a sense of improvement.

The aspiring soul should look on each confession as a momentous affair, to be prepared for, with excitation of faith, hope, and love, as diligently as is the Holy Eucharist. In the first place, one should, whenever it is possible, have a regular confessor to whom one's soul is wholly open. There is great and natural repugnance to manifesting the secrets

---

[4] *Catholic Digest*, April, 1939, p. 9.

of one's heart; yet, this is a price which generally must be paid if one seriously ambitions perfection. By this action we give ourselves into God's hands, recognizing true indications of the will of God in sacramental advice. We are often saved from self-delusion. We acquire the simplicity and docility of the children of whom is the kingdom of God.

We should keep in mind that this sacrament is a remedy not only for serious sin but also for the slightest faults. When a person has only small falls to confess, which however are recurrent, he may be puzzled concerning an effective purpose of amendment. It will be helpful if in every confession he formulate a definite resolution against a particular fault and give expression to it at the conclusion of his confession. Then in the next confession he honestly renders an account of his fidelity to the resolution, expressing sorrow for lapses and remaking the resolution as necessity requires. It is hard to see how one can be constantly faithful to this procedure and not eliminate many faults. For one thing, these resolutions have a sacramental, an *ex opere operato,* value which resolutions made outside the sacrament do not possess. For another thing, it seems psychologically impossible for one to continue accusing himself of a fault to another with explicit promise of amendment and not finally to overcome it. For self-respect demands that either one live up to his word or cease the accusation.

One should also consider how he is the recipient of so many benefits of personal sanctification in the administration of the other sacraments, in the exposition of the word of God, in the carrying out of the liturgy, in the extrasacramental counsel given him, in the prayers which the whole Church offers on his behalf. With never ending awe and gratitude we contemplate God's supernatural economy, the rich and varied means He has provided in the Church for alluring our souls to Him and binding them fast in His love.

Practically all earnest souls try their hand some time or other at fishing actively for souls. For many of them — priests, for instance — fishing for souls is their total occupation. But even if one be not consecrated to this profession by vow or sacrament, yet countless opportunities of at least some species of this work abound which the alert soul can make use of to draw the neighbor to a better life. Whenever we join an association whose purpose is apostolic, or promise our help in some approved work of Catholic Action, or privately set out to effect some supernatural good in the neighbor — bringing back a fallen-away Catholic, persuading a sinner to go to confession, inducing a friend to give up the proximate occasions of sin — we are actively fishing for souls.

How shall we go about these projects? What means shall we use to make them supernaturally fruitful? Three helps are here suggested: cultivation of an intenser faith, prayer, and study of the advice given by Christ to the seventy-two disciples and recorded in the tenth chapter of St. Luke.

No one can fish for souls who does not transcend mere natural considerations. One must view men not with eyes of flesh and blood but with the eyes of the spirit. Now the eyes of the spirit are illuminated from one sole source, the light of faith. The inclination to help souls is in strict proportion to one's life of faith. To live by faith is to live by the unseen and that is no small thing because this world is too much with us. The little things of time cry out so loudly that they drown out much of what faith is telling of eternity. During the brief hour of this existence, these passing mutable things with their bright colors and charming sounds try to simulate Unchanging Immutable Beauty, and they always succeed in captivating the unbelieving heart. Even upon the believer they make too deep an impress. Therefore, whoever would fish for souls must constantly pray with the father of the epileptic boy: "I believe; help my unbelief."[5]

Only intense faith enables us to brush aside external surroundings and pierce to the heart of human affairs. This is always some supernatural problem: the real joys and miseries, evils and advantages of men lie in the unseen, the divine order. With eyes of flesh we may see hungry children: with the eyes of the spirit we should see also souls in whom hunger for truth should be awakened. We may pity a broken battered body: we should see also within it a soul crying more piteously to be healed. We may tolerantly look upon grace and charm of body hiding foul depths of selfishness,

[5] Mk. 9:23.

avarice, or lust: we should also see a poor unregenerate soul for whom Christ shed His blood. We may be disconcerted by the prospect of embarrassment, trouble, thanklessness, and all the other difficulties in the apostolic task we are proposing to ourselves. Let our faith strive to envision the blessed result which our efforts may achieve — a soul at peace with God, a soul growing in the love of God.

The fisher of men realizes that in every man there is a God and a Christ, at least a potential God and a potential Christ. That God and that Christ should not be allowed to perish, but should grow into the fullness of supernatural life destined for it. Like the man who went down from Jerusalem to Jericho and fell among robbers, the wounded souls of men cry for spiritual ministration. The circle of our opportunities and the instruments of our ministration may be quite meager; yet, as far as lies in our power we ought to pour the oil and wine of our mercy into the bruised souls of our fellows.

To have the intense faith of a fisher of souls prayer is indispensable. The vividness of our faith is proportioned to the strength and constancy of our prayer. Prayer is our direct way of getting at God. When we kneel in God's presence in church or the quiet of our room, or when we lift mind and heart to God as we walk about or sit in a bus or trolley car, our conversation with God puts us into the unseen realm of faith; it makes supernatural realities familiar to us; it teaches us the difference between eternal and temporal appeal, between passing and abiding beauty. It sorts out real truth from the appearance of truth. Without prayer no one ever conceived apostolic desires: that would be like trying to run without legs. Without prayer apostolic work will not continue. Suppose one has dedicated himself entirely to apostolic tasks. Without the quiet of prayer, the heat and noise of living deludes and deceives. Without the sustaining power of prayer, the fisher of souls cuts himself off from the source of strength and sweetness which is his right. For in prayer he is entitled to hear the Chief Fisherman consoling, heartening, emboldening, comforting, uplifting. The outward manner of his life closes many natural avenues of happiness to him, but the sweetness of prayer can compensate him for every natural advantage he surrenders. An apostolic life without prayer becomes an empty formalism, futile and pitiable: its burdens are too heavy to be borne alone. Without prayer one attempts to walk alone and carry an impossible load. Suppose one assumes apostolic tasks only from time to time: without prayer to sustain these efforts they will not be persevered in and will quickly disappear like water poured out upon hot sands.

Whether the opportunities of the earnest soul to engage in active tasks are extremely few or many, he should ponder well the words of Christ to the seventy-two disciples. Doubtless, St. Thérèse of the Child Jesus understood them as thoroughly as Francis Xavier.

"The harvest indeed is great, but the laborers are few. Pray ye, therefore, the Lord of the harvest that he send laborers into His harvest." These first remarks are most significant. They afford the underlying clue to the problem of how souls are saved. The clue leads straight to a divine mystery: helping souls supernaturally is a work which originates, is carried on, and is successfully completed by God and in God. First we have the divine complaint, "The laborers are few." How many men and women give themselves day and night, spending their productive energies on the advancement of the kingdom of God? Are they as many and as zealous as the agents of Communism, who spare neither pains nor labor, who have left no part of the inhabited world unorganized, in order to fasten the reign of Satan upon the entire world? And who remedies the situation? Men and women, human plans and human forethought? Nothing of the sort; only the Lord of the harvest can accomplish this. He raises up the necessary laborers. What essential part are we to play in the supply of the necessary laborers? We are to pray. Our prayers will move Him to send the laborers: He has made the sending dependent on our praying.

All the members of Christ are to be solicitous in their proper sphere for vocations to the apostolate. Unless suitable candidates are selected, trained, and set to work, the vigor of the Church is impaired. England lost the faith because the English State was able to destroy the Catholic episcopacy and priesthood. One shudders to think what will be the condition of the clergy and religious orders in the countries behind the Iron Curtain a generation hence, after the youth have been exposed to Communistic education. All, absolutely all are to pray and make sacrifices to the end that this need of the Church be fully met.

The fostering of vocations, however, is not to be left exclusively to the Holy Ghost. God expects human co-operation in the fulfillment of the works of grace. Co-operation consists in the alertness of priests, teachers, and parents to detect the makings of an apostle in a promising young man or woman, and in the time, energy, and human interest they devote to developing such promise. This duty is especially incumbent upon the active apostle who should ambition to live beyond his time in the lives of other apostles, the fruit of his labors, who take up where he leaves off. Since his active years are few enough and the needs of the Body of Christ are perennial, his prayers, example, and solicitude should prepare his successors. For solicitude for vocations to the apostolate is part of his apostolate.

But the great responsibility belongs to God. He will raise up great men and women as the needs of the Church demand. This is His work. He will not fail it. Our assigned part is prayer. What an awe-inspiring comment on the value of prayer! It seems, does it not, that by assigning us this role in the salvation of men, God is teaching us that our prayers have greater supernatural efficacy than our toil and sweat.

"Behold I send you as lambs in the midst of wolves." Whether the apostolic task we set ourselves be the conversion of a nation or a friend, the fundamental elements of the problem are the same. They are these: God indicates an impossible goal, which is to be achieved by hopelessly inadequate means. The end proposed is something distasteful to the natural man to be benefited: the lamb is to triumph over the wolves. Certainly the Roman world of apostolic times wanted no part of Christianity. Were there ever more helpless lambs sent among more ferocious wolves than the Apostles who brought their witness of the resurrection into Mediterranean civilization? So also when I try to persuade my friend to give up sin and go to confession, by natural standards my proposal is unattractive and repelling. If I tell one who is suffering grievous pain to unite his suffering with Christ on the cross, I am quite aware that he is more inclined to rebel and rail against his pain. When I first explain some revealed doctrine to a nonbeliever, I can almost see my words rebound from his mind.

And the means I am counseled to use! In place of my personal brilliance, repression of self; in place of a high, and perhaps violent, hand, mildness and meekness; in place of human strength which is seen, divine weakness which is unseen. In each undertaking I am to be simple as the dove but wise as the serpent. St. Gregory has given us a detailed description of the mildness and simplicity which accomplishes the impossible tasks. "The simplicity of the just man is scorned. It is the prudence of this world to hide one's intent with tricks, to veil one's meaning with words, to parade as true that which is false, to demonstrate as false that which is true. Verily this is the astuteness in which youth is trained, which young people pay money to learn. They who possess it look down with disdain on others; they who lack it, cravenlike, marvel at it in others. For these people highly regard this iniquitous duplicity, under a euphemism of course, calling a perversion of the mind urbanity. Now urbanity commands her votaries to seek the heights of honor, to rejoice in whatever wordly honors they have received, to repay with interest injuries inflicted by others; if they are able, to yield not an inch to their opponents; if they are helpless and cannot achieve their malicious designs, to pretend their weakness is semblance of conciliatory virtue. On the contrary, it is the wisdom of the just to accomplish nothing through bluff, to make manifest their meaning in their words, to love the true as it is, to avoid the false; to do favors for nothing, willingly to tolerate evil rather than inflict it; to seek no revenge for injury, truly to esteem contumely as profit. But this simplicity of the just is laughed at; for virtue's integrity is deemed foolishness by the wise of this world. For whatever is done with upright intention is considered by these people to be stupid; and whatever action truth approves of sounds foolish to worldly wisdom. For what seems more foolish to this world than to reveal one's mind by one's words, to conceal nothing by trickery, to repay no injuries with contumely, to pray for those who curse you, to seek poverty, to give up one's possessions, to resist not the despoiler, to turn to the striker the other cheek?"[6]

In every undertaking we manifest the simplicity of the dove by the pursuit of a single aim. We are not concerned with satisfying any need of self, with creating an impression, or winning credit. We want nothing from the people we deal with but we want Christ for them: no natural advantage for self, only supernatural assistance for the objects of our ministrations. The wisdom of the serpent means the refusal ever to relinquish that aim or to compromise it; it is ever to have the prudent fear that the wolves may corrupt us and we come to admire them as products of high civilization, and so assume their ways of thinking and doing. We could be influenced to believe that pride and carnal love can carry a person far, but we must remember that we are dealing with that world for which Christ would not pray because prayer would profit it nothing.

We need sometimes to contemplate the sobering thought that if the wolves cannot corrupt us, they will assail us. Sometimes by the kind of public clamor, which embattled Protestantism calls unprejudiced zeal for separation of Church and State. Sometimes by naked force. Sometimes by force masquerading under the robes of public justice. Christ has given the warning: "They will deliver you up in councils, and they will scourge you in their synagogues. And you shall be brought before governors, and before kings for my sake."[7] No one who grew up before World War I ever imagined that these words would be literally verified in the twentieth century. Everyone thought the reference was to old, unhappy, far-off things and battles long ago. The fate of Archbishop Stepinac, of Cardinal Mindszenty, and of millions of good Catholics rotting in concentration camps proves that they who want to bring Christ to their fellow man must sometimes be ready to give up everything — good name, liberty, and life itself — for the sake of the attempt.

---

[6] *Moralium Lib.* X, 29, 48; *PL* 75, 947.
[7] Mt. 10:17–18.

"But how will the lamb overcome the wolf?" asks St. Cyril of Alexandria. "I will be with you, He says, and protect you, transforming the wolves into lambs. For nothing can resist My will. And this we know was verified in the case of Paul; for him who was more rapacious against the faithful of Christ than any wolf, He made milder than a lamb."[8] Here again is the great truth which must always uphold yet humble us. Be the work we plan or do great or small, it is God's work; that is, He produces the supernatural result. Paul may plant and Apollo water, but God alone gives the increase.[9]

"Carry neither purse, nor scrip, nor shoes." The lesson is this: never is the shadow of one's temporal advantage to be cast upon the apostolic task in hand. The person for whom we labor must see that we desire not his things or gifts or presents but himself, not our own lucre but his supernatural improvement. To produce this impression we need detachment of heart from material things. Since we must wrestle with the powers of darkness, who, as St. Gregory says,[10] have no possessions in this world and, therefore, wrestle naked, we, too, must wrestle naked. In so dire a struggle we can afford no worldly attachments which will serve our adversary as the handle of our undoing. Love of riches has hindered the work of God: concern for wealth on the part of lay and cleric was an awful evil of pre-Reformation days. To succeed, then, in our various undertakings scarcely any tool is more effective than contempt of worldly goods. It is difficult to overrate the value of disinterestedness in dealing with souls and this is in direct proportion to our personal detachment. People will learn from us to be just and openhanded because they see we set no store by the trinkets which people love to accumulate. And they will envy us our freedom. They who make their happiness depend on having many things are really slaves to them, but the detached soul is free. His trust is in God. Whatever he gives of his worldly goods to the cause of God will always come back to him a manifold blessing. And even if he

[8] *Comment. in Lucam*, c. X; *PG* 72, 665.
[9] Cf. 1 Cor. 3:7.
[10] Cf. *Homiliae*, 32, 2; *PL* 76, 1233.

should give everything, he has no worry about a livelihood. God will provide it: the workman is worthy of his meat.[11]

"Salute no man by the way." The meaning is not that in our apostolic endeavors we are to behave like unfeeling sticks, who know not how to deal with people in a human, friendly way, but that we are to be detached in heart from the people for whom we labor. "Turning aside to others," says St. Cyril, "harms zeal."[12] Just as Eliseus commanded Giezi, "Gird up thy loins, and take my staff in thy hand, and go. If any man meet thee, salute him not: and if any man salute thee, answer him not; and lay my staff on the face of the child."[13] So also in our every undertaking we move straight to the divine objective with the same single-mindedness. We are not, therefore, to be concerned whether or not our efforts meet with gratitude, affection, or credit. If we find these things, we may accept them and be glad that the people we have helped are duly practicing virtue, but we may not seek these things on their own account, directing our efforts as means to obtain them. This kind of detachment is more difficult to practice than the kind outlined above: unconsciously we want, as the saying is, "our little cut" in the form of these advantages. If we exercise this kind of petty spiritual graft, we are to that extent failing in due disinterestedness. If we look for gratitude and credit, we may find disappointment and disappointment breeds resentment. If we seek affection, we may create envy and jealousy. Our zeal, then, would not measure up to that charity which seeketh not her own.[14]

"Into whatsoever house you enter, first say: Peace be unto this house." A great incentive to apostolic effort is consideration of the immediate goal to be sought, which is human order. We offer our fellow man some kind of medicine for the healing of the wounds of sin and the production of order in his being. Order means that he is one with himself and with God. Out of this order comes peace, the tranquillity which results from observing the law of the sons of God and from having one's things in their proper place. What a

[11] Cf. Mt. 10:10.
[12] Loc. cit.
[13] 4 Kings 4:29.
[14] Cf. 1 Cor. 13:5.

surpassing blessing is the peace of a well-ordered conscience!
What a privilege to bring unhappy men something of the
peace of God!

"If the son of peace be there, your peace shall rest upon
him." The son of peace is the man of good will who uses our
efforts on his behalf to co-operate with internal grace. Each
time we undertake a project God says to us: it will succeed
with men of good will. The earnest soul does meet people
of good will, lovers of the truth, and in them his labor for
souls bears eternal fruit. They are the people to whom the
angels sang on the first Christmas morning: "On earth peace
to men of good will."[15] It is not, however, the fisher of souls
who produces this good will. He only sets up some favorable
occasion which allows the good will to become manifest.
Nor is it to these people themselves that their good will is
attributable. It comes from God, "for it is God who worketh
in you, both to will and to accomplish."[16] All the supernatural
good will of men flows from the cross of Calvary.

But what a consolation to be the divine instrument in the
production of eternal values! Augustus rejoiced to found
an empire but the barbarians destroyed it. The money barons
of the nineteenth century looked with complacency on their
huge fortunes but their grandchildren dissipated most of
them. The saving of a soul is an everlasting accomplishment
worth every sacrifice. A Jesuit missionary wrote from his
station on Lake Superior to his Father Superior in France:
"Should the priest succeed in adding only one neophyte to
the number of the Elect, he would have no reason to regret
the sacrifice he has made. He would recall to mind the
sentence of St. Francis Xavier: 'To get to the world's end to
save a soul, and then die, is an enviable fate.' "[17]

"But if not, it shall return to you." The earnest soul will
be rebuffed by bad will. His erring friend will not go to
confession. His neighbor will not go to the priest and
straighten out the bad marriage. Sometimes bad will is only
temporary; sometimes it is enduring. He must then accept with
equanimity the awful power of the human will to say no to

---

[15] Lk. 2:14.
[16] Phil. 2:13.
[17] *Annals of Prop. of Faith,* July, 1854, Vol. XV, no. 91, p. 199.

God. He cannot penetrate the mystery of free will, a mystery latent in every sin committed and grace rejected. He will be tempted to despond, but despondency will dry up all his efforts. He must go on hoping and trying. Who but God knows at what moment the most seemingly hopeless work will become efficacious and the most obdurate sinner begin to show good will? And even if his hardest work is unsuccessful, his effort has not been in vain; the peace of Christ which he offered his neighbor returns to him as his own merit. God is the one employer who pays not for efficiency and results but for good will and effort.

The text of St. Luke continues with Christ's admonition to the seventy-two to observe the laws of hospitality of which they will be beneficiaries. The obvious point is that whoever chooses to preach the Gospel will surely live by the Gospel: he is to take what is offered him by way of temporal subsistence and not to look for what he wants. But there is also another lesson for everyone, namely, timorous regard for one's health should not deter one from apostolic effort. Overcautious consideration of health keeps some people from doing what actually does lie within their power. As usual the saints show us how to solve these problems. In the spring of 1913 the health of St. Pius X was seriously impaired. Influenza was followed by symptoms of bronchitis. Although he was seventy-eight, he made a quick recovery. No sooner was he convalescent than he began to receive prelates and settle business. The chief physician remonstrated with him: "Just think of our responsibility before the world!" "Just think of mine before God," was the energetic reply, "if I do not take care of His Church."[18]

"And heal the sick that are therein and say to them: The kingdom of God is come nigh you." Undoubtedly Christ gave the seventy-two power to work miracles and bodily cures. Where faith is nonexistent, signs and miracles are required to rouse it. The power of healing, however, is not promised with every exercise of apostolic effort which indeed is to be directed not at the sick body but at the sick soul. The souls of men have many infirmities. They are ignorant of God's revelation; they are moon-struck by the form and figure of

[18] F. A. Forbes, *Life of Pius X* (New York: Kenedy, 1918), p. 156.

decaying flesh; they are often well aware how they might amend their lives, but, from weakness or obstinacy, they refuse to do so.

A powerful remedy for these sicknesses is the declaration which John the Baptist expounded to prepare men for the Messias, the same declaration which Christ our Lord made: "The kingdom of Heaven is come nigh unto you."[19] It is dreadfully nigh. The longest life is no more than a dream that fleeteth away, as a vision of the night.[20] Every moment a man lives he is hurrying to eternity. How little often stands between him and sudden expulsion from life into eternity — another few inches and the same accident which brought death to his fellow passenger sitting on the same seat would have victimized him also. And yet how many live as though there were no eternity, as though they were never to give an account of their deeds. There are always occasions for reminding this, that, or the other man that the kingdom of God is nigh. Let us never fear to be ridiculed for seizing it. Some will mock, some will turn away, but some will listen.

Christ next tells the seventy-two how they are to act toward those who refuse to accept their teaching. "Into whatsoever city you enter, and they receive you not, going forth into the streets thereof, say: Even the very dust of your city which cleaveth to us, we wipe off against you." These are among the strongest words Christ ever spoke. Their obvious meaning is that in the Church of God there can be no communion with them who believe not. When the kingdom of God will be finally established, it will be more tolerable for Sodom, the city of sinners, than for those who cut themselves off from Christ by heresy and unbelief. Isaias has predicted what will happen: "For behold the Lord will come with fire, and his chariots are like a whirlwind, to render his wrath in indignation, and to rebuke with flames of fire."[21] In our present context Christ speaks another of His terrible woes against those who scorn the light. "And thou, Capharnaum, which art exalted even unto heaven, thou shalt be thrust down even unto hell." So also in this life it is a grievous crime to

---

[19] Lk. 10:9.

[20] Cf. Job 20:8.

[21] Isa. 66:15.

separate oneself from the Church, to reject her teaching, to close one's ears to the truths of Christ.

These words of Christ provoke two thoughts. First, meditation upon the punishments of God is a tremendous stimulus to apostolic zeal. It is to save our fellow man from this awful fate that we fish for his soul. Second, the Church can never compromise a revealed doctrine. Nothing is more characteristic of the Church's action through the ages than her refusal to deviate from Christ's doctrine. The same adamantine quality should exist in all her children. In order to make the Church attractive to outsiders one may never water down a principle of faith or morals. In dealing with troubled souls the temptation arises of offering them solutions to their problems which are pleasing to them but not in accord with the traditions of the Church. These solutions are worthless. Only the truth will help the needy soul.

This principle of no compromise must be applied with both prudence and charity. In Christ's gradual manifestation of His messianic mission, He shows us that we must at times withhold the full truth until our hearer is capable of receiving its impact. Thus, in offering counsel, we sometimes do not tell the party the full extent of his moral obligations when we foresee that the information would only prove an occasion of sin. We leave him in his good faith. Charity demands that we do not misunderstand these words of Christ. When He says, "the very dust of your city which cleaveth to us, we wipe off against you," He is repeating the declaration of the Psalmist: "I have hated the assembly of the malignant: and with the wicked I will not sit."[22] So long as any group of men or any individual is not joined to Christ by true faith, he can have no part with Christ, he must be to Him as a wanderer and an outcast. But Christ is not condemning persons, only their lack of belief. He is not saying that these people are already doomed, that He does not desire their salvation. As long as life is in them, they have hope of reconciliation; they are fitting objects of apostolic solicitude. So also we should never despair of helping another. We should entertain no resentment or sentiments of condemnation against those who refuse our aid. For indeed the fault may lie with

[22] Ps. 25:5.

us — our lack of good judgment or dexterity to summon forth their good will.

Christ makes clear why the threatened punishments will be utterly just. By rejecting His disciples they reject Himself, for His disciples are empowered to speak in His name, and with His authority. "He that heareth you, heareth me; and he that despiseth you, despiseth me; and he that despiseth me, despiseth him that sent me." These words are spoken to the Church and constitute a divinely given commission. They give substance to her words and acts and are divine warrant that the almighty power of God is behind her. We can apply these words to ourselves, and take great comfort from them, if we are always one with the Church. Oneness with the Church implies two things. First, there is union of our will with the ruling power of the Church. The things we undertake are in the Catholic tradition. They bear the approval of the Holy See or the local Ordinary or some other duly constituted authority. Whatever activity the Church frowns on we sedulously avoid. Second, our intellects must be one with the teachings of the Church. Unless we take pains to say only what the Church says, the light which is in us will be but darkness.

When the seventy-two returned from their little mission, they were full of joy and said: "Lord, the devils also are subject to us in thy name." Jesus answered them: "I saw Satan like lightning falling from heaven." St. Gregory[23] and St. Jerome[24] interpret this passage to mean that the disciples were puffed up with elation and pride, and Christ took occasion to recall them to humility by reminding them of what happened to Lucifer. Undoubtedly a danger of pride lies in apostolic achievement. For the earnest soul can be tempted to attribute to his own industry the good which grace works in the souls of others. An opportunity of appearing to be superior often occurs. But instead of accusing the disciples of pride, let us rather look at the incident from the viewpoint of St. Cyril. "Lest they should think that of their own authority they undertook their preaching, the grace given them by the Spirit bore witness. For, on account of the miracles which

---

[23] Cf. *Moral. Lib.* 23, 6, 13; *PL* 76, 259.
[24] Cf. *Comment. in Is.*, VI, 14; *PL* 24, 219–220.

accompanied their teaching, no kind of calumny could prevail against them. They rejoiced, therefore, that they were held worthy to work miracles and overcome demons. That he had fallen like lightning means that Satan had been cast to the ground from on high, from glory to ignominy, from power to weakness. Before the coming of our Savior, Satan had dominated the world, worshipped by nearly everyone. But he finally fell like lightning who had as adorers those who were deceived by error and now he lies at the feet of his former adorers."[25] It is as though Christ said to the disciples: "You are telling me nothing new. Before I sent you, I had already seen him falling for I had overthrown him."

God calls every zealous Christian to assist in that overthrow, to labor and sweat that the demon does not rise again for the destruction of the unwary. "For our wrestling is not against flesh and blood; but against principalities and powers, against the rulers of the world of this darkness, against the spirits of wickedness in the high places."[26] By prayer we can curb malignant spirits; by the blessings which the Church imparts to sacramentals we can put them to flight. Contemplation of our adversary convinces us of the utter seriousness and otherworldliness of fishing for souls. We must never lose sight of, nor despise, that adversary. The keenest of angelic minds is pitted against the Church: a whole world of malignant wills rage against it. Like a roaring lion, that adversary goeth about seeking whom he may devour.[27] Even now, he seems to have all the advantages. The governments of Christian men have cast God and His Christ from public life. They have removed many of the social barriers by which a wiser generation had hoped to restrain men's unruly inclinations. By so-called laws of divorce, remarriage, license of contraceptive knowledge, they have widened the broad highway which leadeth down to destruction. They have allowed the taint of the flesh to infect many innocent activities, impiety to be applauded, attacks upon the foundations of morality to go unchallenged. What pulling power has a prayerbook in comparison with a slick magazine? Compared to the millions who

---

[25] *Comment in Lucam*, C. X; *PG* 72, 668.
[26] Eph. 6:12.
[27] Cf. 1 Pet. 5:8.

daily drink in television, movies, radio, how few attend divine services of supererogation? How popular is fasting? And what seemingly foolish weapons has the Church to defeat this adversary? Against the twinkling lights of the seen, the Church proffers what no eye hath seen. Against the success stories men daily hear, She can promise only what no ear hath heard. Against earthly love and the joys men can savor now, She offers what the mind of man hath not conceived. Stalin wanted to know how many divisions the Pope had. His Holiness can muster only faith, which is the evidence of things which appear not;[28] only hope, which lays hold of a distant immortality; only charity, which lays down its life for a friend. The Gentiles rage and the people devise vain things. The kings of the earth stand up and the princes meet together against the Lord and against His Christ, but He that dwells in heaven shall laugh at them and the Lord shall deride them.[29] The gates of hell shall not prevail for "behold I have given you power to tread upon serpents and scorpions, and upon all the power of the enemy: and nothing shall hurt you."

"Rejoice not in this that spirits are subject unto you; but rejoice in this, that your names are written in heaven." In conclusion Christ gladdens the zealous soul with the thought of the apostle's reward. Even among men meritorious labor wins its fitting recognition. The great commander in the field receives his four or five stars. The graduate who brings credit to alma mater is called back for an honorary degree. And the workman of the Lord who needeth not to be ashamed,[30] what shall he have? Certainly nobody can reward with an aptness and generosity comparable to God's. Because the Levites served an earthly tabernacle, God blessed them with the tithes of Israel. Far greater is the reward given for acts of supernatural faith, for God said to Abraham: "I am thy reward exceeding great."[31] There must be a special reward for helping to save souls because Proverbs says: "To him that soweth justice, there is a faithful reward."[32] The prophet

[28] Cf. Hebr. 11:1.
[29] Cf. Ps. 2:2–4.
[30] Cf. 2 Tim. 2:15.
[31] Gen. 15:1.
[32] Prov. 11:18.

gives some vague notion of what that will be: "They that instruct many to justice [shall shine] as stars for all eternity."[33]

Christ enlarges that promise and makes it very definite. In our present context He tells the disciples that they have the greatest possible reason for elation — their names are written in heaven. What does this mean? Is an apostolic vocation a sign of election? In order that a man may dedicate himself wholly to the salvation of souls without being hindered by worry over his own salvation, does God give him a certainty of his own salvation?

The Evangelists all record a special divine promise. Peter asks: "Behold we have left all things, and have followed thee: what therefore shall we have?"[34] In reply our Lord assures His twelve Apostles of a very special reward for themselves: "Amen, I say to you, that you, who have followed me, in the regeneration, when the Son of man shall sit on the seat of his majesty, you also shall sit on twelve seats judging the twelve tribes of Israel."[35] They who were the first to leave everything for His sake, who were His companions and the foundation of His Church shall have the primary places of honor in His eternal kingdom, being associated in a very special way with His judicial power, assisting Him on the last day to judge the nations. Then he says of everyone who imitates the Twelve in giving up all things for the sake of the Gospel: "And every one that hath left house, or brethren, or sisters, or father, or mother, or wife, or children, or lands for my sake, shall receive a hundred-fold, and shall possess life everlasting."[36]

Here Christ enumerates the possessions which are most generally loved in this world and for whose sake the service of God is liable to be slighted. Whenever these things become an obstacle to salvation, or to leading the kind of life to which God clearly calls, then they must be generously surrendered. That a soul may make the surrender willingly, the munificent God promises, for this life, a hundred times the value of what is given up, and for the next life, everlasting happiness. The

---

[33] Dan. 12:3.
[34] Mt. 19:27.
[35] Mt. 19:28.
[36] Mt. 19:29.

hundredfold promised for this life is very real but insignificant in comparison with eternal life. Both rewards are conditional and the conditions are two.

First, the sacrifice must be consummated in deed and in affection. There must be the actual giving up of these impediments and no sinful hankering after them once they are given up. What counts is not so much the actual value of the things surrendered as the good will and generosity with which the surrender is made. Even though Peter and Andrew gave up nothing but a fishing boat and a few nets, St. Gregory has this comment on the magnitude of their sacrifice: "We must emphasize affection of the heart rather than the size of a man's wealth. He surrendered much who kept nothing for himself. He left much who gave up absolutely all his possessions however small they were. Truly we cling with affection to what we have and covet what we have not. Peter and Andrew, therefore, gave up very much when both of them surrendered the desire of possession. He gave up very much who together with possession surrendered the desire thereof."[37]

Second, the sacrifice must be continuous, persevering to the end. There can be no resumption of what was surrendered. "For no man putting his hand to the plough, and looking back, is fit for the kingdom of heaven."[38] If then, the apostle does what is required of him, the divine promise is fulfilled to him. But is he so sure that he will fulfill his part that he can now say that his name is written in heaven? On the one hand, God has not exempted him from the situation common to all the faithful that he work out his salvation not knowing whether he is worthy of love or hate.[39] Hence he cannot say that by entering the apostolic life he has received an inalienable right to heaven. On the other hand, he must have something which other men have not. The promise made to him must be real and meaningful: otherwise Christ's words are vain and illusory. He has the promise of a benign providence which will guide him unto the end. We cannot say infallibly that in every individual case a faithful end is absolutely assured; nevertheless, every apostle can go tranquilly forward

---

[37] *Homiliae,* 5; *PL* 76, 1093.
[38] Lk. 9:62.
[39] Cf. Eccles. 9:1.

relying upon the divine promise that a generous God will see Him safely through.

He has a genuine promise of success now and of felicity hereafter. He will accomplish what the Lord sent him into His vineyard to do — he will gather the harvest appointed to him. And, when the heavens are moved, and He comes again in great power and majesty to plant forever the banner of His cross, he will rejoice with the Master in the merriment of the harvest: both he that soweth and he that reapeth will rejoice together.[40]

And even if we can work for souls only from time to time as our physical weakness or dearth of opportunity permits, nevertheless we can be comforted by the promise: "And whosoever shall give to drink to one of these little ones a cup of cold water only in the name of a disciple, amen I say to you, he shall not lose his reward."[41]

---

[40] Cf. Jn. 4:36.
[41] Mt. 10:42.